Stop Thief!

Stop Thief!
Anarchism and Philosophy

Catherine Malabou

Translated by Carolyn Shread

polity

Originally published in French as *Au voleur! Anarchisme et philosophie* © Presses universitaires de France/Humensis, 2023

This English edition © Polity Press, 2023

This book is supported by the Institut français (Royaume-Uni) as part of the Burgess programme.

This work received support for excellence in publication and translation from Albertine Translation, a program created by Villa Albertine and funded by FACE Foundation.

Excerpt from Michel Foucault, *The Government of Self and Others: Lectures at the Collège de France 1982–1983*, published 2010 by Palgrave Macmillan, reproduced with permission of SNCSC.

Excerpt from Jacques Rancière, "Ten Theses on Politics," *Theory & Event*, 5/3 (2001) © 2001 Jacques Rancière and The Johns Hopkins University Press. Reprinted with permission of Johns Hopkins University Press.

Excerpt from Giorgio Agamben, *Omnibus Homo Sacer* used with permission of Stanford University Press, 2017; permission conveyed through Copyright Clearance Center, Inc.

Polity Press
65 Bridge Street
Cambridge CB2 1UR, UK

Polity Press
111 River Street
Hoboken, NJ 07030, USA

All rights reserved. Except for the quotation of short passages for the purpose of criticism and review, no part of this publication may be reproduced, stored in a retrieval system or transmitted, in any form or by any means, electronic, mechanical, photocopying, recording or otherwise, without the prior permission of the publisher.

ISBN-13: 978-1-5095-5522-2 – hardback
ISBN-13: 978-1-5095-5523-9 – paperback

A catalogue record for this book is available from the British Library.

Library of Congress Control Number: 2023934858

Typeset in 11.5 on 14 Adobe Garamond
by Fakenham Prepress Solutions, Fakenham, Norfolk NR21 8NL
Printed and bound in Great Britain by CPI Group (UK) Ltd, Croydon

The publisher has used its best endeavours to ensure that the URLs for external websites referred to in this book are correct and active at the time of going to press. However, the publisher has no responsibility for the websites and can make no guarantee that a site will remain live or that the content is or will remain appropriate.

Every effort has been made to trace all copyright holders, but if any have been overlooked the publisher will be pleased to include any necessary credits in any subsequent reprint or edition.

For further information on Polity, visit our website: politybooks.com

"Even those who do not consider themselves anarchists feel they have to define themselves in relation to it and draw on its ideas."[1]

David Graeber

Contents

Translator's Note   viii

1. Surveying the Horizon   1
2. Dissociating Anarchism from Anarchy   7
3. On the Virtue of Chorus Leaders: Archy and Anarchy in Aristotle's *Politics*   25
4. Ontological Anarchy: Traveling from Greece to the Andes with Reiner Schürmann   38
5. Ethical Anarchy: The Heteronomies of Emmanuel Levinas   61
6. "Responsible Anarchism": Jacques Derrida's Drive for Power   83
7. Anarcheology: Michel Foucault's Last Government   111
8. Profanatory Anarchy: Giorgio Agamben's Zone   145
9. Staging Anarchy: Jacques Rancière without Witnesses   178

Conclusion: Being an Anarchist   210

Notes   222
Index   257

Translator's Note

Anarchy in Translation, or Can Translation be Anarchist?

Having translated seven of Catherine Malabou's books, I have argued consecutively that translation is plastic, differently feminine and not secondary to a binary, that the accident is its condition, that translation is textual epigenesis, that translation morphs with our intelligence in the age of A and that – oh yes – translation can be a clitoridian pleasure. Will I now ascribe anarchism to translation? No. That's not possible. Anarchism cannot be attached as predicate to its substance. Its existence is other. To think anarchism philosophically, as Malabou explains, we'll need to unseat foundations, starting with Aristotle's *archē*, and all the principles, beginnings, commands, and orders that have ensued. We'll have to move from vertical pyramids of hierarchy and control to the relief of horizontal planes. A new mapping will emerge from the translational topography in anarchist geographers' sights.

Even if ascription is not possible, between translation and anarchism, there's certainly something to be said. Let's start with the history of disavowals of anarchism that Malabou parses here as she works through the thought of philosophers from Reiner Schürmann to Emmanuel Levinas, Jacques Derrida, Michel Foucault, Giorgio Agamben, and Jacques Rancière, every time picking out with that astute eye we have come to trust and admire, the fault in the fabric of their thinking, the place where the light of anarchism shines too bright for them to see. Again and again, Malabou shows how even the most radical philosophers could not think … not the un-governable, that's simple enough – could not think … the non-governable. Following her tracking, readers will recognize that gentle indocility of Malabou's own thought, her refusal of mastery and masters, her penchant for looking toward the space of transformations brought about not by an unruly refusal to obey, but rather by quiet indifference. Anarchism is not about the ungovernable – that's just distraction to keep some inside, others out, everyone and everything in their defined place on the colonizing map of hegemony. This is not about in and out; anarchism is a plastic world of its own.

But if anarchism is a critique of representation, a critique of the hierarchy of representing because to represent is to speak in the place of and for another, then how can translation be anarchist? That is, how is translation something other than representation? Walter Benjamin asked a similar question of photography in the age of mechanical reproduction. In the age of artificial intelligence, the question is about how in translation does there lie a potentiality beyond transfer: the plastic power of transformation. A type of translation that is not about speaking for, not a strategy of domination (translation has been used in this diminished manner far too often); it is about amplifying and regenerating an authorial voice with a translator's own, working it in another idiom for more times and places. Taking anarchist practices to imagine liberation via language, I'll posit that translation offers a plastic *porte-parole*, one that occasionally allows anarchism to emerge. This is precisely because translation here is not secondary and subservient representation, and not even deferred reformation; it is, rather, anarchism in action. Too often, translation is placed in a position of exception, cordoned off from writing – why? Because sometimes in its plasticity there is anarchist expression.

Anarchism is a powerful word. It turns heads. Then, usually, all too soon it is dismissed as anarchy, misconstrued and maligned as disorder, excluded from the realm of possibilities. As Malabou writes here: "Not for a moment do philosophers consider the possibility that we might live without being governed." An anarchist imaginary sees the radical and transformational reordering the world calls for: climate crisis and the attendant wounds of capitalism compounded by slavery require what Joseph Proudhon reframed as the highest form of order – no other reparation is enough.

There is anarchism. In translation there is anarchism. Malabou concludes her meticulous reading of anarchism in philosophy by discussing the ever-renewed demand that anarchism offer proof that it exists. I suggest that, sometimes, that is just what translation does. I won't claim that this translation is anarchist – it's too ready to take on Malabou's order, even when it is artfully plastic. But, like every translation, this Malabou in English does partake in the potentiality of translation that is always anarchism. It defends that plasticity as its condition of possibility and its world. The translational is what opens us to the transformation that is anarchism.

1

Surveying the Horizon

I propose the term geographicity to parallel historicity.[1]

Yves Lacoste

If Marxism is a passion for history, anarchism is the love of geography. All historical approaches, whatever their methodology, inevitably reproduce hierarchical interpretations of dominant positions. Anarchist geography, on the other hand, avoids vertical readings, although this does not mean it exists on the flat. Élisée Reclus, author of *The Earth and Its Inhabitants: The Universal Geography*[2] and *The Earth: A Descriptive History of the Phenomena of the Life of the Globe*,[3] articulates better than anyone the lines drawn across distance that make up a landscape shaped by the harmonious juxtaposition of mountains and dales, rivers and valleys, the teeming life that lies behind every map: "Gushing springs, rivers disappearing deep into the earth, waterfalls, floods, fissuring glaciers, erupting volcanos, emerging sand bars and islands, waterspouts, hurricanes, and tempests."[4] To refuse verticality is not to walk in the plains. It is, instead, an entirely different way of knowing how to boldly face the expanse. It is a knowledge that is another means of presenting the relief. Each of the six volumes of his later *L'Homme et la terre* – the earth that Reclus explored so far and wide, largely on foot – bears the epigraph: "Geography is none other than history in space, in the same way that history is geography in time."[5]

Reclus coined the French neologism *entraide* [mutual aid] for his friend and fellow geographer Peter Kropotkin, contributing a key element to the French translation of the 1902 masterpiece *L'Entraide, un facteur de l'évolution*.[6] An indefatigable observer of Manchuria and Siberia, and author of three significant works on physical geography (a treatise on the orography of Asia, a theory of glaciation, and a study of desiccation[7]), Kropotkin, too, understood the ground we stand on not merely as inorganic fact but rather as the tangled traces of life. All across the Eastern steppes, palimpsests of evolution offer brilliant, frozen memories of relations between the animal world, humans, and the desert.

A forebear of social geography and ecology, anarchist spatialization works tirelessly to achieve a political vision of horizontality. It is no mere pun to say that both geography and politics establish this groundwork together. As a geography of emancipation, as opposed to a geography of domination, anarchism refers verticality back to what it is, namely, a governing logic that reduces every diestema to subordination. Yet organization does not necessarily require subordination. As Reclus puts it: "Our political aim ... is the absence of government, it is anarchy, the highest expression of order."[8]

The absence of government. This book was sparked by the question of how to understand this phrase. It invites readers to look at anarchism anew, forgoing hegemonic habits and the evaluative gaze.

This is a book of philosophy, however, not geography. It comes from a dawning awareness that philosophy is lagging behind geography. An awareness that philosophy is tardy when it comes to physical geography and a politics of horizontality. In short, that philosophy is belated in addressing anarchism.

The time has come to make up for this delay. To undertake the reckoning between philosophy and anarchism that has not yet taken place.

*

I explore the concept of anarchy in the work of six key contemporary philosophers: Reiner Schürmann, Emmanuel Levinas, Jacques Derrida, Michel Foucault, Giorgio Agamben, and Jacques Rancière. Although they all accord anarchy a critical value – be it ontological, ethical, or political – they fail to truly engage in a philosophy of anarchism. Even as they adopt the geographical language of surface, fold, and the demise of overviews to counter the diktat of pyramid models, ultimately, they are unable to rid themselves of the logic of government. My goal is to interrogate the anarchist failure of philosophical concepts of anarchism.

*

Why stage this reckoning now? Because horizontality is in crisis: dissociated, split, torn asunder by its uniformity, its geography is disoriented, the compass of differentiation lost.

Our current crisis in horizontality comes from the global coexistence of de facto anarchism and dawning anarchism. Their coexistence makes it difficult to establish a rigorous distinction between resignation and initiative, forced as they are now to tread the same ground.

As far as de facto anarchism is concerned, the state has already disintegrated. It is no more than a protective envelope for various oligarchies that have divided up the world between them.

It's clear as day: there's nothing more to wait for from on high. Everywhere, the social world is condemned to a horizontality of desertion.[9] In economically privileged "democratic" countries, the effects of the longstanding collapse of the welfare state continue to circulate endlessly. No state institution, no common parliamentary organization (think of the dysfunctional European Union) has shown itself able to respond to the challenges of poverty, migration, or ecological and health crises in any way except through pitiful emergency measures.

As far as dawning anarchism is concerned, the actual collapse in the social meaning of verticality coincides with an emergent planetary consciousness signaled by the dramatic rise in collective initiatives and experiments in alternative political visions.[10] In France in recent years, for example, Occupy strategies, the Yellow Vests movement [*Gilets Jaunes*], and the creation of 'Zones to Defend' [ZAD: *zone à défendre*] have introduced the very real existence of organizations and modes of decision-making based on self-generated, collective care for an environment, territory, or structure within the political landscape. There's clearly a connection between anti-globalization views of anarchism that date back to events in Seattle in 1999 and the explosion of the many phenomena taking place outside unions and political parties even though they do not openly align themselves with anarchism. In this context,

> the circulation of information in fact occurs more through channels that, if they are not in competition with unions, at least exist in parallel, in forms of horizontality that contest the information "silos" of national organizations ... This alters communications between individuals and activist groups and established actors who seek to offer collective expression.[11]

These alternative modes of communication are contemporaneous with what must be described as the anarchist turn in capitalism itself, for capitalism is the prime actor in de facto anarchism. Emerging from the financial crisis of the 2000s, this turn marks the shift from neoliberalism to ultraliberalism. In the critique of neoliberalism discussed by many contemporary philosophers, capitalism's current anarchist turn can no longer be ignored. The development of post-Fordist capitalism at the end of the twentieth century was not yet fluent in the language that economic actors now practice openly and that has become the hegemonic language of anarcho-capitalism.

I hear the objection loud and clear: aren't we witnessing a global hardening of political interventionism that is inseparable from a new form of centralized economic power? Aren't we faced with intensified political authoritarianism, the consolidation of wealth and profit in the hands of just a few companies and conglomerates? Yes, certainly. But when political commentators declare in all seriousness that Donald Trump is an anarchist,[12] they are not using words lightly. They are trying to express what the entire world is experiencing as a major crisis: *the combination of government violence and an infinite uberization of life*. Authoritarianism does not oppose the disappearance of the state; rather, it acts as its messenger. It masks this so-called "collaborative" economy that continuously erodes all fixed regulations by putting professionals and users in contact directly via online platforms.

Researching the world of cryptocurrency transactions and the circulation of non-national currencies heightened my awareness of this phenomenon. Cryptocurrencies leech off state currencies and compete in the usual circulation of funds by commercial and central banks.[13] More generally, as Alain Damasio comments, "the fundamentally horizontal and libertarian architecture of the net" gives rise to a "polymorphic" anarchism that is just as libertarian as it is liberational.[14] In the end, I concluded that cyber-anarchism is one of the most visible symptoms of the existing anarchy that is now a dimension of our reality, like it or not.

How can the horizontality of alternative formations be distinguished from the veinstone of anarcho-capitalism? How do we dig for the relief of difference at the surface? This is the new geographical, political, and philosophical challenge of the twenty-first century.

It might be argued that this difference, not to say incompatibility, is blindingly obvious:

> "Anarcho"-capitalism is not part of the anarchist tradition and ... has falsely appropriated the name ... [We] present the case why "anarcho" capitalists are not anarchists ... indicating where they differ from genuine anarchists (on such essential issues as private property, equality, exploitation and opposition to hierarchy) ... [and] present a general critique of right-libertarian claims from an anarchist perspective ... we show up why anarchists reject that theory as being opposed to liberty and anarchist ideals.[15]

This distinction is convincing, but is increasingly overshadowed. César de Paepe noted as much back in 1874: "The word *an-archy* ... raises the hackles of our bourgeois, whereas the idea of indefinite whittling away of government functions and ultimately the abolition of government is the last word among the laissez-faire economists favored by these brave bourgeois!"[16]

There's nothing new in the coexistence of revolutionary anarchism and market anarchism, but nevertheless the expansion of what Rifkin terms the "Collaborative Commons"[17] has created an unprecedented situation that forces us to examine the polymorphism of anarchism in order to identify its limits. This is the arena where philosophy must intervene.

*

The problem is that even if some of the most significant continental philosophers of the twentieth century viewed anarchy as a deconstructive and transformative resource, rejecting the limitations of more established political theories (notably Marxism), not one of them managed to breach the distance that they argued separates anarchy from anarchism. This separation remains conceptually underdeveloped. Philosophy must therefore explore the anarchism of its various forms of anarchy. In return, anarchism must open itself up to philosophical dialogue to create the instrument of a differentiation that is lacking on our current horizon.

*

I hear the ready objection: but there's no single anarchism! It has so many forms! How can we ignore the tremendous diversity of its aspects, cultures, languages, pragmatic modes? How can we flatten the long trail of its history, from the invention of its name, its status as a movement forged in the 1870s, the subsequent developments of anarcho-syndicalism, autonomy, anarcho-feminism, the anti-globalization turn of the 1990s, the emergence of post-anarchism, Occupy movements, the current rise of social uprisings without leaders …? How can we ignore the local specificity of Zapatista autonomy, Kurdish anarchist resistance, Anarchists Against the Wall in Israel, and Black Lives Matter in the United States?

Endlessly emphasizing the diversity of anything is also a way to avoid thinking it. As Jacques Derrida put it: "To pluralize is always to provide oneself with an emergency exit, up until the moment when it's the plural that kills you."[18] Yet, contrary to what the enemies of thought always claim, the multiple is not the enemy of the idea. Responding to the journalist who asked, "What is anarchism?" in response to his documentary *Ni Dieu ni maître* [no gods, no masters], Tancrède Ramonet replied that one cannot say "what" anarchism "is"; one can only say "there is" anarchism, which does support a certain use of the singular.[19] "There is anarchism" means "anarchism is in evidence" or "anarchism reveals itself," both here and there.

A thing can reveal itself without becoming one and without dissolving into fragmented phenomenal occurrences. After several years of researching anarchism and many long months spent in the unreal exploration of the world via the confinement experience of technological a-geography, I'm taking a shot now at the singularly diverse exploration of the statement: "there is" anarchism.

2

Dissociating Anarchism from Anarchy

Exploitation and government, the first affording the means whereby to govern and representing the prerequisite as well as the object of all government, which, in turn, guarantees and legalizes the power to exploit, are the two indivisible terms of all that goes by the name of politics. Since the beginning of history, they have indeed constituted the stuff of the life of States: theocratic, monarchical, aristocratic, and even democratic.[1]

Mikhail Bakunin

[Anarchism is] the rupture of the axioms of domination: a rupture, that is, in the correlation between a capacity for rule and a capacity for being ruled.[2]

Jacques Rancière

To distinguish de facto anarchism from dawning anarchism, we must first shed light on the other difference that separates philosophical anarchy(ism) from political anarchism. This difference has not yet been taken sufficiently into account, even though it signals their strange mutual ignorance amid a shared skein of tangled questions.

Although Schürmann, Levinas, Derrida, Foucault, Agamben, and Rancière all inscribe anarchy at the heart of their thought, they all insist nonetheless that anarchy is irreducible to political anarchism.

Political anarchism, too, is often hostile to philosophical reflection.

In *L'Anarchisme aujourd'hui* [anarchism today], Vivien García writes "Reading anarchist texts, one is inevitably struck by the constant affirmation of the immanent relation between theory and practice. Proudhon himself wrote: 'know therefore that action is the idea.'"[3] Nowadays there are endless assertions of the primacy of practice over theory, extending Proudhon's rejection and Bakunin's unwillingness to recognize himself as the philosopher that he is. Spanish anarchist Tomás Ibáñez, one of the creators of *A cerclé* [A in a circle, the anarchist symbol], recently stated:

To my mind, there is no anarchist philosophy and anarchism cannot be approached as if it were a philosophical reflection or system of philosophy. Even if we consider only its discursive aspect, it is clear that anarchism has no counterpart as a type of philosophical discourse, at least in the dominant tradition instituted by Plato. One reason for this is that its mode of production is not at all of the same order as the mode of production of philosophic discourse. Anarchist discourse is not solely the result of a pure intellectual activity, oriented towards analysis or understanding, nor even to the invention of concepts, as Deleuze defined the task of philosophy.[4]

This mutual avoidance is all the more confusing given that philosophical anarchy(ism) and political anarchism have a shared goal: the irrevocable critique of all phenomena of domination. Domination is not – at least not simply – mastery, authority, or power. These three terms are ambiguous because they have both negative and positive connotations. The power to do something, pedagogic authority, mastery of an instrument or discipline are not, in themselves, inherently coercive. By contrast, domination is bereft of any constructive resources. It relates unequivocally to subjection and alienation, blurring the line between power and abuse of power.[5] Philosophical anarchy(ism) and political anarchism agree that domination is the *power problem*.

Consider the etymological proximity of the words "domination" and "danger." "Danger" derives from the Late Latin *dominarium*, used in Northern Gaul for *dominium* and signifying "property, right to property," hence "domination, power, right." Subsequently, in feudal law "danger" became a lord's right over his forests, meaning that landowners could neither sell nor manage them without his permission and without paying the tithe, under pain of confiscation. By extension, "*estre en dangier d'aucun*" eventually came to mean "to be at the mercy of someone," and then "to be in danger" (*estre en dangier*).

Anarchism is not, and never has been, *simply* an attack on the state, as is claimed far too often. In fact, the destruction of the state is perhaps not even, or no longer, its leading light. Anarchism is first and foremost a fight against mechanisms of domination, which exceed the sphere of the state strictly speaking and affect all domains of life – public, private, collective, individual. Emma Goldman, for instance, lamented the fact that feminists in her time only ever called out "external tyrannies," while the "internal tyrants" ruling over more intimate spheres such as businesses, homesteads, or the marital bed, continued their abuses with impunity. In "The tragedy of women's emancipation," Goldman writes:

> The explanation of such inconsistency on the part of many advanced women is to be found in the fact that they never truly understood the meaning of emancipation. They thought that all that was needed was independence from external tyrannies; the internal tyrants, far more harmful to life and growth – ethical and social conventions – were left to take care of themselves.[6]

Goldman reminds us of the obvious fact that domination is never petty and there's no such thing as insignificant domination.

Marxists criticized anarchists for separating domination from exploitation. But the critique does not stand. Without renouncing their critique of capitalism for a moment, anarchists recognize that the question of power infiltrates all areas of life – domestic, institutional, academic, psychic – and that this phenomenon must be the subject of specific attention and study.

"Domination" describes all forms of control that subject an individual or group to continuous subordination, often through terrorist tactics. Even when it is apparently at the furthest remove from the political sphere, subordination originates both psychologically and politically in what Proudhon calls the "governmental prejudice."[7] The critique of the state begins with the fact that the state is only a pretext for forms of governing, that is, the establishment of the unequal sharing between rulers and ruled. Such is the logic, or "prejudice," of government: some command, others obey.

State sovereignty does not exist without the governing logic, and there is no governing logic without domination. Any individual mandated to represent another person is inevitably led to will in their place. As Proudhon puts it:

> This external constitution of the collective power, to which the Greeks gave the name *archē*, sovereignty, authority, government, rests then on this hypothesis: that a people, that the collective being which we call society, cannot govern itself, think, act, express itself, unaided, like beings endowed with individual personality; that to do these things, it must be represented by

one or more individuals, who, by any title whatever, are regarded as custodians of the will of the people and its agents.[8]

His conclusion is damning:

> To be GOVERNED is to be kept in sight, inspected, spied upon, directed, law-driven, numbered, enrolled, indoctrinated, preached at, controlled, estimated, valued, censured, commanded, by creatures who have neither the right, nor the wisdom, nor the virtue to do so ... To be GOVERNED is to be at every operation, at every transaction, noted, registered, enrolled, taxed, stamped, measured, numbered, assessed, licensed, authorized, admonished, forbidden, reformed, corrected, punished. It is, under the pretext of public utility and in the name of the general interest, to be placed under contribution, trained, ransomed, exploited, monopolized, extorted, squeezed, mystified, robbed; then, at the slightest resistance, the first word of complaint, to be repressed, fined, despised, harassed, tracked, abused, clubbed, disarmed, choked, imprisoned, judged, condemned, shot, deported, sacrificed, sold, betrayed; and, to crown it all, mocked, ridiculed, outraged, dishonored. That is government; that is its justice; that is its morality! And to think that there are democrats among us who pretend that there is any good in government; Socialists who support this ignominy, in the name of Liberty, Equality and Fraternity; proletarians who proclaim their candidacy for the Presidency of the Republic![9]

*

What does philosophy have to say on the matter? In a brilliant dissertation titled "The primacy of resistance: Anarchism, Foucault and the art of not being governed," Derek C. Barnett, an early career researcher in critical theory at the University of Western Ontario, suggests that we name the *philosophical* version of "governmental prejudice" the "*archic paradigm.*"[10] The archic paradigm refers to the structure that, right from the beginning of the Western tradition, links state sovereignty and government to one another. The name of this structure is *archē*, a term whose philosophical meaning comes from Aristotle, who defined it as both "beginning" and "command." As Barnett explains it, "*archē* ... is the principle that locates the question of politics at the intersection between power exercised as government and the logic of state sovereignty."[11] This paradigmatic unity remains the touchstone of all political philosophy right up to the second half of the twentieth century. There's not a treatise in classical political philosophy that does not begin with joint consideration of sovereign and governmental authority, considered as absolute starting points.

While dismantling this paradigmatic unity is of interest both to philosophers of anarchy and to anarchists, for philosophers it requires far more than a hasty denunciation of a "prejudice." Philosophers of anarchy must first determine where exactly prejudice inheres in the "governmental prejudice."

These philosophers recognize that the logic of the governing body, as the foundation of traditional political thought, is a fundamental motif in Greek philosophy, especially in Aristotle, who argues that the constitution (*politeia*) or Republic – what we call the state sovereignty today – cannot exist without a form of government (*politeuma*). Moreover, in Book 3 of *Politics*, Aristotle goes so far as to establish their synonymy: "The governing body *is* the constitution."[12] Later he continues: "'Constitution' and 'governing body' signify the same thing, since the governing body is the authoritative element in cities."[13]

For contemporary philosophers, anarchy is therefore already inscribed in the heart of the logic of forms of governing defined by Aristotle. Anarchy is to come only because, paradoxically, it is already here. Indeed, a critical examination of the archic paradigm reveals that *anarkhia* haunts *archē* upon its emergence, as its necessary flaw. Anarchy is originary, inscribing contingency in political order.

But at first sight, nothing signals this flaw. In *Politics*, the *archē*, as the excellent form of the constitution (*aristè politeia*), is invested with a triple meaning: sovereign or supreme power (*to kurion*), the distribution of particular powers or magistratures (*arkhai*), and the exercise of government (*politeuma*). This structure is supposed to guarantee that the Republic is protected from disorder (*anarkhia*).

So, where's the contingency? Originary anarchy is based on a secret twist in *archē*: the archic paradigm grants the value of a principle to something that is actually derivative.

The political order cannot be, and can never be, purely political. That which is pre-judged in the "governmental prejudice" is the indestructible relation between forms of governing and domestic domination. Although Aristotle clearly asserts that *archē politikē* is born of the divorce from *archē despotikē* – the domination of father over wife and children, master over slaves – he fails to uncover a purely political normativity, one that is entirely *sui generis* and takes nothing from the domestic economy. *The law of the master remains the disavowed model of all government.* The law of the home, *oikonomia*, thus has an ambiguous relationship with *archē politikē*, that is, it is the paradoxical cement of the archic paradigm. The reversibility of commanding and obeying, which is the specific mark of citizenship, since Aristotle says that all citizens must be able, alternately, to command and to be commanded, is inevitably fractured by the fact that in the end only some people – those who are supposedly more apt to govern than others – give commands. This hegemonic betrayal of the equality of citizens reveals the indelible trace of the figure of the master of the house in a sphere from which it is supposedly excluded.

The anarchic virus infecting *archē* from the start is the inability of political order to found itself. This order thus reveals its dependence on that from which it is supposedly cut off and which Rancière, taking *oikos* outside the walls of the home, describes as "the natural order of the shepherd kings, the warlords, or the property owners."[14]

Even though it is concealed, the contingency of *archē* thus derives from a paradoxical revelation of its *heteronormativity*.

Philosophers argue that this problem requires a more radical elucidation than the one offered by anarchist critiques. Even if the philosophers discussed here do not all consider themselves "deconstructionists," this clarification draws more on a Heideggerian *Abbau* or *Destruktion* of metaphysics than on revolutionary thought. Moreover, in *Heidegger on Being and Acting: From Principles to Anarchy*, Schürmann explicitly connects Heideggerian "deconstruction" to anarchy.[15] The dismantling of the archic paradigm can occur only at the price of the deconstruction of metaphysics, which alone is capable of undertaking a deconstitution of *archē*. A deconstitution that is *ontological* (Schürmann, Derrida), *ethical* (Levinas), and *political* (Foucault, Rancière, Agamben). Starting from a genealogy of philosophical tradition, each of these three directions follows the vacillations of the principality of principles through to the exhaustion of their legitimacy and authority.

The first, "*ontological* anarchy,"[16] interrogates the archeo-teleological domination that imposes the derivative schema – according to which everything starts with a beginning and is arranged toward an end – onto thought and practice. The second, "an-archic responsibility,"[17] unseats the domination of the same and the subordination of alterity. The third, undertaking the "anarcheological" critique of "apparatuses" (Foucault),[18] reveals "the anarchy internal to power" (Agamben)[19] and claims that "politics has no *archē*, it is anarchical" (Rancière).[20]

*

How are we to understand the fact that, despite everything, philosophers *never* refer to the anarchist tradition? The explanation given is often the same: for them, classic political anarchism is only a moment in metaphysics. Anarchists have a substantialist view of power and oppose the politico-metaphysic principles that have reigned up to now only to replace them with others such as human nature, moral good, and reason. In the opening pages of *From Principles to Anarchy*, Schürmann declares: "Needless to say, here it will not be a question of anarchy in the sense of Proudhon, Bakunin and their disciples. What these masters sought was to *displace* the origin, to substitute the 'rational' power, *principium*, for the power of authority, *princeps* – as metaphysical an operation as has ever been."[21]

Philosophical anarchy thus adopts the paradoxical form of an anarchy without anarchism. This helps explain why no serious reading of the work of Proudhon, Kropotkin, Bakunin, Malatesta, Goldman, Bookchin, not to mention more contemporary anarchists, is used to support the philosophical deconstruction of the archic paradigm. The sarcasm with which Marx and Engels ridiculed and marginalized anarchism has not yet been subject to deconstruction.

Moreover, for a philosopher, if there's no shame, and never has been, in declaring oneself a Marxist, calling oneself an anarchist is almost indecent, since anarchism is immediately associated with the impossible, the unachievable, a confounding mix of terrorist violence and naivety. As Alain Badiou put it: "We know today that all emancipatory politics must put an end to the model of the party, or of multiple parties, in order to affirm a politics 'without party,' and yet at the same time without lapsing into the figure of anarchism, which has never been anything else than the vain critique, or the double, or the shadow, of the communist parties, just as the black flag is only the double or the shadow of the red flag."[22]

But Schürmann, Levinas, Derrida, Foucault, Agamben, and Rancière are undoubtedly closer to anarchism than to Marxism. Why didn't they develop the anarchist dimension of their interventions, ridding the anarchist posture of all the clichés with which it is so widely associated?

*

Some will say they did just that. The "post-anarchism" movement, first named by Hakim Bey (*Post-Anarchism Anarchy*, 1987) and bringing together several mostly anglophone anarchist thinkers, was inspired by Foucault, Rancière, and Agamben inasmuch as they outlined the possibility of an *other* anarchism. Important theorists such as Todd May, Saul Newman, and Lewis Call argue that the dichotomy between anarchy and anarchism instituted by continental or "poststructuralist" philosophers was not reactionary at all, contributing instead to a rejuvenation of classic anarchism.

In his Introduction to *The Political Philosophy of Poststructuralist Anarchism*, May writes: "The purpose of this essay is to sketch the framework of an alternative political philosophy, one that differs from its dominant predecessors," in other words, the works of traditional anarchists.[23] This "alternative political philosophy" presents as "tactical thinking,"[24] whose characteristics May borrows from Foucault and, indeed, must succeed the "strategic thought" of earlier anarchism, based as it is on an overly simplistic opposition between power and resistance. Today, "power is decentralized ... sites of oppression are numerous and intersecting."[25] Traditional anarchism remains dependent on a pyramid view of the state and forms of governing. For instance, many militant anarchists believed in "terrorist attacks against heads of state, to eliminate power at a perceived source."[26] But the notion of a single source of power is a recent target of poststructuralist critiques.

Poststructuralist thought is considered to have the advantage of opening political philosophy in general, and anarchism in particular, to a theoretical and practical perspective freed of a monolithic view of power. It frees anarchism from the idea that each individual is a representative of "human essence."[27] Ultimately, May's claim is that poststructuralist political theory is more anarchist than anarchism itself.

For post-anarchists, it's as if the history of anarchism were secretly oriented toward a future that could be confirmed only by deconstruction.

The three main periods in this history – the anarchist movements of the late nineteenth and early twentieth century; the anarcho-syndicalism of the 1930s; the anti-globalization movement of the 1990s – would eventually lead to a renewal in revolutionary practices more inspired by philosophical concepts of anarchy than the now unusable core ideas of historical anarchism. Lewis Call concludes that it "is becoming increasingly evident that anarchist politics cannot afford to remain within the modern world. The politics of Proudhon, Bakunin and Kropotkin ... have become dangerously inaccessible to late twentieth-century readers."[28]

Indeed, it is always with reference to poststructuralist philosophers that post-anarchists announce the disappearance of militant universalism and its splitting into many different fronts of resistance: local, plural, changing, heterogenous fights that no longer come together under the single category of "class." At the same time, the knots of conflict composing the social fabric signal discontinuity: the demands of unions, feminists, ecologists, decolonial militants, the fight against racial and gender discrimination, homophobia, transphobia[29] ... "Human essence" can no longer be the basis of all these agonistic fields. Contemporary philosophers have thus actively contributed to demonstrating that "the problem of essentialism is the political problem of our time."[30]

I'm convinced that post-anarchists are missing the point. Philosophers of anarchy have never conceptualized the anarchist dimension of their concepts of anarchy. This analysis is not undertaken with a view to engaging anarchism in a new, postmodern phase; rather, first and foremost, it seeks to *dissociate* from it.

*

It is this internal dissociation within philosophical thought on anarchy that I intend to analyze as a triple cleavage that engages all at once an *unthought*, a *theft*, and a *disavowal*.

An unthought

The origin of philosophical concepts of anarchy is still unthought. In fact, the very possibility of these concepts depends entirely on a fundamental event: Proudhon's mid-nineteenth-century semantic revolution of the word "anarchy." A revolution about which the philosophers say not a word.

In *What is Property?* (1840), the ancient word "anarchy" inherited from the Greek *anarkhia* suddenly became a *neologism*. When Proudhon declared for the first time "I am an anarchist," connecting the word "anarchist" directly to the question of forms of governing, he conferred on it a meaning it never had before:

> What is to be the form of government in the future? I hear some of my younger readers reply: "Why, how can you ask such a question? You are a republican." "A republican! Yes; but that word specifies nothing. *Res publica*; that is, the public thing. Now, whoever is interested in public affairs – no matter under what form of government – may call himself a republican. Even kings are republicans. –
>
> "Well! you are a democrat?" – "No." – "What! you would have a monarchy." – "No." – "A constitutionalist?" – "God forbid!" – "You are then an aristocrat?" – "Not at all." – "You want a mixed government?" – "Still less." – "What are you, then?" – "I am an anarchist."
>
> "Oh! I understand you; you speak satirically. This is a hit at the government." – "By no means. I have just given you my serious and well-considered profession of faith. Although a firm friend of order, I am (in the full force of the term) an anarchist."[31]

Linguists explain that while a neologism usually refers to a newly created word, a prototype, it may also refer to impressing a new meaning on an old word,[32] which is exactly what happened here. "Anarchist," along with "anarchy," became, so to speak, "an-archaisms."

"Under the name of Anarchy, a new interpretation of the past and present life of society arises, giving at the same time a forecast as regards its future," Kropotkin later wrote.[33] The neologism is a play with time itself: "anarchy" no longer refers to disorganization as it did in the past; instead, it signals a new type of organization: "Anarchy is order without power."[34] Even if Proudhon did not yet describe his doctrine as the "anarchism" that was to become a fully formed movement some forty years later,[35] his redefinition of anarchy identifies it with a political project for the first time.

DISSOCIATING ANARCHISM FROM ANARCHY

What was the archaic meaning of the word "anarchy"? Its history begins in Greece with *anarkhia* (ἀναρχία), referring to

> "the state of a people regularly without a government" (Herodotus, *Histories* IX, 23) or "the occasional absence of a leader" (Xenophon, *Anabasis*, III, 2, 29), "the lack of authority" (Sophocles, *Antigone*, v. 672) or "the refusal to obey" (Aeschylus, *Seven against Thebes*, v. 1030). In Plato (*The Republic*, VIII, 565e 2–5 et IX, 575a 2), where it is contrasted to *eleutheria* ("freedom"), *anarkhia* is associated with *anomia* ("the absence of law"), *anaïdeïa* ("impudence"), *asôtia* ("debauchery") and *hubris* ("excessiveness"). In *Politics* (1302b 29), Aristotle makes *anarkhia* synonymous with *ataxia*, disorder.[36]

For many centuries the word "anarchy" retained these negative connotations, as is evident, for instance, in Diderot's article "Anarchy," written for the *Encyclopedia*: "Disorder in a state, deriving from the fact that no one has enough authority to command and to impose the laws and consequently, the people acts as they will, without subordination and without police."[37] Until the mid-nineteenth century, "anarchy" referred to chaos caused by an absence of governmental authority.

> [Chaos] as much in the political realm (liberalism and universal suffrage were labeled anarchic by Maine de Biran in 1817 and by Saint Priest in 1831), as in the socioeconomic realm. In 1830 Fourier spoke of "anarchy of the press" and "mercantile anarchy"; in 1845 Louis Blanc referred to "industrial anarchy"; in 1890 Jaurès described the "anarchy of the market"). Even in the social realm ("social anarchy," Villeneuve-Bargemont, 1845) and religion ("atheism is religious anarchy," Pastoret, 1797, *Sur la liberté des cultes et leurs ministres*).[38]

Today, in the same vein, cancer cell development is described as "anarchic proliferation."

Even if this negative semantic constellation has not disappeared, it is impossible to ignore the *other* meaning of anarchy: the meaning that no longer views the absence of principle or leader as a catastrophe:

> *Anarchy* – the absence of a master, of a sovereign – such is the form of government to which we are every day approximating and which our

accustomed habit of taking man for our rule and his will for law, leads us to regard as the height of disorder and the expression of chaos.[39]

Far from entropic fate, the absence of master and sovereign appears instead as the condition of possibility of new organization. For anarchists, it is the "archic" order that is a disorder precisely because it is not founded on free consent. And if, as with Reclus, anarchy can be described as "the highest expression of order,"[40] it is precisely because it gives no orders. Likewise, for Malatesta, order without orders characterizes "the condition of a people who live without a constituted authority, without government."[41]

Without this revolution in meaning, none of the philosophical concepts of anarchy developed in the twentieth century could have seen the light of day. Indeed, they all assume that the archaic meanings of the notion – disorder or chaos – have been superseded. Ontological anarchism in Schürmann, "arche-writing" in Derrida, anarchic responsibility in Levinas, "anarcheology" in Foucault, destituent power in Agamben, "democracy" in Rancière – all are indebted to Proudhon's semantic transformation.

A theft

Contemporary philosophy thus *took* something from anarchist thought. Perhaps unwittingly, perhaps without admitting to itself that it was doing so.

"What is property? … It is theft."[42] When Proudhon wrote these words, he took aim not only at material confiscation. His sights are not only set on the fact that private property entails the dispossession of most of humanity, nor is he thinking only about the exploitation of workers. He is also describing the way in which a theft always conceals itself. Thus, private property, which comes from an abduction, is protected by the law and covered up by a suit of legitimizing instances. Theft always occurs twice over. To steal is first to despoil, then to conceal – both the stolen object and the theft itself. "The etymology of the French verb *voler* is … significant. *Voler*, or *faire la vole* (from the Latin *vola*, palm of the hand), means to take all the tricks in a game of ombre."[43] In the thief's game there is a dual activity of capturing (taking charge of) and disappearance (passing from hand to hand). This dissimulation is the best way to keep the stolen object ("the things that … you have such fear of losing,"[44] Proudhon retorts to the defenders of property).

Is it too much to claim, then, that there has been a *philosophical theft* of anarchy from the anarchists? A theft concealed, knowingly or unknowingly, by an apparent concern for theoretical and political distance? Something dangerous, shameful, explosive, enclosed in the underside of consciousness, something that philosophers have shifted from hand to hand?

How else can we understand their silence? The concept of anarchism is not just any concept. One cannot claim to invent it, to play on the privative prefix (*an-arkhia*) or simply borrow it from the dictionary without knowing how it was innovated by political anarchism.

A disavowal

The unconscious motive for such poaching cannot be ignored. Most likely this theft is related to a disavowal. Need I recall that in Freud disavowal refers to a defense mechanism in which a desire is spoken, even as it is signaled by negation? The argument presented in his article "Negation" [*Die Verneinung*][45] is well known:

> The manner in which our patients bring forward their associations during the work of analysis gives us an opportunity for making some interesting observations. "Now you'll think I mean to say something insulting, but really I've no such intention." We realize that this is a rejection, by projection, of an idea that has just come up. Or: "You ask who this person in the dream can be. It's not my mother." We emend this to: "So it is his mother." In our interpretation, we take the liberty of disregarding the negation and of picking out the subject matter alone of the association. It is as though the patient had said: "It's true that my mother came into my mind as I thought of this person, but I don't feel inclined to let the association count."[46]

What then are we to make of philosophers who announce "I am not an anarchist" even when "anarchy" is everywhere to be found in their work and has the last word? What are we to think except to assume that philosophical reservations about anarchism are also the expression of a form of a partially successful repression?

But a repression of what exactly? A repression of the issue at the heart of the anarchist question, namely, the political viability of the absence of government. In referring to a disavowal, I certainly have no intention of suggesting a psychoanalytic session for the contemporary philosophical critique of the "governmental prejudice." If it is necessary to have recourse to the language of psychoanalysis, as I often do here (how can you avoid the psychoanalytical when it's a matter of domination?), it is because anarchism and the unconscious have a special relationship. A relationship whose terms Derrida laid out, exploring the space of a beyond principles with and contra Freud, especially in *The Post Card*.[47]

The reservation philosophers have about the idea of not having a governing body – and which is shared by Derrida despite it all – is probably largely unconscious. They accept a dismantling of the archic paradigm and welcome the deconstruction of domination – but the possibility that humans might live without being governed and without governing themselves? Unthinkable! The possibility that we simply rid ourselves of the very concept of governing? Out of the question! The former meaning of anarchy hangs over us still. Without the logic of governing, without the sharing of command and obey, wouldn't it be … wouldn't that be, how shall I put it … anarchy?

*

Hobbes is never far from this line of thinking and his indelible mark continues to shape contemporary thought. Need I remind readers that in *Leviathan*, Hobbes describes the state of nature, "mere nature," precisely as "*anarchy*"? "That the condition of mere nature, that is to say, of absolute liberty, such as is theirs, that neither are sovereigns, nor subjects, is anarchy and the condition of war … that a commonwealth without sovereign power, is but a word without substance and cannot stand."[48]

Philosophers have never managed once and for all to differentiate anarchy – the state of a people without a government – from the state of nature. Remember, it is Hobbes whom Freud cites in *Civilization and its Discontents* when he describes the "inclination to aggression,"[49] harbinger of the death drive, the "anarchy drive,"[50] as Derrida puts it, as even more dominating than *archē* in its many compulsive manifestations – the drive for control, the addictive taste for power, sadism, violence, cruelty ...

How can we set this aside when in France a radical Left persists in associating anarchy with a mortal and criminal frenzy of passions? In a virulent indictment of anarchism, for instance, Frédéric Lordon claims:

> the characteristic shortcoming of "horizontalist" thinking is to systematically overlook the fact that associations which are freely entered into (and touted as the seed of a new form of politics) would not quite be able to support themselves since they would be incapable of creating the conditions of their own viability ... the stateless world is not a world of associations but of gangs. By its nature, only the vertical can restrain violence in a large group.[51]

For many thinkers, anarchism will always be gang philosophy. But it would be misleading to limit the reservations expressed by philosophers of anarchy regarding anarchism to this type of conclusion.

We need only think of how Foucault interprets Hobbes in an "unorthodox" manner, inverting the logical and chronological order that seemingly rules relations between the state of nature and civil state. In the seminar *Society Must Be Defended*, Foucault demonstrates that the "state of nature" is in fact a political state, a state of rebellion, civil war, a dynamic of resistance to the state. He writes:

> Hobbes does not simply claim that this war of every man against every man gives birth to the State on the morning – which is both real and fictional – on which Leviathan is born. It goes on even when the State has been constituted and Hobbes sees it as a threat that wells up in the State's interstices, at its limits and on its frontiers.[52]

The primary meaning of *anarchy* is thus resistance.

Consequently, even though Hobbes is one of the fiercest adversaries of anarchy, for Foucault he nonetheless opens up the possibility of an alternative understanding of politics. Rather than starting from *archē*, this interpretation takes its starting point in resistance to *archē*, in "anarchy." It is therefore possible to read the chronology of the state of nature–civil state to counter-*archē*, and to find in anarchy an alternative origin of politics. Foucault demonstrates the ordinary narrative of modern political theory as "an agonistic conception of … politics."[53] This conception displaces politics "from *archē* to *agōn*."[54]

Following the path forged by Foucault, Agamben also views the Hobbesian state of nature as a permanent *stasis* that signals resistance to *archē*: "The state of nature is a mythological projection into the past of civil war; conversely, civil war is a projection of the state of nature into the city."[55] Agamben's view is shared by Tiqqun in *Contribution à la guerre en cours* [contribution to the current war]: "The history of the modern state is the history of its battle against its own impossibility, in other words, its excesses by the set of means deployed precisely to ward off these very same excesses."[56]

The role of Hobbesian thought in dismantling the archic paradigm is therefore more complex than I initially suggested.

I'm still convinced, however, that whatever their understanding of Hobbes, philosophers who discuss anarchy tend to consider anarchism as an economy of disorder paradoxically anchored in authoritarian principles. It is this view that holds philosophers back at the edge of the radicalness they advocate. It turns out that it is not enough to speak about resistance, revolt, or rebellion, to speak about *stasis*, *différance*, or disagreement, if we are to dismantle the logic of government. The legitimacy of commanding and obeying has yet to be philosophically toppled.

Let me repeat my point: not for a moment do philosophers consider the possibility that we might live without being governed. Self-management and self-determination are not serious political possibilities for any one of them. In the final analysis, government is always safe, even if it takes the form of self-government. This is why the concepts of anarchy presented by Schürmann, Levinas, Derrida, Foucault, Agamben, and Rancière all run up against a limit that compromises the force of their arguments, causing them ultimately to take refuge in the protective wings of *archē*.

Don't get me wrong: I'm not criticizing philosophers for not being anarchists. Besides, I think that even if the anarchists have described possible alternatives to government (short mandates, federations, communes, self-management, platforms, and decision syntheses), they have not yet sufficiently explored the space that the transgression of sharing commanding and obeying opens up, and they have not been fully convincing in their attempts to truly distinguish anarchism from turmoil, deviation, and death.

*

To launch this discussion, I shall introduce – not as a solution, but as a question – the concept of *non-governable* as a space of encounter and communal efforts between philosophical anarchy(ism) and political anarchism.

The non-governable is not the ungovernable. The ungovernable refers to something that is out of control, like a vehicle that cannot be driven. In terms of morals and politics, it evokes a lack of discipline and disobedience, insubordination. The ungovernable is, and remains, nothing but the opposite of the governable. It resists and opposes what it assumes, namely, the priority of government. By contrast, non-governability refers neither to a lack of discipline, nor to errancy. And it does not refer to disobedience; rather, it refers to that which remains radically *foreign* to commanding and obeying in both individuals and communities.

The non-governable is neither the opposite, nor a contradiction, of the logic of government. It is other. The other *to* (not *of*) government. The mark of its impossibility. The anarchist critique of government is not, in fact, a bias. It is not based on the idea that governing is "bad" but rather that governing is not possible. This impossibility is inscribed differently in the real, as a network with connections that are at once ontological, psychical, practical, artistic, and biological. Its landscapes are not those of a state of nature, nor of a space of uncontrolled outbursts of passion. Nor can they be summarized as a cartography of resistance. They correspond to regions of being and psyche that governing can neither reach or manage.

Faced with the ungovernable, with revolts, protests, and civil disobedience, there are two ways for a government to respond: either by negotiating and perhaps consenting to a change of politics, or with repression. In this sense, the ungovernable is that which can be either heard or dominated.

By contrast, the non-governable can only be dominated. The only way to treat it is not to negotiate with it, either by actively ignoring it, or by oppressing it, crushing it, even putting it to death. But governing it is definitively impossible since, to repeat, it is the mark of the impossibility and failure of all government.

Recent spontaneous popular protest movements make it difficult to distinguish confidently the part in them that participates in the ungovernable and the part that is non-governable. The difference between the two is not a prior given. There is no clear line between disobedience and that which is a stranger to obedience. Hence the difficulty experienced by political parties, unions, and the media in identifying and categorizing these movements. The non-governable sits right at the border that separates it from the ungovernable. A fragile demarcation.

Yet this line is precisely what marks the distinction between de facto anarchism and dawning anarchism. As Foucault demonstrated so effectively in *The Birth of Biopolitics*,[57] anarcho-capitalism certainly calls into question the intervention of state and government in the market, but, for all that, it remains a *profoundly governed* ideology. Indeed, and this is what proves that it is no more than a branch of neoliberalism, anarcho-capitalism is still based on a confidence in "governability." Not the governability of institutions, but that of "transactional realities,"[58] the new governmentalities of "civil society."[59] Foucault clearly foresaw the moment when these "transactional realities" (for which the uberization of life today is the perfect expression) would determine new systems of regulation for economic subjects. In this sense, de facto anarchism, which is deaf to the question of the non-governable, remains an offshoot of the logic of government. For this reason, it has nothing to do with dawning anarchism.

*

If it is so difficult to shed light on it, how then can we draw out the non-governable? The only way is via contrast. The developments discussed in what follows, all of which are devoted to the philosophical dissociating of anarchy from anarchism, reveal the non-governable as that which is left out of discourse.

This book starts with a presentation of aporias in Aristotle's *Politics* that instigates a systematic analysis of each of the concepts of anarchy mentioned. Then, taking a sharp turn, the reading lays bare the counter-revolutionary part concealed in several philosophical texts, thereby suggesting the contours of a real alterity to the logic of government.

3

On the Virtue of Chorus Leaders
Archy and Anarchy in Aristotle's *Politics*

> Therefore we must say that the rulers and the ruled are the same, and in a sense different. So education too must necessarily be the same in a sense and in another different.[1]
>
> Aristotle

When contemporary philosophers emphasize the contingency of political order as described by Aristotle, they are not referring to the proper Aristotelian concept of contingency, which is the non-necessary. Aristotle defines politics as contingent inasmuch as it belongs to the shifting realm of human affairs. Despite this contingency, in this moving, versatile realm, politics has its own space, the "community of citizens," that endows it with a particular necessity and autonomy. Although the concept of *politeia* encompasses the plurality of different types of regimes in the empirical realm, it also refers to an ideal form, the form of the "best regime" (*aristē politeia*), which is the principle – *archē* – of all individual regimes. Due to its principled dimension, *politeia* is subject not only to descriptive but also to normative analysis. Politics is not simply a sphere of activity; it is also a science. This duality explains why Aristotle's *Politics* is composed of both "realist books" and "idealist books."[2]

Even if politics were not a branch of metaphysics, the legibility of politics derives from the primordial order whereby accidents obey substance. As Schürmann notes, for Aristotle, "individual ends and actions are ordered to those of the city, as accidents are to substance and, in general, predicates to the subject."[3] The *archē politikē* is thus ordered by the logical and ontological principle that controls the ordering of all things.

The contingency identified by contemporary philosophers is entirely distinctive and secretly undermines this necessity, ideality, and principleness due to the heteronormativity that they simultaneously conceal and reveal. This is how *anarkhia* appears as the collapse of order inscribed

25

in the heart of order. The collapse is visible in the interstices opened by the aporias in *Politics*.

The aporias of Aristotle's Politics

As Pierre Pellegrin puts it in the preface to his French translation of Aristotle's *Politics*, this foundational text of Western political philosophy is "hermeneutically unstable" because it is highly aporetic.[4] Scholars of Aristotle agree on its ambiguities, which are sometimes downright contradictions. These contradictions are partially due to misfortunes in the history of determining the text, which give rise to questions about the ordering of the books that editors tried to render coherent. Furthermore, the text was initially composed of notes taken by students, a fact that also explains some of the uncertainties associated with its current composition.[5]

But are the aporias of *Politics* merely circumstantial? Translator and commentator Pellegrin concedes that these uncertainties, which are "sometimes surprising in the work of a philosopher known for his commitment to matching language to things,"[6] cannot "be blamed on editorial accidents" alone.[7] He goes on to argue that "when we examine *Politics* closely, we are not so much confronted by *real problems* demanding *solutions* … as by *uncertainties* or what might be called 'undecidables.'"[8]

This observation in no way diminishes the seriousness of these "uncertainties." After all, these "undecidables" did no less than determine the fundamental decisions of Western political philosophy.

There are three major aporias in *Politics*, all of which are found in Book 3, the lynchpin of the work. As we know, an aporia is the presentation of two contradictory theses without a solution. The first aporia appears in Chapter 4 of Book 3: (a) by definition, all citizens are capable of both giving orders (*hegeomai*) and receiving orders (*hupakouo*); (b) only the "principle of the best" should preside over the choice of those who rule, so it turns out that some citizens are better than others at ruling.

The second aporia, found in Chapters 6 and 7 of Book 3, asserts that: (a) the governing body only ensures the exercise of power in an executive role; (b) *politeia* and *politeuma*, state sovereignty and forms of governing, are synonymous.

The third aporia concerns the subject matter of the book: which topics should receive priority? Which are most important: the "idealist" books (1–3) or the "realist" books (4–8)? Is it (a) the idealist conceptual books devoted to the best regime or "constitution," (b) the realist books that describe the different regimes and that outnumber the idealist chapters? This aporia stamps uncertainty on democracy: is the structure of democracy at one with the structure of the best regime? Or is democracy nothing but a particular governing body that has in fact proven to be one of the most defective?

First aporia: citizens, rulers, ruled

Aristotle defines the regime (*politeia*)[9] as "a certain arrangement of those who inhabit the city."[10] This arrangement is the *archē* that confers state sovereignty onto the city (*polis*).

Since *politeia* is defined in terms of *polis*, first and foremost (*prôtē skepsis*), the city must be studied. Of all the communities, the most eminent "is what is called the city or the political community."[11] Right from the beginning of Book 1, Aristotle tries to make clear the essential distinction between this political community and the domestic community organized around the power of the "master" as "head of the family" or "slave master."[12]

Second, and consequently, defining a city implies that "what the citizen is must be investigated."[13] What is a citizen? The city corresponds not only to geographical territory; likewise, the citizen is not only an inhabitant of the city: "nor is the citizen a citizen by inhabiting a place, for aliens and slaves share in the habitation."[14] Other exclusions from the city include "those who have been deprived of their prerogatives or exiled," who are thus "incomplete" citizens.[15] Aristotle is categorical in this regard: "We are seeking the citizen in an unqualified sense, one who has no defect of this sort requiring correction."[16]

The citizen "in an unqualified sense" is defined by the right to participate "in decision and office"[17] (*archē*), that is, to sit on both a jury and in the assembly (*ekklesiastes*), to thereby act in the administration of justice and to vote.[18] Aristotle distinguishes temporary offices, whether civil or military (where "the same person is not permitted to hold them twice"[19]), from "indefinite" offices (*aoristos archē*), specifically "that of juror or assemblyman."[20] "Whoever is entitled to share in an office [*archē*] involving deliberation or decision, is, we can now say, a citizen."[21] To the extent that any citizen possesses, and maintains for a lifetime, the right to participate in the deliberations of the assembly and to be re-elected as a member of a jury, all share in the *archē*, which thus appears as the sovereign authority (*tous kuriôtatous*) that today we would call the state.[22]

Archē, "command, authority, power," thus refers both to any specific public function ("office") and to the authority of the state as a whole, in which all active citizens participate.

However, there is another meaning of "power," namely, power *over* (*hegemonia*). *Archē* also belongs to the leader. Political order is all at once "order as arrangement" (*taxis*) and "order as command" (*epitaxis*), given order. On first glance, in the best regime the two forms of power coincide. Aristotle declares, "But there is also a sort of rule in accordance of which one rules those who are similar in stock and free. For this is what we speak of as political rule."[23] To rule people of the same stock as oneself implies also accepting their rule. The citizen only has power over others inasmuch as others have power over them, such that no one dominates anyone else.

All citizens are thus equally capable of ruling and obeying and demonstrate that they are endowed with both dispositions.

> The ruler learns it [how to rule] by being ruled – just as the cavalry commander learns by being commanded, the general by being led, and similarly in the case of the leader of a regiment or company. Hence, this too has been finely said – that it is not possible to rule well without having been ruled. Virtue in each of these cases is different, but the good citizen should know and have the capacity both to be ruled and to rule, and this very thing is the virtue of a citizen – knowledge of rule over free persons from both points of view.[24]

Greek citizenship, Derrida remarks, thus adopts "the alternating form of the *by turns*, the *in turn*, the *each in turn*," adopting the rhythm of a "circular or spherical rotation."[25]

Yet the topic of Chapter 4, which is "the virtue of the good man and the excellent citizen,"[26] is ambiguous. Having posited the circularity of giving and receiving commands, Aristotle then adds: "Both [aptitudes of ruling and being ruled] belong to the good man too."[27] How do we explain the appearance of this moral figure, "the good man," among the citizens? Why does the inquiry into citizenship take a sudden turn to become an inquiry into virtue (*arété*)? Because the problem of the capacity to govern is still not settled. Contrary to expectations, the circular definition of citizen did not exhaust the question.

Aristotle compares the city to a ship. Like a ship, the city is a unity. But also like the ship, it is governed by a diverse crew, in which each member exercises their own function (*ergôn*).

> Just as a sailor is one of a number of sharers, so, we assert, is the citizen. Although sailors are dissimilar in their capacities (one is a rower, another a pilot, another a lookout …), it is clear that the most precise account of their virtue will be that peculiar to each sort individually, but that a common account will in a similar way fit all.[28]

Sailors, who excel in their individual functions, all pursue the same end, namely, a safe crossing. Yet each of them has a circumscribed role: some work the machines, others maintain the ship, still others are in the kitchen.

Likewise, citizens also pursue the common goal that is the preservation of *politeia*, starting from individual excellence. Each citizen offers the community different services appropriate to individual talents. For this reason, citizens see the whole only from a partial perspective. Hence, Aristotle concludes: "That it is possible for a citizen to be excellent yet not possess the virtue in accordance with which he is an excellent man, therefore is evident."[29] The virtue of the good man is not circumscribed by any specific function; it exists in all circumstances. This is why Aristotle insists that "in absolute terms, the virtue of the excellent man is different from the virtue of the excellent citizen … It is possible to possess the excellence of the good citizen even as one is without the excellence of the virtuous man."[30]

One virtue is indivisible into specific types: prudence (*phronesis*).[31] From this virtue, Aristotle returns to the question of the exercise of power. Ultimately, he demonstrates that the ideal ruler is the good man, the prudent (*phronimos*) man. The aporia becomes glaringly apparent: "We assert that the excellent ruler is good and prudent, while the excellent citizen is not necessarily prudent."[32] From which we are led to believe that only one category of citizens – the "prudent" ones – are apt to rule:

> Prudence is the only virtue peculiar to the ruler. The others, it would seem, must necessarily be common to both rulers and ruled, but prudence is not a virtue of one ruled, but rather true opinion: for the one ruled is like a flute maker, while the ruler is like a flute player, the user [of what the other makes].[33]

Prudence thus stamps a seal of irreversibility onto the circularity that initially bound rulers and ruled. Prudence is not only the art of deliberating in a critical situation, but also the ability to decide on the rule of deliberation. To be prudent, that is, excellent, in the art of commanding requires knowing how to determine the rule and give orders (*epitaxis*) according to the choice of rule. This is the meaning of the flute-maker metaphor. The flute-maker knows how to make flutes and why he does so. By contrast, the one who receives orders does not choose the rule of his obedience. He does not command his obedience. He follows the order, he plays, but he does not make the flute. Due to the reliability of his upright opinion, the ruled citizen knows the rule but does not invent it. Thus, "the man who follows the good path without seeing it walks blindly: he does not direct himself; he does not decide on his life course … He is guided by a sort of natural instinct, as if he were on a leash by another person: his temperance derives from his temperament."[34]

The aporia regarding the question of whether the aptitude to command is the reserve of some, or whether it is shared by all, is developed over the course of several chapters that serve only to emphasize, through successive reversals, its undecidable nature. Aristotle begins, therefore, by claiming that the citizen's relation to commanding and obeying is circular. He then states that the virtue of the citizen and that of the good man are different. Yet in Chapter 18 he still states that he has established that they are the same: "In our earlier discourses it was shown that the virtue of man and citizen is necessarily the same in the best city."[35] In Book 7, he concludes that education resolves the problem, since both "excellences" of rule and being ruled, that is, of being a good man, can be learned. If first one is ruled, "later" one can become a ruler: "The legislator would have to make it his affair to determine how men can become good and through what pursuits, and what the end of the best life is."[36] However, educating to obey and educating to rule do not require the same skills. Aristotle therefore concludes: "In one sense, therefore, we must say that the rulers and the ruled are the same, and in another sense different."[37] A circular argument if ever there was one.

Second aporia: "regime" and "governing body" as synonyms

In Chapters 6 and 7 of Book 3, Aristotle posits that regime (*politeia*) and governing body (*politeuma*) are synonymous, even though the previous chapters rigorously distinguish between the two terms. The "community of citizens in a regime"[38] (*koinonia politon politeias*) or state sovereignty was clearly placed above the exercise of governmental authority and was distinct from it. Yet Aristotle now states: "The governing body is the regime."[39] And: "'regime' and 'governing body' signify the same thing … the governing body is the authoritative element in cities."[40]

It might be objected that this synonymy between state and governing body is not, in fact, aporetic at all given the fact that, for Aristotle – the first thinker to introduce the concept of *politeuma* into political philosophy – "governing body" refers to the organization of powers within the state, that is, the ordering (*taxis*) of different offices. The governing body is thus legitimately involved with sovereign power. Even today, the term "regime" involves the governing body understood as an instance of distribution of power. Aristotle asserts that whatever the regime, the distribution should consist of three parts:

> Of these three things, one is the part that is to deliberate about common matters; the second, the part connected with offices – that is, which offices there should be, over what matters they should have authority, and in what fashion the choice of persons to fill them should occur; and the third, the adjudicative part.[41]

These "three parts" correspond to the bouleutic, archic, and dicastic powers. The governing body must therefore be understood as having a legislative function since, again, it organizes the distribution of sovereign authority.

However, as we have seen, governing body also refers to *archē*, understood as executive power, hegemony. Aristotle develops this point immediately after presenting the "three parts" necessary for any regime. The question of exercising power is introduced by a set of discussions about how, in fact, the three parts are organized internally: "How many? For how long? How often? Where? Within which group? Who? How?"[42] All these questions invariably lead to an investigation into not only the criteria for a just sharing of political authority[43] but also – and this is the critical question – *who* has the capacity to rule and what relation exists between ruling and being ruled. The executive meaning of the governing body thus renders problematic the synonymy between *politeia* and *politeuma*.

In previous chapters, the investigation of the virtues necessary to rule (Chapter 3) and the role of the "lawgiver"[44] or nomothete (Chapter 4), laid the groundwork for an investigation into the executive role of the governing body. In fact, it is in the moment of transition between presenting the governing body understood as an organizing instance and presenting it as command or hegemony that, in retrospect, the question of the difference between those who rule and those who are ruled assumes its full meaning.

The aporia thus relates to the status of the synonymy between state sovereignty and the exercise of power in the archic paradigm. Should this connection be construed as continuous? If so, then there is only a minimal difference between sovereign authority and governing authority, a difference that ensues from imperatives to spatialize power. This difference is comparable to the different rooms in a house. Or should this connection be construed as a safety valve? The exercise of governing power would then fill in a blank within sovereign authority since citizens are not all able to occupy any given office, and still less, able to rule. In the conflictual space opened up by the synonymy between *politeia* and *politeuma*, the legislative and executive meanings of governing body clash: the equality required by the legislative is replaced by the implicit hierarchy of the executive. Collective sovereign authority gives way to the emergence of a *ruling class*.

Third aporia: the subject of *Politics*

The second aporia leads to the third: what is the subject of *Politics*? Is it the "best regime"[45] or is it the different types of particular regimes? Is it a study of sovereign authority or an inquiry into the ruling class? Which ruling class are we talking about? All the people, some of the people, or one person? Democracy, oligarchy, or monarchy?

We recall that *politeia* refers to both a general and a particular regime. This dual meaning explains the ambivalence of Aristotle's treatise. The work is composed of eight books split into two distinct moments. Books 1–3 examine regime from the point of view of the fundamental concepts of "city," "citizen," "excellent man," "archon," and "nomothete" while Books 4–8 are devoted to studying different regimes or "constitutions." The ambiguity arises from the question of which section should be given priority.

Right at the beginning of Book 3, Aristotle defines the task of the political philosopher: "to investigate the regime(s) [*peri politeias*]."[46] *Politeias* can be an accusative plural. In this case, the sentence would read: "The first thing that must be investigated relates to *the regimes.*" And if this is the case, the books on "concepts," which establish the definition of the *polis* and the criteria of citizenship, are secondary to those comparing different types of regimes. *Politics* would therefore have a similar goal to *The Athenian Constitution*, in which Aristotle examines in detail the different forms of constitutional regimes.[47]

But *politeias* can also be a genitive singular, which would imply that it be read as: the first thing that must be investigated is "*the regime.*" In this case, the first books are the core of the subject and the investigation into types of regime becomes secondary. If the phrase is read as a genitive, as is usually the case, then *politeia* refers to the community of citizens in general, rather than any given political regime or constitution. An excellent regime is one in which "all the citizens fulfill their tasks excellently."[48] In other words, the excellent constitutional regime is the transcendental form of all political community irreducible to any given type of governing body.

So, what does it mean for citizens to "fulfill their tasks excellently"? We have seen that it involves sitting on a jury and participating in the assembly as well as possessing equally both the ability to rule and the disposition to obey. If such is the case, the "excellent regime" coincides with democracy. The transcendental form of the regime is the democratic form. Indeed, Aristotle sometimes uses *demokratia* in place of *politeia*.[49]

On the other hand, if the primary subject of the treatise is an examination of all regimes, democracy loses its transcendental status. The excellent regime, defined in the "conceptual" chapters, then appears as a principle that is more or less mismanaged by the reality of the different political regimes, including the democratic regime. Each regime has its "right" form. In this sense, there is something of the excellent regime in every specific type of regime. But each regime also has a deviant form and therefore there is only a little – and sometimes very little – of the excellent regime in each of them. Democracy is one of the regimes containing the least transcendental democracy.

The aporia that concerns the subject of the book ultimately relates also to the status of democracy. On the one hand, Aristotle presents democracy as an ideal form of constituent power:

> Election to all offices from among all the citizens; rule of all over each, and of each over all in turn; having all offices chosen by lot, or those not requiring experience and art; having offices not based on any assessment, or based on the smallest possible; the same person not holding any office more than once, or doing so rarely, or in few cases, apart from those relating to war; having all offices of short duration, or those where this is possible; having all adjudicate or persons chosen from all, and concerning all matters or most, and these the greatest and most authoritative (for example, concerning audits, or the regime, or private transactions); the assembly having authority over all matters or the greatest, and no office having authority over any, or having it over as few as possible.[50]

On the other hand, Aristotle describes it as one of the worst regimes due to the abuse of power of the majority over the minority, and as a regime in which the poor impose their law on the rich, who have birth and wealth: The "majority ... on the basis of number ... will act unjustly by confiscating the property of the rich few."[51] In this case, democracy is no longer the pure expression of equality, nor is it the reversibility of ruling and being ruled. The poor are now the ones ruling. The dissymmetry between commanding and obeying thus appears in every type of regime.

If, in the end, the main subject of *Politics* is the investigation into particular regimes according to their history, geographic roots, right and deviant forms, then the irreversibility of ruling and being ruled, rulers and ruled, is an inescapable reality within the ideal.

Politics and domination, the return of oikonomia

What is the effect of these aporias on the solidity of the archic paradigm? Scholars usually mention these ambiguities in Aristotle's work without according any real importance to them. For them, the archic paradigm is intact. Despite the "uncertainties" of the text, Aristotle supposedly revealed the foundations of the *archē politikē*, defined the excellent regime, and demonstrated how it was present in the right form of particular regimes despite significant empirical variation. According to these readings, like any self-respecting Greek philosopher, Aristotle is of course hesitant about the status of democracy, but ultimately the logical connection between state sovereignty, governing body understood as the distribution of offices, and governing body understood as the exercise of power is flawless. The aporias in no way tarnish the force of *archē*.

But there is another interpretation, one in which the wavering elements, the indecision, the aporias of *Politics* are intrinsic to the archic paradigm, revealing the fragility of its edifice. An anarchic threat inevitably lodged in the core of *archē*. This threat is connected to the first aporia, from which the other two aporias follow: the impossibility of maintaining the reversibility and circularity of ruling and obeying.

It is as if *archē politikē* must always return to what it dismisses, *oikonomia*, the law of the house or domestic economy, in order to establish this fateful impossibility. Indeed, the dissymmetry and irreversibility of ruling and obeying finds its first structure in domesticity. In the end, it is domesticity that imposes its form on the concept of governing body – a ruling that then becomes difficult to rigorously separate from "natural" domination.

In the earliest books of *Politics*, Aristotle certainly asserts strongly that *archē politikē* is irreducible to *archē despotikē*, domestic power, defined as follows: "There are three parts of the art of household management

– mastery ..., paternal rule, and marital rule."[52] Why question this clear-cut distinction?

It appears irrevocable: the master of the house rules but does not have to obey. The two functions are perfectly separate for him. In the domestic economy, the subordination of those who obey is constant precisely because it is irreversible.[53] The master gives orders which he does not necessarily know how to obey: "There is rule of a master, by which we mean that connected with the necessary things. It is not necessary for the ruler to know how to perform these, but only to use those who do."[54] There is no need for the master to know how to execute the lowly tasks he orders his slave to complete for him. Domestic domination is absolute: he who rules has no need to obey; conversely, those who obey cannot rule.

Unlike the master, the ruling citizen does not rule to rule; he must also know how to obey. He does not obey to obey since he can learn to rule.[55] The city is not, therefore, anything like a family; instead, it is a community of free men.

However, when he presents the different functions of citizens within the city-ship, differentiating them from the prudence that is the reserve of the excellent man, Aristotle refers to domestic power as a model, thereby preparing the thesis on the inevitability of political subordination. He writes:

> For if it is impossible for a city to consist entirely of excellent persons, yet if each should perform his own task well, and this [means] out of virtue, since it is impossible for all the citizens to be similar, there would still not be a single virtue of the citizen and the good man.[56]

We are already familiar with this line of reasoning. Aristotle goes on: "Further, since the city is made up of dissimilar persons ... the virtue of all the citizens is necessarily not single, just as that of a head and file leader in a chorus is not single."[57] We might think that the difference between the chorus leader and a member of the chorus is precisely reversible – the chorus member could always try to become chorus leader one day, since the leader must have started by being a member of the chorus. But the circularity is immediately interrupted. There really is a difference between chorus leader and chorus member: "As an animal is made up of soul and body, for instance, soul of reason and appetite, and a household of man and woman and master and slave," so a chorus is composed of a leader and its members: "In the same way a city is made up of all of these."[58]

The dissymmetry between the ruling and the ruled is thus ultimately reduced to a series of subjectivations, the last of which (the subordination of slave to master) is particularly significant. *Archē despotik* – initially excluded from the political scene – now serves as a tool for explaining unequal aptitudes. Inequality becomes the instrument for legitimizing the order and the direct transition between factual hierarchy and political hierarchy. The dissymmetry between ruling and ruled is justified by an implicit theory of governability: to be governable is to be naturally destined to obey, it is to be the somatic instance of the political psyche, the city's help, if you like.

After being initially excluded, *oikoinomia*, the law of the house, intervenes here to naturalize *archē politikē*. The heteronormativity of *archē*, which is simultaneously political and domestic, also defines its solidity and vulnerability, along with its anarchy.

Accounting for this an-archic element is the central theme of some of the most significant contemporary philosophical interpretations of the Western political *archē*. I turn now to a discussion of these readings.

4

Ontological Anarchy
Traveling from Greece to the Andes with Reiner Schürmann

Deconstruction is to set free ... an origin less compromised by command and domination.[1]

A cessation of principles, a deposing of the very principle of epochal principles and the beginning of an economy of passage, that is, of anarchy.[2]

Reiner Schürmann

Anarchy, metaphysics, and "deconstruction"

If politics depends on the logical and ontological development of *archē*, and thereby reveals its constitutive heteronormativity, then the anarchic dimension of metaphysics must also be elucidated. This elucidation is the core of Reiner Schürmann's most important work, *Heidegger on Being and Acting: From Principles to Anarchy*. Over the course of a unique trajectory that was prematurely interrupted, Schürmann developed a significant analysis of the structural relation that has always existed between anarchy and philosophy.[3]

Schürmann's *From Principles to Anarchy* threads together the Aristotelian *archē*, an interpretation of its deconstruction by Heidegger, and anarchy as a political question in a systematic analysis.

Schürmann claims that, as a whole, metaphysics stands upon an "ontological anarchy," which it represses but in which it ultimately expires. This belated withering, marking the last moments of what Heidegger thought of in terms of history of being,[4] arises when all the principles that ruled this historical era decline, gradually, one after another, evacuating all meaning from the idea of principle: "The destiny of metaphysics is, throughout, the destiny in which principles wither away."[5]

While political anarchism dates back to the late nineteenth century, ontological anarchy is a twentieth-century phenomenon. As Schürmann put it: "It is in the epochal constellation of the twentieth century that the ancient procession and legitimation of *praxis* from *theōria* comes to exhaustion. Then, in its essence, action proves to be an-archic."[6] The question of anarchy appears at the very moment when "action" and, more generally, *praxis*, can no longer be legitimized by *archē*.

Paradoxically, anarchy becomes a concept when it ceases to be "theoretical": "Anarchy … does not become operative as a concept until the moment when the great sheet of constellations that fix presencing in constant presence folds up, closes in on itself."[7] Anarchy as *praxis* should not, however, be confused with "anarchism." Throughout his work, Schürmann maintains a rigorous distinction between anarchy and anarchism. The future liberated by "deconstruction" cannot be anarchist given that, despite its revolutionary extremism, anarchism too must be entirely deconstructed, since it cannot mask its belonging to metaphysics and, therefore, the paradox of its subordination to *archē*.

But are we sure that ontological anarchy borrows nothing from political anarchism? At the very least, doesn't it take its name from it? To describe Heideggerian deconstruction as a "principle of anarchy"[8] is a bold philosophical gesture, but where does this concept of anarchy, which is not present in Heidegger, come from? How can Schürmann develop it while setting aside any reference to anarchism?

Critiques of anarchism

From Principles to Anarchy contains three critiques of anarchism. The first, mentioned above, denounces the assumed bond of anarchist thought to metaphysics. We recall Schürmann's statement:

> Here it will not be a question of anarchy in the sense of Proudhon, Bakunin, and their disciples. What these masters sought was to *displace* the origin, to substitute the "rational" power, *principium*, for the power of authority, *principes* – as metaphysical an operation as has ever been. They sought to replace one focal point with another.[9]

Ontological anarchy posits that any "answer" to the question "What should I do?" is pointless, for to answer would again be to invoke an *archē*, an explanatory principle.

But this does not imply that ontological anarchy is a mere utopia. This is the second critique of anarchism, for the idea of utopia is also owned by metaphysics. The relation between metaphysics and deconstruction has nothing to do with the contrast Thomas More makes between "the England of Henry VIII" and "the blissful isle of Nowhere."[10] Schürmann responds:

> Here, the answer has to follow the same line as my earlier remark regarding anarchists: Utopianism, whether conceived as the theory of the perfect city or as the philosophy of history attaining its future culmination in some universal harmony, is as "metaphysical" as theoretical anarchism. In either case, political thinking consists in weighing the advantages and drawbacks of one theory or another.[11]

Moreover, there is "nothing of the kind" here.[12] Indeed, "utopia is the most fanciful and imaginary instance of the substantialist relation to the One."[13]

The third critique of anarchism follows from the previous one: even if not a utopia, ontological anarchy offers no response either to the practical "criteria" invoked "by Proudhon (the substitution of science for man's domination of man) or Bakunin ('spontaneous life,' 'passion,' the 'revolt of life against science')."[14]

The sole authority, then, capable of legitimating the concept of anarchy is "a concept of phenomenological ontology. It has nothing to do with the ancient debate about the best form of governing: the three forms traditionally judged good, monarchy, aristocracy, and democracy and their respective perversions, tyranny, oligarchy, and anarchy."[15] Ontological anarchy has nothing to do with a debate about regimes: "To confuse the amalgam of these three perversions – the anarchy of power – with [ontological …] anarchy is to be mistaken about the starting point, the method, and the result of the phenomenology of reversals in presencing."[16]

This phenomenology makes evident the fact that "the principle of cohesion, be it authoritarian or 'rational,' is no longer anything than a blank space deprived of legislative, normative power. Anarchy expresses a destiny of decline, the decay of the standards to which Westerners since Plato have related their acts and deeds in order to anchor them there and to withdraw them from change and doubt."[17]

These three critiques of anarchism do not, however, lead Schürmann to depoliticize anarchy. On the contrary, he claims that, "with the turning [of the closure], a certain way of understanding the political becomes impossible and another way becomes inevitable."[18] Action henceforth suspended in the void is political in an entirely new sense that our transitional era is just beginning to envisage.

This new meaning can only appear on the horizon of a radical meditation on principle, which alone enables the discerning of its practical stakes.

Anarchy and meditation on principle

What is a principle? In Book 5 of *Metaphysics*, Aristotle declares that a principle or "'beginning' means that part of a thing from which one would start first … It is common … to all beginnings to be the first point that either is or comes to be or is known."[19]

The beginning principle is "that from which" or "that starting from which" something is what it is. To meditate on principle is thus first and foremost to think about the places of origin. All things have their *hoten*, that from which they come, "as the keel of a ship and the foundation of a house, while in animals some suppose the heart, others the brain."[20] This is what seemingly renders all anarchy vain. If everything has a source, then nothing is anarchic.

The problem is that source and beginning are not one and the same. The proper philosophical understanding of the "that from which" immediately transforms antecedence into priority and superiority. For Aristotle, that which sources begins and that which begins commands. A temporal hiatus – the gap between coming before and coming after – becomes hierarchical. That which comes before has authority over that which comes after. The philosophical history of sources is thus confused with the genesis of government. "Intelligibility and authority are … structurally as well as genetically identical."[21]

On Aristotelian teleocracy

Traditional thinking on action borrowed from early philosophy the concept of a beginning "to which the multiple can be referred and thus be made true and verified. Likewise, in order that there be action and not merely activities there must be a first that provides action with sense and direction."²² Aristotle presents the paradigmatic form of "boss," literally *archē*, in "metaphysics as logic," defining the relation of substance to its predicates "according to the attributive πρὸς ἕν [*pros hen* ...] relation."²³ "The *archē* always functions in relation to action as substance functions in relation to its accidents."²⁴ The attributive relation is thus the archetype of power.

To explain the relation of substance to accident, Aristotle

> compares the constitution of a principle for action to an army in full retreat, propelled by fear, but in which first one, then several soldiers stop, look to the rear where the enemy is approaching and regain their courage. The entire army does not stop because two or three master their fear, but suddenly it obeys orders again and the activities of each become again the action of all. Aristotle views command (*archē*) imposing its order on the runaways just as he views substance, as *archē*, imposing its unity upon the accidents.²⁵

There is, therefore, an isomorphism between metaphysics and politics, between ontology and military command.²⁶ Schürmann posits that this dual relation forms an economy. The *oikos* is not only the law of the house, the headquarters of *archē despotikē* from which *archē politikē* secretly draws its model, but the place of a more extensive heteronormativity, a composition of meaning and facts that bears witness to all that Aristotle had to assemble and force into it in order to produce the philosophical meaning of *archē*. *Archē* proceeds then from "a group of premises foreign to their domain of application."²⁷

"How much of genuine attention to the phenomena and how much metaphysical construction is there in the Aristotelian notion of *archē*?"²⁸ Schürmann argues further that, since the time of Homer,

> the common meaning of the verb ἄρχειν had been "to lead," "to come first," "to open," for instance a battle or a discourse. In the epic tradition, ἀρχή [*archē*] designates what is at the beginning, either in an order of succession in time, like childhood, or in an order of constitutive elements, as flour is the basis of dough or as the organs are the elementary parts of the body. The other meaning, that of command, power, domination, although absent in Homer,

is found in Herodotus and Pindar. Aristotle also uses the word in this sense. But the Aristotelian innovation consists in uniting the two senses, inception and domination, in the same abstract concept.[29]

By melding the two meanings of beginning and commanding into an indissoluble unit, Aristotle projects the horizontal properties of space and time onto the incline of ontological hierarchies. Henceforth, to precede in time and space means to overlook and subordinate.

The logical reason for the dissymmetry between those who govern and those who are governed is therefore as follows: the distance between subject and predicate is not a straight line; rather, it slopes. The predicating form (S is P) is defined by Aristotle as a slope, whereby "'*enklisis*' means to fall, to incline."[30] Attribution is the leaning of substance, which determines an order for start and end. The subject of the proposition is a promontory, the relief (*exogè*) that accidents and predicates run up against. They are not added to the substance from the outside: rather, they *come* from it: "Aristotle's proposition is that when *logos* is organized around the distinction within it of subject and predicate, especially when the 'slope' of such a *logos* is indicative [S is P], the thing thus being said by it … is as if it came from it."[31]

This declivity is the origin of governability. The relation of the general to his soldiers, just like that of the governing to the governed, is the objective translation of the predicative relation, which affixes the *pros hen* schema in relation to power.[32] Predicates and accidents stoop before the instance from which they are derived.

It is not enough to critique the "governmental prejudice" on its own account. It must be acknowledged that governmental subordination is first and foremost the tracing of a logical and ontological oblique that signals the complicity of thought and domination.

In the archic paradigm that articulates the relation between sovereignty and government, everything lies on a slope. Let's start with cause. Principle draws its power from the causal relation it institutes between premises and consequences: "The alliance between the notions of inception and domination is possible *only once the metaphysics of causes is constituted*."[33] It is from the overlook from which its effects derive that the causal principle destines things to endlessly traverse the distance that both separates them and brings them closer to themselves.

This causal provenance necessarily corresponds to the orientation toward the end. *Archē* assumes the teleological organization of the causal regime, which explains why the archic paradigm is a "teleocracy": "*Telos* 'reigns,' 'commands' and therefore exercises the function of *archē*."[34] *Archē* and *telos* appear "in their strange mutual identification."[35] Strange indeed, since *archē* is inception and *telos* completion. In reality, as origin, "the *telos* 'does not put an end to the thing; rather out of [the *telos*] the thing begins to be what, after production, it will be."[36] The thing begins to be only once it is oriented toward its end. Moving toward its own being, it cannot deviate from its trajectory. The thing is thus condemned to its completion, falling down toward it. For Schürmann, teleocracy has reigned uninterrupted throughout the history of metaphysics.

The articulation of *archē* and *telos* conforms to the schema of production, to a certain relation between *praxis*, *poiesis*, and *tekhnē*.[37] Schürmann reminds us that Heidegger demonstrated that "theoretical teleocracy" comes from a reflection on the indissoluble link that brings these three domains together. The end of a thing, its completion, is thought through the model of work, a product. This explains the privileging of examples of the artist and artisan in the ontological explanation of provenance and destination.[38] Coming into being – birth, growth, becoming – is construed in terms of a production schema, including for living beings. "The field of phenomena to which causality is appropriate … its home territory,"[39] are manufactured beings. The transition from potentiality to actuality, even entelechy, is governed by poetic reason. Why? Because "the view set on the *eidos* is 'dominated' by the '*telos*' for as long as the latter is not achieved, as long as it lies ahead to be pursued."[40] Like a work, being is never anything but being toward an end.

The articulation of the different values of the oblique explains how "the legitimation of the city in relation to its constituents [the different magistratures] is gained by substantialist criteria that belong properly to the analysis of fabrication. It is in making things that all acts of the artisan, all materials and 'accidents,' must be directed 'toward the one' [*pros hen*], that is, the finished work."[41] Thus, kings, magistrates, and governors are, first and foremost, architects: "Magistrates, kings, and tyrants are named under the same rubric as the architectonic arts."[42] The archic paradigm is an architecture in the true sense of the word, for, in a single edifice with its sloping walls, it holds together the attributive schema, the concept of cause (*aitia*), the teleocratic link, the techno-poetic schema, and political hegemony.

From archē *to* principium

This architectural supremacy endures throughout the metaphysical tradition, adopting a different form for every era. The "incessant internal rearrangements"[43] of *archē* are proof both of the force of its continuity and of its fissuring, namely the decrepitude of its occurrences. Initially, anarchy appears as the phenomenon of return, both ontological and political, that architecture suffers at the end of an era. This phenomenon is all the more paradoxical in that each time, moving from one metaphysical age to the next, *archē* seems to become more solid.

Schürmann offers the example of the shift from Greek *archē* to Latin *principium*. The concept of *principium* is developed "from Cicero to Leibniz"[44] and already, in medieval ontology and particularly with Duns Scotus, finds its guiding meaning, prefiguring the principle of reason:

> In the phrase *principium rationis sufficientis*, it is not the word *principium* that translates ἀρχή [*archē*]; it is the word *ratio*: "nothing is without reason," *nihil est sine ratione*. The "principle of reason" then seems to amount to a simple tautology: "principle of ἀρχή [*archē*]" "principle of the principle." From the ἀρχή [*archē*] as primordial element constitutive of sensible substances, we have passed to *principium* as evident proposition from which other propositions derive that are not evident themselves. Leibniz is telling us of a proposition about the *archē*: everything, he says, has a principle (understood as *archē*), such is my great principle (understood as first and evident proposition).[45]

On the one hand, then, the transformation of *archē* into principle, and from principle into principle of the principle, reinforces the architecture of the paradigm. By doubling itself, *archē* becomes a hyper-principle, governor supreme, the medieval *Deus Pantocrator*: "The domain from which the medievals understand the origin is no longer man-made change, but *gubernatio mundi*, the government the supreme entity exercises over things."[46] With the updating of the principle of reason, this authority becomes the "ground upon which is based, hereafter, all certitude and all truth."[47] The principle – all the power of rationality

– thus establishes its ontological and political empire (*imperium*): "The metaphysic of principle ... invests the origin as a *princeps*, prince and governor."[48]

On the other hand, a heightened fragility produces a crack in this increase in solidity. Certainly, the principle of the principle obeys nothing and no one. This is equally evident in politics. In his article "Legislation-transgression," Schürmann takes the later example of Machiavelli: "The Machiavellian prince thus binds others but remains unbound himself. Should he commit himself to his prescripts, he would no longer be master. For a type of will to be strong, it must legislate for others, for the 'herd,' but not for itself."[49] Yet it is precisely here that the crack emerges: the hyper-principle is, of necessity, beyond principle.

Since it has no principle, the principle is destined to leave its own field. Theology already demonstrated this: "The world is ordered toward God, but God is not part of that order. He is not ordered toward the world. He is eminent, that is, heterogenous to the order whose principle he is."[50] The ever-steeper incline expels the principle from itself. Becoming a hyper-principle, it moves away from its subordinates and loses itself as it moves higher, becoming the principle of nothing, prince of no one.

As Stanislas Breton puts it in reference to Schürmann, the meditation on principle is a "continual return to that which shows through the principle in the very game of the question that always returns."[51] The question is the following: is the principle to be found in what it is the principle of, or outside it? Has the correct distance between principle and what is derived from it ever been metaphysically established? The fissure is found right there, in the heart of the problem of the difference between the principle and the principled. If it is too distant, the principle leaves its field, losing its meaning by becoming estranged from what is derived from it. If it is too close, too equal to its derivative, too democratic, then it also loses its aspect as principle.

Let us return for a moment to the Aristotelian definition of principle. "It is common then to all beginnings to be the first point from which a thing is or comes to be or is known; but of these some are immanent [*enuparkousai*] in the thing and others are outside [*ektos*]."[52] This seemingly simple statement (some beings have their principle within them, others, such as manufactured objects, have it outside themselves), contains the seed of the antinomy of principle. The principle is by necessity linked in some way to the things of which it is the principle, otherwise it would not be their principle. It must form a logical, ontological, political community with them. But it must also differ radically from them if it does not wish to become assimilated with things over which it has command. Having to be both at the same time, the principle cannot be either within or without that of which it is the principle.

Principle – of nothing

Archē lost power because it was constituted from an abuse of power that is now exploding in the raw light of day. No longer can hyper-principality mask the fact that there never was a "pure" principle, a radical beginning without contradiction. As we have seen, this is the case because, on the one hand, the Aristotelian meaning of *archē* is an assemblage and, on the other, this assemblage of beginning-command condemns the principle to being either too far from, or too close to, that which it governs. There has never been a pure rule, an imperative sufficiently authoritarian to mask its own contingency and settle the correct distance between governing and governed.

Order in metaphysics is determined not by leaders, but rather by "forms of domination."[53] It is not first and foremost the archons who hold power, but, rather, the "codes."[54] It is not primarily the citizens who obey, but, rather, "things, actions and words."[55] Assemblies and conceptual bricolage are the true principles of principles. Governors, laws, decisions, and acts all draw their authority from the constellation or economy of the presence of that to which they belong, which organizes itself every time around a center devoted to anarchic dissolution.

It is striking that Schürmann also describes the constitution of the archic paradigm – that inclined slope of governability – as *theft*. He writes:

> From the genealogical perspective, the historical constellations of entities appear as orders arranged under an ordering first. But once the phenomenological gaze moves back from the quality and interplay of things present toward their presencing, the line of descent in which these constellations were put into place by figures of an epochal first proves to have itself sprung from an initial concealment.[56]

The Aristotelian conceptualization of *archē* harbors – that is, both purloins and dissimulates – the anarchic element of its own provenance by transforming it into absolute beginning and command.

The distinction between Schürmann's harboring and Proudhon's theft soon becomes evident, however. From Schürmann's perspective as a philosopher, property is firstly what is proper, that is, the way in which the identity of things has been philosophically assigned to them by stripping them of their originary consistency. Far from being the "mythical source of all things,"[57] the origin does not begin, is articulated with no end, and has command over nothing: "The pair of notions *archē-telos* does not comprise the entire phenomenon of origin."[58] Ontological property, like material property, thus proceeds from an obscuring of the source. But Schürmann claims – and in this lies his critique of anarchism – that deconstruction of the proper has priority over the abolition of private property.

The emergence of anarchy as a political question

For Schürmann, to accord this type of priority does not obliterate, but rather liberates, the aspect and political future of ontological anarchy.

Once action is no longer dependent on *archē*, politics loses its obsession with the governmental: "The pair ἄρχειν-ἄρχεσθαι, to rule and be ruled, expresses quite clearly which thought pattern is bound to wither away at the end of metaphysics."[59] Consequently, Schürmann continues, "deconstruction is to set free … an origin less compromised by command and domination."[60] If the origin appears "'at bottom' … as an-archic" then "its patent expression, the political, will … be deprived of its foundation." And "if it appears without a principle, then the only principle of the political will be the principle of anarchy."[61]

The time of anarchy

Anarchy has several different times. There is the time of its momentary breakthroughs, that is, the reverse phenomena described above between two epochs of principles. There is the time of transition anarchy that typifies Heidegger's thought. Heidegger did not reach the anarchist conclusion up to "anti-principial … actions."[62] This is why his thought remains in an in-between space, "still implanted in the problematic of *τί τὸ ὄν* ('What is being?'), but already uprooting it from the schema of the *pros hen*, which was connate to that problematic … Still a principle, but a principle of anarchy."[63]

Lastly, there is the time of anarchy that lies ahead on the horizon of the definitive withering of principles after deconstruction. Schürmann does far more than constitute anarchy as a tool to read Heidegger; he also removes Heidegger from his position of master: "'Heidegger' … will take the place here of a certain discursive regularity. It will not be the proper name, which refers to a man from Messkirch, deceased in 1976."[64] This "regularity," this rule with which Heidegger finds himself associated here, is the thought of being. But Schürmann delocalizes this rule, taking the Heideggerian corpus "in a direction the man Martin Heidegger would not have wished to be led."[65] This "direction" is, of course, anarchy.

The coming anarchy is both the same as and other than the anarchy of previous eras. It is the same because it appears in "the place deserted by the successive representations of an unshakable ground,"[66] while "no new representation of a supreme entity is there to take over."[67] It is other because it opens the possibility of "going beyond the origin as *archē* and as principle … taking the keys of the field as one reclaims one's freedom."[68] We live in the era of emancipation of "liberties under principial surveillance."[69]

This emancipation elucidates the difference between politics and the political. If politics has no existence outside the archic paradigm, then the political is the anarchic form of community, that is, connection without subordination. Since the Greeks, and throughout Western history, the political has disappeared in politics. The "obverse" dimension of the political appears today through its "confusion."[70] Now, if the origin shows itself "'at bottom' … as an-archic, its patent expression, the political, will then be deprived of its foundation. If it appears without a principle, then the only principle of the political will be the principle of anarchy."[71]

So how exactly does Schürmann envisage the political meaning of anarchy? Two important reference points guide his political thinking: his readings of Plotinus and Foucault. Although it is powerfully original, the reading of Plotinus still evinces the influence of Heidegger, while the reading of Foucault is a sidestep if ever there was one.

Reading Plotinus: politics as event

The political is the phenomenological region in which "things, actions, and words enter into mutual presence."[72] A unity without an archon, without a prince, does therefore exist. This "One" is what Plotinus envisaged in its irreducibility to any archic, centralized, overseeing unity. "Henology" (literally *logos* of the One) is already the deconstitution of teleocracy.

In an article entitled "L'hénologie comme dépassement de la métaphysique,"[73] Schürmann demonstrates that although in Plotinus the One is often named "principle," it should not be equated with *archē*. However, Plotinus' thought was often interpreted as a radicalization of the Aristotelian concept, a supreme expression of the "transcendentalist" thesis. Plotinus considered that the *archē*, the principle, establishes its domination by keeping itself infinitely at a distance from that of which it is the principle: "Such is the received opinion of Neoplatonists: since the One transcends Intelligence and beings, it is 'above them.'"[74] According to this "opinion," the principle remains inaccessible to its derivatives. Or, as Schürmann puts it: "Henology proposes a metaphysics of radical transcendence."[75] Yet nothing could be more foreign to Plotinus' thinking than this debate between transcendence and immanence.

When Plotinus says that the One "is not," that it is not the principle of that which it is the principle, he is not simply positing a relation of distance; rather, he opens the space of ontological difference. The One is not – a being: "For negative henology, ontological difference separates the One from being."[76] However, difference is not hierarchy. The One thus conceived generates no "schema *pros hen*," determines no derivation. "It cannot be said of it that it does something, that it acts. If it unifies, that is not its act in the sense that thinking or speaking are the acts of a human substance, an agent."[77] Later we read: "Unification is not the act of the One, but the One is entirely unification."[78]

But what is unification without action? A unification that is neither beginning nor commanding? A unification that does not govern? Schürmann answers: "If the One is not a being (*mé on*) but rather being itself (*to einai*), then it must be understood as an event."[79] In light of the Heideggerian concept of *Ereignis* (appropriating event), Schürmann proposes an *event-based reading of the principle, that is, a reading of the principle that is not foundational*.[80] The event is that through which things hold together, adjust to one another, *horizontally*.

> An *archē*, a principle, is nothing in itself, is merely an ordering factor … As a principle of order, a differential principle among things, "it has not come, it is there! It is nowhere and there is nothing where it is!" The One is the factor through which all things coordinate and in the absence of which they disintegrate. It is their pure constellation, unifying the bricks in a house, the soldiers in an army, the cities in an empire. But far from holding the pinnacle of power, as a mode of phenomenal interaction, it is what is most tenuous, the most precarious.[81]

Negative henology "thwarts the collusion between what comes first and what functions as foundation."[82] In other words, *sometimes a principle does not command, sometimes a principle does not begin*. A principle can come first without dominating. Schürmann goes on to explain that if "the non-metaphysical notion of the One is difficult, that is because it calls for its dissociation from all causal representations."[83] The One is that through which things organize themselves amongst themselves, an ordering without orders given. The principle is thus neither outside, nor within, things, it is neither "transcendent" nor "immanent." This is a weakness only if the One is defined as the supreme cause. Not if it is thought of as an event, as the way in which the elements take shape in a whole, in which each thing finds its place, without obeying anyone, in one fell swoop: "Suddenly the anarchic economy."[84] Plotinus, the first anarchist.[85]

Ontology and politics finally meet in the place of anarchy when the question of a unification that is not dependent on government finds its answer in the event. It is the event that signals the possibility of coordinating individuals, a set of differing elements that assemble without a central authority.

Reading Foucault

Once the ontological provenance of the "governmental prejudice" is identified, once the idea of the correct distance from principle to principled has been deconstructed, once the hierarchy has been dismantled, Schürmann, as an avid reader of Foucault, can then also engage in a critique of governmentality by relating the event-based interpretation of the principle to the political dimension of anarchy.[86]

Following Foucault, Schürmann emphasizes the increasingly composite and multiform nature of political authority, signaling the dusk of sovereignty: "Michel Foucault has observed that the age of Kant is also the age where 'mobile, polymorphous, circumstantial techniques of power' begin to replace techniques confined to the hands of the sovereign alone."[87] Governmentality now fritters away to become a set of micro-procedures of control that undermine "the *archē*-metaphysical concept of power as something one possesses and eventually delegates" – a concept that shored up "all contract theories with their corollaries."[88]

Schürmann proposes an interpretation of the Foucauldian theme of experimentation of the transcendental developed in "What is enlightenment?"[89] Foucault writes: "The Kantian question was that of knowing what limits knowledge has to renounce transgressing, it seems to me that the critical question today has to be turned back into a positive one … The point, in brief, is to transform the critique conducted in the form of necessary limitation into a practical critique that takes the form of a possible transgression."[90] Thus, he continues: "This historico-critical attitude must also be an experimental one."[91]

Schürmann radicalizes this point. For him, the experimental attitude, the crossing of limits, is already at work in Kant's practical thought. To legislate is to impose order. But do we ever know the origin of the law? Doesn't it remain always undetermined?[92] So, if then it is imposed by a law incapable of explaining its origin, practical order remains secretly illegitimate. It therefore follows that the logic of governing – commanding and obeying – is destined to transgress itself.

On the one hand, command must sit above law, more authoritarian than any law since the origin of law is indeterminate: "Inasmuch as the nomothetical type remains above its laws, they are transgressed by that type as they are laid down. The simultaneous formal transgression of the imperatives by the imperator is even the condition for the validity of norms, for their being values. If he does not exceed his creations his will ceases to be normative."[93] On the other hand, obeying, "the counter-strategy of transgression in constructs of power-delegation,"[94] is also transgressive. Insofar as subjects delegate their power "voluntarily," they command their own submission. Their obedience is thus an act of sovereignty. Subjects command themselves to obey.

There is, therefore, command in obedience and obedience in command. In subjectifying themselves, individuals have always already governed their obedience and transgressed their governability by power. The practical determination of politics as Kant posits it tends toward its opposite, since "it cannot stop short of strengthening the counter-strategy towards 'direct democracy' within the strategies of representative democracy."[95] For Schürmann, Foucault clearly demonstrated that, one way or another, being a subject always amounts to "constituting oneself as a subject" and thus too, one way or another, "as an anarchist subject."[96]

Freed of a teleocratic understanding, freed too of "an epochal enclosure"[97] of the forms of domination that must be escaped,[98] the political finally locates its meaning between Plotinus and Foucault, born of the coming to light of the self-transgression of all commanding and obeying. Echoing the "experimental attitude" of Foucauldian critique, Schürmann produces a fine definition of anarchy as the "inception of experience."[99] The political reveals what politics conceals, the "without reason" – that is, the non-governable.[100]

"What should we do today?"

So why doesn't Schürmann ever cross the line that separates anarchy from anarchism? He does not do so because, as he puts it, "transgression does not denote here the passage beyond some closure, not some step across the line (*trans lineam*)."[101] Moreover, the question "What is the anarchy to come?" can never elicit a response worthy of anarchy. The freedom that emerges with the withering of principles is a strange freedom, one "that gives us little to choose, to will, to legislate, to ordain"[102] and that "has nothing to do with Aristotelian deliberative 'choice', Augustinian 'will divided against itself,' Kantian causality and 'moral self-determination,' or Sartrian 'fundamental choice in which I decide my being.'"[103] To say "I am an anarchist," to choose to say it, to want to say it, would contradict anarchy itself, transforming it into a position, hence into a new *archē*.

Double bind

But in the end, isn't this a way for Schürmann to disavow the subterranean anarchism of his approach? Starting with "borrowing" the term "anarchy" from the political tradition from which he is so keen to dissociate himself?

The strong argument he would use to counter this objection – as well as my systematic research into the secret hiding place of the disavowal of anarchism in philosophical thinking – is that a*narchy and anarchism are by necessity committed to mutual dissociation*. Indeed, anarchism is the ontic version of ontological anarchy. It is impossible to say "I am an anarchist" without contradiction, without obfuscating ontological difference. To identify as an anarchist or to try to expose what anarchism "is," annuls the very thing one is trying to identify and expose. If there "is" anarchism, it cannot be confused with the logic of disavowal and dissociation. Negative-heno-anarchy.

"The No is greater than the Yes."[104] Position and transgression coincide. The contemporary form of negative henology, its anarchy(ism), is the double bind, the "dual constraint."

> The phrase *double bind* was first coined in 1956 by Gregory Bateson, as far as I can tell. I am retaining the three formal traits by which Bateson characterizes this concept … : a primary injunction declaring the law; a secondary injunction declaring a counter-law, hence conflicting with the first; and lastly a tertiary injunction "prohibiting the victim from escaping from the field" constituted by the first two injunctions.[105]

The double bind – that is, a dual or contradictory injunction – jams the logic of governing and renders commanding and obeying simultaneously impotent. To obey a contradictory injunction such as "Be spontaneous" is immediately to disobey it. To command with a contradictory injunction is to be commanded by it since it cannot be obeyed. In some ways the dual constraint brings together the impossible autonomy of the Kantian subject and the suffering of the tragic hero, forever condemned to obey two conflicting laws. Indeed, the tragic hero stands "at the intersection of two transgressions."[106] Hence, at the intersection of two laws: "Whether he [Agamemnon] chooses to desert his commander's post or to disrupt his lineage, there remains no way out of the situation without incurring guilt."[107] Later Schürmann writes: "*A tragic denial is necessary if a univocal law is to be born* … The hero sees the laws in conflict. Then – this is the moment of tragic denial – he *blinds himself* toward one of them, keeping his *gaze fixed* on the other."[108]

The impossibility of calling oneself an anarchist does not contradict anarchism; it respects it. The dissociation between anarchy and anarchism forms this double bind ("be an anarchist"), which, in its impossible possibility, is a powerful weapon against the governmental prejudice. The double bind cannot be governed. In the end, the schism between ontological anarchy and political anarchism – which cannot coexist without gouging each other's eyes out – is the anarchist signature of Schürmann's *From Principles to Anarchy*.

Delegitimizing philosophy, disarming the contradictory injunction

Schürmann's conclusion is even more compelling in that he is careful not to constitute the double bind as principle. At the very moment where it seems he will definitively lock up political anarchism in the philosophical prison house of negativity, philosophy itself becomes anarchical.

Denouncing the danger that deconstruction become petrified by deconstruction itself, infinitely ensnared in the double bind, Schürmann announces that *deconstruction must be delegitimized*, that is, it must *delegitimize delegitimizing itself*. To finally become anarchist perhaps? The "two instances of legitimation" must be distinguished from one another: one that "establishes the legitimacy of a regulation of obedience"[109] (traditional philosophy), the other that, following a program of "exceeding metaphysics" is "deconstructive, repealing the principial representations on which inherited forms of regulation have rested."[110] It is not enough to identify the heteronormativity and self-transgression at work in the archic structure of metaphysics; this orientation gesture must also be stripped of all governmental authority. Indeed, "in his abandonment of any origin that commences and commands – of any standard as standerbefore, as θέσις or position – Heidegger proceeds as in an annulment. His revocation of the titles of rule so generously dispensed by metaphysics follows criteria … To cancel the juridic instruments of power having passed as legitimate for too long is again to bring legal jurisdiction to bear."[111] Hence, once the legitimacy of deconstructive delegitimation is recognized, it must, in turn, be delegitimized itself.

Anarchic delegitimation thus implies, once and for all, the "annihilation ... of philosophy's legitimating, justificatory function."[112] This annihilation presupposes the development of a third type of reading: after traditional reading, after deconstructive reading (delegitimizing traditional reading), lies the delegitimizing reading of deconstructive reading itself.

Philosophy makes it possible for anarchy to undertake the work that anarchism did not do: the work of meditating on the principle without which anarchy is only another version of the reign of *archē*. But this meditative work leads to an exiting of philosophy since, even in its post-metaphysical form, philosophy remains a nomothetic enterprise.

Does Schürmann really achieve this exit? Isn't the very moment when he thinks of philosophy as the emergence of anarchy the moment of his greatest disavowal?

The (Greek) temple in the sun

What type of reading, what type of action is liberated by Schürmann's delegitimation? At the heart of *From Principles to Anarchy* lies an archipelago of meaning that is somewhat isolated from the rest of the remarks even as it is set within them. Its surprising subject matter appears to open the continent of the book to an elsewhere. Schürmann leaves Greece for Peru to discuss the conquest of the Inca Empire, one of the three great empires of the pre-Columbian Americas. Around 1530, Pizzaro became governor of what is now Peru, making his domain there the center of Spanish colonial expansion. Suddenly, we set off on a voyage into the Andes, to Cuzco, the "Puma-Shaped City," nestled at the foot of the mountains: "The city is encased between two mountain ranges which rise to twenty thousand feet."[113]

Schürmann proceeds to analyze the dislocation of the Inca Empire, the submission of the colonized, the loss of their world. He draws on famous ethnologist and anthropologist Nathan Wachtel, who, in *The Vision of the Vanquished: The Spanish Conquest of Peru through Indian Eyes, 1530–1570*, restituted the point of view of the Indigenous peoples who were traumatized by the arrival of Pizarro and his armies.[114]

Following Wachtel, Schürmann analyzes the colonizing "despoliation."[115] "What happens in the transition from the pre-colonial to the colonial era is primarily a dispossession. The Indians are deprived of their gold, their goods, their land, their peace, their means of production and consumption, their sites, their rites, their administrative and spiritual organization, their progeniture, their life."[116]

What is the relevance of this critique of colonization? Of course, initially it appears to align with the critique of metaphysics even if it goes beyond the Eurocentric limits of deconstruction. It appears to delegitimize deconstruction's claims by equating philosophy with a form of colonialism. Moreover, with this traveling, isn't Schürmann imagining another sense of the word "theft" – one that is more "material," social, or economic than the theft concealed by metaphysics? Isn't he relating the colonial catastrophe to capitalism, extending the present state of Cuzco and Machu Picchu as they become "a commodity on the international tourist market"?[117] Isn't he moving out of the Western "enclosure" of concepts? Developing *another* critique of power?

Writing about the world before conquest, Schürmann also states: "We must admit that we understand almost nothing about it … How did things come to presence, how did they appear, before the conquistadores? That is what will forever escape us."[118] Does this failure to comprehend prepare a form of revolt against philosophical government, against the logical imperialism that bars access to that very critique of governing and imperialism?

It does not. It soon becomes evident that Schürmann simply applies the categories developed in his reading of the Greeks and Heidegger to the context of the Inca. The conquest of the Inca Empire and its contemporary extension in the marketing of sites are interpreted solely in terms of the shift from one form of domination to another, as if the Inca Empire had the status of a moment in the metaphysical tradition and as if its devastation were that of a "reversal." The philosophical conceptuality dominating the analysis of domination remains intact.

For Schürmann, the move from Inca splendor to the world of Pizzaro is a shift from one *archē* to the next. Prior to colonization, the Inca Empire is also structured by an archic paradigm: "Cuzco bears its principle inscribed within it."[119] Just like the Greek *archē*, this principle is simultaneously authority and intelligibility.

Authority: Cuzco is the center "of this, the most centralized empire ever."[120] Indeed, "Inca" is the name of the ruling class. It can also designate the leader of that class, the emperor. His insignia is the puma, which represents the principle in its function as authority, *princeps*. Paved roads ran from the central plaza, following the ridge lines. Along them, couriers transmitted the summonses, directives, decrees, and verdicts as far as what is today Argentina, to the south and Quito, to the north.[121]

Intelligibility: The principle of intelligibility of the Inca civilization is the decimal system: "The population, the animals, the labor, the soil itself, were parceled into decimal units."[122] This system "made it possible to subject heteroclite tribes to the central power."[123] And finally, "the Inca empire could be pan-Andean because it was a system, a pyramid with a decagonal base. The origin of the system, 'origin' both as archē and as princep-principium, allows one to understand this society and its achievements."[124]

The ethnocentrism of this reading is even more shocking when Schürmann characterizes conquest and colonization in terms of "epochal transition."[125] "When an entity like the city of Cuzco was inhabited solely by the descendants of the emperor, to the exclusion of any other clan, the web of being was pre-understood otherwise than when Pizarro had churches and convents built on the partially razed Inca dwellings."[126] Later, we read: "No epochal break has been more incisive than that undergone by the American civilizations at the time of the Spanish conquest."[127]

Colonization, once again a "reversal" suffered by the Inca, was the prelude to an epochal reconfiguration: "The dividing line that separates the Incan apparatus from its colonial displacement appears as traced by a tactic of reinterpretation."[128] The fact that the "acculturation" of the indigenous peoples by the Spanish "has … run aground deplorably"[129] serves only to show all the more clearly what epochal anarchy, the withering of the principles of an epoch, consists of: "The disjunction opens a rift that sets apart two eras … to give autonomy to life strata."[130]

Schürmann briefly considers whether the actual categories of epoch or *archē* are relevant either for the description of the Inca world or for an analysis of the colonial phenomenon. Instead of an anarchist liberation of the land, in this Andean excursion, we witness a *hyper-legitimation* of philosophical analysis.

The difference between the *political realm* and *politics* emerges at this point, suggesting that it might enable a dismantling of this interpretative framework or that it could open up a space for another vision of the community of colonized peoples: "Everything is not told about the rise of Inca civilization once its conquests, its superb usage of the decimal system, its disdain for the particular and the individual have been described."[131] This civilization must be grasped through another type of rise than the archic beginning, through the "presencing" that "requires a type of thought other than that which traces the reversals in historical principles."[132] But this other type is immediately caught between Plotinus' non-foundational unity and Heideggerian *Ursprung*, which suddenly become protective authorities, imposed without nuance onto a reality that has no connection to them.

Inca civilization is thus visible in light of "a 'clearing' in which a given community can live. A historic community is recognizable by the rise of an epochal first … Inca urbanism, the tattoos, the hats, the aide-memoires made of small cords called *quipu* – each speaks in its own way of the referent that gives coherence to that culture."[133] Negative henology and ontological difference take possession of Cuzco.

It is clear that "we understand none of it" paradoxically encounters no obstacle to onto-deconstructive interpretation of Inca political organization and colonizing epochal change.

What meaning can "clearing" or *Ereignis* have in pre-Columbian America? What status, except one of symptoms of coloniality? Admittedly, Schürmann was writing at a time when the notion of "coloniality" was not yet widely known. Introduced in the second half of the twentieth century by Peruvian sociologist Anibal Quijano, this idea is distinct from "colonialism." Coloniality describes the pursuit of colonization after decolonization. It refers to the survival of the colonial system and ideology after their official termination in a modified, but fully intact, form.[134] The neologism "coloniality" was forged from the terms "colonization" and "modernity," both of which are inseparable and which, in Quijano's view, were brought together in the conquest of the Americas. On the cusp of modernity, the philosophical sovereignty of the subject goes hand in hand with European imperialism, land theft, and slavery. As Argentinian philosopher Enrique Dussel puts it: "The Cartesian 'ego cogito' of 'I think therefore I am' is preceded by 150 years of the imperial '*ego conquiro*' of 'I conquer, therefore I am.'"[135]

In retrospect, how can we not read Schürmann's Andean tropism, his analysis of the Spanish conquest, in light of coloniality? How can we not detect the persistence of inception and command in his discourse, the absolute confidence in the transferable, exportable nature of the epochal schema, along with the mark of all-powerful deconstruction? The dominating resource not only of the principle of anarchy, but also of the anarchy of principle, interpreted solely in terms of negative henology?

For Schürmann, anarchy fails to go beyond the ontological frontiers, which consequently renders it archaic. Anarchy seeks its delegitimation by traveling to an elsewhere that turns out to be nothing but an exotic version of the same world and same legitimacy.

"Why should [the] ford of philosophy be a single stone?"[136] Schürmann asks, via René Char, on the final page of his book. Why, indeed, wouldn't there be several stones, several fords? Meanwhile, it seems that the uncemented stones in the walls of Cuzco, those stones that hold together by themselves and whose mystery has never been fully solved, are, for Schürmann, still essentially, in principle, caught up with the foundations of a Greek temple.

To understand…

I wrote earlier that to declare "I am an anarchist" is to contradict anarchism itself. Yet:

> [If] to understand poverty, one must be poor. [If] to understand detachment, one must be detached. [If] in Heidegger, to understand the turn, one must oneself turn about. [If to understand the primitive leap that is originary, one must leap oneself.] [If] to understand authentic temporality, one must exist authentically. [If] to understand the directionality, *Sinn*, of being, one must become *besinnlich*, meditative. [If] to understand the fourfold's play without why, one must live without why. [If] to understand releasement, one must be released …[137]

… then to understand anarchy, one must surely be …

5

Ethical Anarchy
The Heteronomies of Emmanuel Levinas

The Good ... is an anarchy.[1]
No one is a slave of the Good.[2]

Emmanuel Levinas

To love God is the only way not to have a master.[3]

Paul Claudel

On dissociation

Schürmann and Levinas apparently never met, yet their "anarchies" share at least one commonality, namely, a clear demarcation from political anarchism.

This separation is probably one of the reasons why Levinas sometimes writes "an-archy" in a hyphenated form to distinguish it from its usual meaning. As he explains: "The notion of an-archy we are introducing here has a meaning prior to the political (or antipolitical) meaning currently attributed to it."[4]

Miguel Abensour comments:

> The idea of *anarchy* in Levinas cannot be reduced to its political signification. Levinas is keen to distinguish an-archy or the an-archic in the sense that he understands it – as the plot of the human, the plot of responsibility – from anarchism. Anarchism, as political doctrine, is constituted and asserted by means of a principle and through recourse to principle, namely the invocation of the principle of reason against the principle of authority. For an-archy, it is an entirely different matter.[5]

Consequently, there is no direct reference to anarchism in Levinas's work. He refers neither to traditional political anarchism nor to the messianic anarchism of thinkers such as Scholem, Landauer, and Benjamin.[6] For

Levinas, an-archy is certainly not devoid of political meaning, but this meaning owes nothing to anarchism theorists.

The similarity with Schürmann's thought ends here, however. Levinas's anarchy is not about deconstruction; it resists the logic of the double bind. To reach the secret area where his disavowal is woven, we must therefore follow a special path.

It may seem that the reason for the dissociation between anarchy and anarchism is entirely obvious: Levinas is not an anarchist because such a position is not compatible with his defense of the state of Israel and his support for a certain form of Zionism. In this view, Levinas's disavowal of anarchism would allow him to avoid the supposed contradiction between his concept of an-archy and his acceptance, not to say support, for Israel's nationalist, colonialist, territorial policy. This is not a bad explanation, but it is too quick and simple. While it should not be discounted, it is important to understand that it is only the tip of the iceberg. My view is that the theme of anarchy conceals an obscure area of Levinas's thought that has not yet been addressed.

Beyond deconstruction

Levinas does not situate his thought in the wake of deconstruction, which is why he does not try to clarify the relation between metaphysics and anarchy. For him, "metaphysics" already signifies an exceeding of both traditional metaphysics and "transcendence."[7] The "true exteriority" of "his" metaphysics is the fact that it is irreducible to ontology.[8]

As early as 1930, in *The Theory of Intuition in Husserl's Phenomenology*, pursuing this strangeness and exoticism within his own thought, Levinas announces an exit from Greece – a departure that also involves leaving deconstruction behind. The Heideggerian undertaking of *Destruktion* or *Abbau* might be an overthrow of teleocracy, as Schürmann claims, but it is not a deep breach of the structure of the archic paradigm.

Indeed, Levinas writes, "the 'egoism' of ontology is maintained even when, denouncing Socratic philosophy as already forgetful of Being and already on the way to the notion of the 'subject' and technological power, Heidegger finds in Presocratism thought as *obedience* to the truth of Being."[9] Heideggerian thought thus remains a thought governed. In Heidegger there is no an-archy, not even in principle.

Ontological difference is nothing but a new version of the relation between commanding and obeying and consequently remains prisoner to archic totality. By contrast, Levinas claims that "if the notions of totality and being are notions that cover one another, the notion of the transcendent places us beyond categories of being … The transcendent is what cannot be encompassed."[10]

This is why any voyage that does not go beyond ontological categories is "allergic," reacting against alterity, colonialist, and imperialist voyaging. Any expedition oriented by "certainty, which remains the guide and guarantee of the whole spiritual adventure of being," will be only an odyssey. Even deep in the Andes, it is still Greek in exile. Levinas might have replied to Schürmann: "This is why this [your] adventure is no adventure. It is never dangerous; it is self-possession, sovereignty, $\dot{\alpha}\rho\chi\dot{\eta}$ [*archē*]. Anything unknown that can occur to it is in advance disclosed, open, manifest, is cast in the mold of the known, and cannot be a complete surprise."[11]

The possibility of deposing the archic paradigm can no longer come from either the fragility of its foundations or an inner exhaustion. The paradigm, in and of itself, is never exhausted. This possibility comes from an elsewhere, from this outside that is the ethical injunction as exposure to an Other [*Autrui*]. An absolute outside without negotiation or compromise: "Bits of thread cut by the Parque [never knot] together again."[12] It is impossible to re-knot connections cut from ethics and ontology.[13]

The anarchy that haunts Levinas's texts from his early writings right up to the last Talmudic readings thus becomes, from around the 1960s, the actual name of the ethical question. An anteriority more ancient than the a priori, a continued passivity of a past without a present, the exposure to the Other [*Autrui*]: all mark the spot where ethics and anarchy coincide – responsibility. *Anarchic responsibility.* That's the oxymoron of transcendence.

Substitution without dual injunction

The outside is, of course, experienced from within. While exposure to the Other is never a fact of consciousness and is more ancient than the self, it is nevertheless felt within me: "It is with subjectivity understood as self" that "the relationship with the other" is established.[14] The desubjectivation caused by the call of the outside is thus, initially, a subjective experience. But, at the same time, responsibility reveals the secondary nature of subjectivity, its delay with regard to this Other who precedes it by living within it. This is why the subject, taken hostage, "does not appear, but immolates itself."[15]

The chapter "Substitution" in *Otherwise than Being*, which picks up from the 1965 text, proposes what must be the most striking analysis of this experience, couterposing the archy of the self and the anarchy of the other, inasmuch as, from the outside, they share the same interior. They are together in the same body, the same tight skin: "In responsibility as one assigned ... – from outside, assigned as irreplaceable, the subject is accused in its skin, too tight for its skin. Cutting across every relation."[16] In this skin, "the relationship with the other precedes the auto-affection of certainty."[17]

Substitution is paradoxical, and Levinas knows it. This is evident when he refers to a potential "skepticism." Isn't substitution simply a form of alienation? The diachronic and non-synthetic coexistence of Self and Other in the Self, is thus an "ambiguous ... way of speaking," one that requires "as much audacity as skepticism shows, when it does not hesitate to affirm the impossibility of statement while venturing to *realize* this impossibility by the very statement of this impossibility."[18]

However, the enigma of substitution is not enigmatic for ontological thought, which is based, despite everything, on "the eternal presence to oneself"[19] of the self. In fact, "the oneself escapes *relations*,"[20] it does not enter into relation with the other, but lets it come to it. Thus, "it is perhaps here, in this reference to a depth of anarchical passivity, that the thought ... differs from ontological thought."[21]

Substitution takes shape in consciousness but is not founded in it, nor does it derive from it. It is precisely the non-principled and non-derivative nature of substitution that makes it a radical anarchic phenomenon. What can the mode of being be of that which therefore "is not," for that which is neither grounded nor deduced? Levinas's answer is: obsession.

> We have called this relationship irreducible to consciousness obsession. The relationship with exteriority is "prior" to the act that would effect it. For this

relationship is not an act, not a thematizing, not a position in the Fichtean sense ... Obsession traverses consciousness countercurrentwise, is inscribed in consciousness as something foreign, a disequilibrium, a delirium. It undoes thematization, and escapes any *principle*, origin, will, or ἀρχή [*archē*], which are put forth in every ray of consciousness. This movement is, in the original sense of the term, an-archical.[22]

It is not therefore clear that the complexity of this relation between outside and inside, which holds the other and the same together and infinitely separated all at once, should be seen as a logic of the double bind. Nor that Derrida is right when he claims, "this thinking *of* substitution leads us toward a logic that is hardly thinkable, almost unsayable, that of the possible-impossible, the iterability and replaceability of the unique,"[23] "the terrible ineluctability of a double constraint," even if "Levinas never puts it in these terms."[24]

That's exactly the point: Levinas never refers to it this way.

Between Self and Other there is a movement similar to the one at play in the tension between the Saying and the Said. Admittedly, this tension evokes an economy of "possible-impossible." Levinas asks how do we say the an-archic in the absence of an anarchy of language? The predicative proposition, the "Said" "apophantic," is the first form of language, even if "*apophansis* does not exhaust what there is in saying."[25] It cannot be exhausted; yet there is but one language. It is impossible to find an outside to the word, a sentence entirely irreducible to propositional form. Consequently, an-archy can only be said at the price of an affront to the predication in predication, an "abuse" of language within language. Levinas "exacerbates" and "abuses" by dramatizing, in the strong sense, the anarchic puncture of thematic word into established order.[26] The lexicon of suffering – persecution, traumatism, hostage, "expulsion outside of being"[27] – that accompanies substitution does not destroy the sentence, but does make it waver on account of its excessiveness. As if substitution "exacerbated" the tightness of the Self without destroying it.

If anarchy could speak its own language, it would betray "the fact that it is impossible for the anarchical to be constituted as a sovereignty – which implies the unconditionality of anarchy."[28]

Anarchy, at war with predicative logic and its authoritarian incline, can leave only a wake in it, "a trace which speech, in the pain of expression, seeks to state. But there is only a trace."[29] Imperceptible, but outrageous, this trace nonetheless changes everything, for it is the striation of "the thought ... that differs from ontological thought."[30]

Anarchy does not therefore show itself through fissures in the archic paradigm. Nor can it be assigned to the schizoid mechanism of disjunction. The fact that the self can be substituted does not immobilize it in the trampling of the impossible.

If there is a fault in the archic paradigm, it is this very absence of fault line, its rampart being, its blindness "into which we can be led by logic and against which Western philosophy had not sufficiently insured itself."[31] The logic that leads to the "bloody barbarism of National Socialism." But this is not to say that the archic paradigm is the "elementary Evil." Nor that philosophy has in some manner "eluded" evil at the very moment when it thought it was doing what was right. Evil does not come of a failure in the construction of the *archē* any more than it comes of "some contingent anomaly within human reasoning, nor in some accidental ideological misunderstanding."[32] In this sense, it is impossible to deconstruct evil.

If "elementary Evil" is a "possibility ... inscribed within the ontology of being,"[33] in other words, in all the history of philosophy before it eventually culminates in Heideggerian thought, it is not because philosophy is the possibility of evil. It's because the possibility of philosophy is, from the outset, an indifference to the Other, and hence an indifference and insensitivity to evil. Being is the wall of indifference built by philosophy. This is why it is difficult to know whether, for Levinas, philosophy is guilty because it commits evil or because it does not care about evil.

Yet the distance of the ethical, its transcendence, offers an infinite resistance to this indifference. The ethical injunction has a form so unique that it cannot be definitively stifled. Its exteriority is irreducible.

Two, but not double

Levinas nevertheless explains that it is important to distinguish one injunction from another. It is precisely because there are two types of injunction that there is no double injunction. The two injunctions, which differ from each other, are the ordinary injunction (the command to do this or that) and the ethical injunction. The first is structured by the clear partition between the order given and the order executed. By contrast, in the case of the ethical injunction, this relation is dramatically upturned. Indeed, in the ethical injunction, *obedience precedes command*. To be responsible implies answering even before hearing the call, even before it is interiorized, allowing it to enter the economy of auto-affection and representation. Taking too long to hear means not hearing, by which time it is already too late: "I am first a servant of a neighbor, already late and guilty for being late. I am as it were ordered from the outside, traumatically commanded, without interiorizing by representation and concepts the authority that commands me."[34] Everything occurs "as though the first movement of responsibility could not consist in awaiting nor even in welcoming the order ... but consists in obeying this order before it is formulated. Or as though it were formulated before every possible present, in a past that shows itself in the present of obedience without being recalled, without coming from memory, being formulated by him who obeys in his very obedience."[35]

The double bind is a command that can only be obeyed through disobedience. By contrast, the ethical injunction disarticulates entirely any relation between commanding and obeying, and thus between obedience and disobedience, because it simply does not give orders, does not govern. Any imperative in the ordinary sense thus finds itself doubled, outpaced because this "obedience precedes any hearing of the command,"[36] this "obedience to an order accomplished before the order makes itself heard: anarchy itself."[37]

Heteronomies

The interruption of the logic of government, that which is absolutely singular in Levinas's thought, produces one of his most important concepts: heteronomy. Contrary to what one might imagine, "heteronomy" – literally the law of the other – is not alienating. No Other [*Autrui*] dictates a law to me. Indeed, no Other has ever begun to be the other, which is why the Other does not exist in a fixed spatio-temporal point from which to begin to command or from which to begin to be. Heteronomy appears as the mark of "the antecedence of responsibility and obedience with respect to the order received or the contract."[38]

Responsibility responds only to the lack of an order for that for which it is responsible.

The anarchic injunction is heteronomous insofar as it answers those "we do not even know"[39] – an echo of voices that fall silent without ever having been heard officially, victims whose names are not inscribed on any headstone. It answers the silence of those who disappeared. In *Totality and Infinity*, Levinas writes:

> Fate is the history of the historiographers, accounts of the survivors, who interpret, that is, utilize the works of the dead. The historical distance which makes this historiography, this violence, this subjection possible, is proportionate to the time necessary for the will to lose its work completely. Historiography recounts the way the survivors appropriate the works of dead wills to themselves; it rests on the usurpation carried out by conquerors, that is, by the survivors.[40]

His 1934 text on Hitlerism is a sobering assertion that history is the history of the victors but that "speaking absolutely, he [Man] has no history."[41] The Other [*Autrui*] has no history and is without beginning and end.

Responsibility is implacable but not hegemonic – it is anarchic. Responsibility is persecuting but not hierarchical – it is traumatizing. Its law, its *nomos*, is before me, yet I do not come from it, I do not remember it.

Consequential autonomy

But isn't the claim that there is an indissoluble connection between ethics and heteronomy shocking? Levinas reads Kant backwards, since Kant considers heteronomy as the source of all illegitimate principles of morality.[42] For Kant, the *nomos* of heteronomy is not a law, despite its name. Or rather, this law is not truly legislating since it is subordinated to something other than itself. It only has the name of a law and thus remains outside it. In a word, it involves no obligation.

Very early on, with "La philosophie et l'idée de l'infini" (1957), later included in *En découvrant l'existence avec Husserl et Heidegger* (1967 [1949]),[43] Levinas explains the paradoxical ethical privilege that he grants heteronomy over autonomy. He is entirely aware of the fact that the "thesis of heteronomy ... breaks with a venerable tradition"[44] – namely, the primacy of autonomy, the primacy of freedom defined as obeying the law one prescribes to oneself.

We must not forget, however, that there are two forms of injunction. Likewise, there are two forms of heteronomy. Heteronomy is heteronomous to itself: ordinary heteronomy is based on the dissymmetry between commanding and obeying, while, as we have seen above, ethical heteronomy eclipses this dissymmetry as an obedience that follows no order whatsoever.

For Levinas, Kantian autonomy remains archic in that it can be reduced to command, as shown clearly by the definition of the categorical imperative. Autonomy has no content other than itself, merges with the consciousness it has of itself, and is therefore what it is at the expense of the exclusion of alterity: "Such is the [traditional] definition of freedom: to maintain oneself against the other, despite every relation with the other to ensure the autarchy of an I."[45] Consequently, "freedom denotes the mode of remaining the same in the midst of the other."[46]

The ethical injunction is that which cannot be its own source. Otherwise, what would be ethical about it? It is the Other [*Autre*], such that "the face of the other is perhaps the very beginning of philosophy."[47]

Levinas posits that freedom is "difficult" precisely because it does not come first. Responsibility precedes it infinitely:

> The Infinite affects the I without the I's being able to dominate it, without the I's being able to "assume" through the *archē* of the Logos the unbounded nature of the Infinite thus *anarchically* affecting the I, imprinting itself as a trace in the absolute passivity, prior to all freedom, showing itself as a "Responsibility-for-the-Other" to which this affection gives rise.[48]

Election and slavery

We have reached a decisive moment in the analysis. Explaining the distinction between the two heteronomies, Levinas also characterizes it as a difference between *election* and *slavery*: there is the heteronomy of the elected and the heteronomy of the slave.

Being able to obey without any rule being presented to consciousness or to the will is a sign of *election*. Election replaces the logic of government. I am "chosen without assuming the choice!"[49] without ever experiencing it as an order and without needing to bear its weight. Election dispenses with coercion. To be elected means not needing to be commanded or governed. Anarchy and election are sisters. The heteronomy of election is thus absolutely the opposite of the heteronomy of slavery.

Yet aren't they similar in a sense? In "Humanism and An-archy" Levinas asks, "But isn't this servitude? *Not being able* to get out of responsibility? How can this passivity place the subject 'beyond freedom and non-freedom'?"[50] His answer is crystal clear: "No slavery is included in the obligation of the Same for the Other."[51] For the "service [of election] is not slavery."[52] Elsewhere he writes: "the other awakening the same is the other in the same without alienating him, without slavery."[53] There is no question that submission implied by responsibility is total, that there is no possibility of desertion: "Such an antinomy [of a service that is not slavery] bears witness to the Good."[54]

In other words, the heteronomy of election is *free*. This is not to contradict what has previously been said. Freedom is not first; it is not the past of responsibility. That much is clear. But we now understand that freedom is its future. In the heteronomy of election, "the Other ... does not clash with freedom but invests it."[55] Eventually then, ethical heteronomy appears as true autonomy. The command, which comes from the Other, ultimately comes from the self: "The possibility of finding, anachronously, the order in the obedience itself, and of receiving the order out of oneself, this reverting of heteronomy into autonomy."[56] To repeat: heteronomy does not alienate and "no one is enslaved to the Good."[57] The submission implied by responsibility "is canceled by the bounty of the Good that commands. Beneath enslavement the obedient finds his integrity."[58] The bearer of responsibility is not dominated.

In contrast to the "plot [that is ...] anarchic,"[59] that is not a "slave's alienation,"[60] there is also a servile, enchained heteronomy.

By rigorously distinguishing between two types of "service" – anarchic slavery and alienated servitude – Levinas presents the slave as counterpoint to the elected.

The figure of the subject subordinated to the tyrant

Who, then, is the slave? There are two contrasting figures – the tyrant's subject and the proletarian – sharing a single trait, namely, a defining relation to a master. The theme of slavery appears in two key texts, "Freedom and command" (1953) and "Humanism and an-archy" (1972). In a reading of Plato's *Republic* in "Freedom and command," Levinas names the slave the subject for whom "the love for the master fills the soul."[61] What is it to love the master? An individual subject, just like a people, reach this extreme when their consciousness of oppression dissipates. The political slave of the tyrant is the feeble child of the archic paradigm, born when the dissymmetry between commanding and obeying is so great that it collapses into its own abyss.

> To have a servile soul is to be incapable of being jarred, incapable of being ordered. The love for the master fills the soul to such an extent that the soul no longer takes its distances. Fear fills the soul to such an extent that one no longer sees it, but sees from its perspective.[62]

In "Humanism and an-archy" Levinas again claims that "servitude" comes of the presence of an irreducible distance between commanding and obeying, such that "the determined must remain other with regard to that which determines it."[63]

Levinas explains that, at the same time, the slave always has the possibility of remembering the moment when the alienation began, for they "must keep a memory of the present when the determining determined it and was its contemporary."[64] The heteronomy of slavery is thus prisoner to commanding and inception.

The figure of the proletarian

The figure of the proletarian is outlined in *Totality and Infinity*.[65] The worker is free to remember being free in the past.[66] The proletarian is also conscious of the inception of their servitude. In *The Infinite Conversation*, Blanchot reiterates this view when he writes: "The slave has the good fortune of having a master; the master he serves today is the one against whom he will rise up tomorrow."[67] He goes on to argue: "The slave is a man who has already succeeded – an infinite progress – in encountering a master; he thus has this master to rely upon."[68] The fight against the master is indispensable to the conquest of emancipation, the indispensable mediation caught in consciousness, the beginning of revolution.

Although the oppressed political subject and the worker are diametrically opposed, they are first of all slaves to the political and economic situation when they claim their independence from ethics. Indeed, "politics left to itself bears a tyranny within itself."[69] As for the exploitation of workers, it too depends on being limited to the economic circle. This "anomaly called alienation is explained by the structure of the economy, left to its own determinism."[70]

In both instances, the relation to the master – whether "loved" excessively or resisted – marks the absolute dissymmetry between commanding and obeying, that is, the extreme logic of government.

Who is elected?

Let's go back to election. Of course, Levinas writes "There is no enslavement more complete than this seizure by the good, this election."[71] Yet, I repeat, it is important to understand this elective service as anything but slavery.

Sacred history teaches that the chosen people of the children of Israel experienced slavery in Egypt without ever submitting to this servitude. *The chosen ones were successful in not developing a servile soul.* As "the slave of the slaves of the state" in Egypt, Jews never "loved" Pharaoh. The "soul" of the children of Israel is an anarchic soul.

By inflicting the trial of slavery on the Jews, God revealed the irreducible difference between servitude and enslavement, between God and master:

> Verse 55 of Leviticus Chapter 25 reads: "For to me the people of Israel are servants; they are my servants whom I brought forth out of the land of Egypt; I am the Lord your God." As if the human self could signify the possibility of a belonging that is not alienating and be exalted to freedom through this very subjection.[72]

Blanchot concurs here too:

The Hebrews had been only sojourners in Egypt, refusing the temptation of a closed world where they could have had the illusion of freeing themselves in situ by a slave statute ... [T]hey began to exist only in the desert, freed by having taken to the road in a solitude in which they were no longer alone ... [The desert is] that place without place where alone the Covenant can be concluded and to which one must always turn as to that moment of nakedness and separation that is at the origin of true existence.[73]

Election and revolution

Another sign of the election of the chosen people is the possibility of seeing from above, better than slaves themselves, the part of election that exists within slavery and enables its true emancipation. The Jew, "free *qua* affranchised,"[74] can indeed feel "solidarity for all enslaved people."[75]

The Torah illuminates political and economic questions in a more brilliant light, one more raw than politics and economics. For example, in "Judaism and revolution," Levinas writes that the Talmudic Tractate *Baba Mezia* is a "union text before the letter."[76] This Tractate "extends the principle of freedom conditioned by allegiance to the Most High, to the daily problem of rights of the day laborer. As a servant of God, he retains an independence with regard to his employer that even his contract cannot alienate; and he can, in certain circumstances, leave his master right in the middle of the day's work."[77] The Torah prescribes punishment for anyone who renounces their independence in any way such that they remain the slave of a master. Anyone who denies their freedom. The law of the Pentateuch (Exodus 21: 5–6) already instructs that "the slave who, for love of his master, renounces the freedom that is due to him, 'in the seventh [year]', '[shall be brought] before [the court]' and will have 'his ear [bored] through with an awl.'" Levinas comments:

> Mark forever with infamy an ear that will have capable of remaining deaf to the good news ... in which, at the foot of Sinai, the end of the enslavement of man by man is announced. The man who, despite the Revelation, seeks a human master for himself, is not worthy of serving God – in other words, is not worthy of his freedom.[78]

Election, the good news, Revelation: all bear "that one thing that disalienates definitively, beyond any political disalienation."[79] Levinas continues: "As if the notion of Israel, people of the Torah, people as old as the world and as old as persecuted mankind, carried within itself a universality higher than that of a class exploited and struggling; as if the violence of the struggle were already alienation."[80] The Torah also teaches that "humanity is nevertheless not defined by its proletariat … As if all alienation were not overcome by the consciousness that the working class may achieve from its condition as a class and from its struggle; as if revolutionary consciousness were not sufficient for disalienation."[81]

Contrary to what we might first imagine, election is thus not a strictly national affair but rather a global revolutionary ferment.[82] The chosen people of the children of Israel are those who know, far longer than others, that all people are elected, even when they do not always yet know it. "The trauma of the 'bondage in the land of Egypt' which marks the Bible and the liturgy of Judaism would belong to the very humanity of the Jew and of the Jew in every man who, a freed slave, would be very similar to the proletarian, the stranger, the persecuted."[83] Every human is Jewish, every Jew human.

> Echo of the permanent saying of the Bible: the condition – or incondition – of strangers and slaves in the land of Egypt brings man closer to his fellow man. Men seek one another in their incondition of strangers. No one is at home. The memory of that servitude assembles humanity. The difference that gapes between ego and self, the non-coincidence of the identical, is a thorough non-indifference with regard to men.[84]

A blind spot appears

Strangely, just at the point when the political meaning of election seems to be illuminated, we come up against the difficulty that lies within Levinasian anarchy: its dissociation with anarchism at two levels of opacity.

First level of opacity: anarchism of the state

If the heteronomy of election and the heteronomy of slavery eventually meet and potentially annul their heterogeneity in the incondition of the stranger of "all men," and if, beyond a specific chosen people, obedience without command contains a universal promise of emancipation, then why can ethical anarchy not be extended to political anarchism? Why isn't anarchism the good news of the good news?

Why does Levinas consistently claim that the state is necessary? How can he assert, for instance, that the state represents "the necessary conditions" for "the dignity" not only of all people, but also of "the descendants of Abraham"?[85] Isn't the state the return of the master?

We can't help noticing that the two heteronomies meet precisely at the spot where anarchism is excluded. As if they had been differentiated solely to ultimately confirm the necessity of preserving ethical anarchy through a state structure: "Freedom consists in instituting outside of oneself an order of reason, in entrusting the rational to a written text, in resorting to institutions. Freedom, in its fear of tyranny, leads to institutions, to a commitment of freedom in the very name of freedom, to a State."[86]

It might be imagined initially that the state protects the community against the stubborn heteronomy of slavery, against the extremes to which it can lead when the subject accepts the temptation of living in a state of indifference toward values, opened by a freedom defined as an "impetuosity of the current to which everything is permitted."[87] In a word, that the state protects against crime. But that's precisely the problem: the state also protects ethical heteronomy from itself. Ethical heteronomy has its own excess – there is a veritable "ethical madness,"[88] with its own specific immoderation.

Although Levinas consistently claims that politics is derivative ("Politics after!"[89]), he still asserts that without state politics, ethics is excessive.

What does he mean? The excess of the ethical relation comes from a specific form of injustice born, so to speak, of justice itself. This is a common phenomenon: in daily life, those close to us are favored at the expense of those more distant. The other who is near me – parent, child, friend – receives all my attention, usurping the infinite transcendence of the Other [*Autrui*]. The role of the state of justice is to introduce a third into this "mad" relation of favor, thereby ensuring, as Abensour explains, "measure into the incommensurable, the comparison of reason between what is incomparable, reciprocity, symmetry where asymmetry reigns. In short, the entry of the third *seeks to institute order in this disarray, in this anarchy.*"[90]

The role of the state is thus to *institute order in anarchy*. Why? Because the state relation protects ethical anarchy from the excess of horizontality that is proximity. It protects it from the horizontality of immanence, "a stifling imprisonment within," by opening a space for political breath through the intervention of the third.[91] A horizontality of transcendence, if you like.

Which state?

However, for Levinas the state is the antithesis of the Leviathan. Abensour confirms that Levinas is the "author of a veritable 'Against Hobbes.'"[92] He strongly criticizes and clearly rejects Hobbes's wild image of the state of nature, which illustrates the "odious hypothesis"[93] of war of all against all, a "multiplicity of allergic egoisms which are at war with one another."[94] Levinas refuses the exclusive vision of interhuman interactions as power relations: "The Other [*Autrui*] does not oppose one force to another, rather it opposes the unpredictability of its reaction, or better yet, the transcendence of its being in relation to all of power systems."[95]

So which state would provide the horizontality of transcendence?

A new distinction is introduced here to separate the "state of Caesar" from the "state of David." The state of Caesar is the Leviathan: "Jealous of its sovereignty, the State in search of hegemony, the conquering, imperialist, totalitarian, oppressive."[96] "Incapable of being without self-adoration, it is idolatry itself."[97] This state is the one that forges "slave souls."

For Levinas, the state of justice, the state of David, is placed under the sign of being-for-others [*pour-autrui*], peace and "remains in the final stage of Deliverance."[98] It is not, in fact, certain that war was at the inception: "Before wars there were altars."[99] The state of David suspends all possible tyranny and oppression, thus paradoxically recalling the antecedence of election in relation to the institution of the state itself, thereby protecting its subjects against love of the master and protecting in one fell swoop all those in danger of forgetting their responsibility as they cultivate the love of those too close to them.

The state of David inscribes the non-archic promise within the state itself. This "beyond the state in the state" is the title of a famous lesson in the Talmud.[100] There is a state "larger than an excess, or a surplus that exceeds it."[101] *A state that promises no government.*

The state is necessary to save anarchy, to warn against the ever-possible collapse of the heteronomy of election into a form of heteronomy of slavery, or bondage to another in a system of dependence.

Israel in general

We recognize the state of Israel in the state of David. While the possibility of election is open to all people, there is still only one type of state that meets the mark: only Israel is simultaneously a state and beyond the state. As Derrida puts it, Israel is "'*beyond in*': transcendence in immanence, *beyond* the political, but *in* the political. Inclusion opened onto the transcendence that it bears, incorporation of a door [*porte*] that bears [*porte*] and opens onto the beyond of the walls and partitions framing it."[102] But as I said from the outset, it seems to me that the problem lies not so much in this insistence on the specificity of Israel[103] as in the more general idea that a state can be considered, without any contradiction whatsoever, as a bridge to anarchy.

When, for instance, Levinas analyzes the May 1968 uprisings in France, it is not Israel he has in mind, but rather this more general notion of the state as guarantor of anarchy. As a professor at University of Paris Nanterre, he lived through the events of 1968 and understood their determining nature, explaining that "in the flash of a few dazzling moments in 1968," the youth "contested a world long condemned."[104] He saw in this revolution a "word ... that came of sincerity, that is, from responsibility for others." The students' demands were an expression of ethical anarchy. Levinas also stated that "in 1968, all values were 'empty,' except the value of 'others' which demanded devotion."[105] He adds:

> Aside from capitalism and exploitation, it was conditions that were contested: the individual understood as an accumulation in being, through merit, titles, professional competence – an ontological tumefaction weighing on others until it crushed them, instituting a hierarchical society that maintained itself above the needs of existence and that no religious influence managed to make equal anymore. Behind the capital of having weighed a capital of being.[106]

Resisting this accumulation of being, anarchy becomes synonymous with youth: "This adjective [young] indicates the surplus of sense over the being that carries it and claims to measure and restrain it."[107]

But if May '68 succeeded in putting the notion of *archē* into question, it failed in thinking that ethical anarchy could thrive in political anarchism. The conclusion is irrevocable: anarchism led them to "renounce society and drown in the limitless responsibility for others all possibility of answering in fact ... Not caring in the least means flirting with nihilism."[108] Levinas claims that the "nihilist" anarchism of 1968 ended up using a "language just as wordy and conformist as the one it was supposed to replace."[109] And why was that? Because we just can't do without "tradition [and] institutions."[110]

In the end, again, anarchism can exist only as state anarchism.

Second level of opacity: the entirely other heteronomy

The defense of the state as protector of ethical anarchy at the first level of dissociation coexists with a more subterranean level of disavowal. It becomes apparent that the distinction between the two heteronomies — the heteronomy of election and the heteronomy of slavery — is possible only at the expense of the unthought exclusion of *another*, unsaid, heteronomy, that threatens its solidity.

Why? Because the heteronomy that Levinas calls the heteronomy of slavery is *completely unrelated to the reality of the objective legal and social system of slavery*. It bears no relation whatsoever to historical reality. Man may have no history, but slavery certainly does.

Neither of the two Levinasian figures of the slave relate to historical realities such as Greek slavery or the transatlantic slave trade. The subject of the tyrant, the masses fanaticized by Hitlerism, are not, strictly speaking, slaves. Nor are proletarians slaves. To use this term to discuss them is to verge on an abuse of language. In Levinas's thought, the heteronomy of slavery is not connected to any reality other than testimony (the slavery of the Israelites in Egypt is attested only by sacred texts) or metaphor (the Marxist characterization of proletarians as slaves). Levinas's "slaves" are thus outside slavery.

As we have seen, the slave is the shadowy lining of the elected. But this shadow also has its own shadow, an invisible and ghostly one with neither shape nor face: the shadow of the slaves never named. The paradoxical structural solidarity of the two heteronomies crushes a third: the heteronomy of slaves put in chains, transported, separated, bought, and sold. These slaves are indeed *other*: other to free peoples, other to the elected, other, too, to fanaticized subjects, other to proletarians. Other to those others with whom they have nothing in common. Here we have a remnant heteronomy, falling outside heteronomy due to its excess.

Need I recall that if a slave is a slave, it is not for love of a master but because they are property, both exploitable and negotiable? A slave is a slave because slavery is synonymous with social death: "A slave is an individual deprived of their freedom, or part of it, by the applicable rules of a given country or era. A slave is an economic instrument dependent on a master and who can be bought or sold."[111] A slave is defined by the absence of legal personhood. That is why it is always laws, as variable as they are across time and space, that determine the conditions under which an individual becomes a slave, or ceases being a slave. The official emancipation of a slave always comes from the decision of the master or existing legal or state authority. It is never their own.

If we connect slavery to its historical definition now, we might ask what the idea of "slave soul" can mean. The phrase "servile soul" resonates strangely, in contradiction to the traditional philosophical definition of a slave as a being deprived of a soul, or endowed only with the soul of a tool ("an animate tool,"[112] according to Aristotle). The slave is outside the state of choosing their life and achieving happiness, which consists in the active practice of virtue.[113] However, if the slave possesses a certain part of humanity, it is within the strict measure in which they are considered a part separate from the body of the master, not his soul.[114]

Later, in 1748, in *The Spirit of the Laws*, Montesquieu returned to the argument about the lack of a soul in "Of the slavery of the Negroes," writing:

> It is impossible for us to suppose these creatures to be men, because, allowing them to be men, a suspicion would follow that we ourselves are not Christians ... These creatures are all over black, and with such a flat nose that they can scarcely be pitied. It is hardly to be believed that God, who is a wise being, should place a soul, especially a good soul, in such a black, ugly body.[115]

Levinas does not sufficiently interrogate his own concept of "slave soul." He does not consider to what extent this type of concept corroborates the traditional view. Nor does he seem to be prepared to recognize – precisely in order to block this vision once and for all – that *no slave ever has the soul of a slave*. Not because they do not have souls, but because nothing like a "slave soul" exists among slaves. Slaves are not servile. The concept of a "servile soul" is a dangerous concept. It's a master's concept.

In his article "Phénoménologie des identités juive et noire" [phenomenology of Jewish and Black identities], philosopher Abdoulaye Barro reminds us of the archive of "dialogue begun between Jews and Blacks" about their respective fates.[116] "An analogy between the condition of Blacks and Jews in the Old Testament is made frequently in the work of Black intellectuals such as Du Bois, Senghor, Baldwin, and Cone," he writes.[117] Indeed, in *The Souls of Black Folk*, William Du Bois claims that the foundations of Jewish identity offer a model for the identarian construction of Black people.[118]

> The symbol of the veil that covers Moses on Mount Sinai to speak to his people is reinterpreted by Du Bois as the veil that separates white America from black America. To guide black folk in their fight for liberation and unity is to be take inspiration from Moses as an exemplary model who, as a spiritual leader, succeeded in translating the passions, suffering and aspirations of the Jewish people. Du Bois himself identifies with Moses, as a law-making prophet.[119]

Yet, contrary to what we might initially imagine, the assertation by Du Bois of a form of community between Jewish and Black people does not lead to an interpretation of slavery as a paradigmatic form of election. When asked about this, Edouard Glissant explains, in *Poetics of Relation*: "Peoples who have been to the abyss do not brag of being chosen."[120] For Glissant, the idea of a slavery of election is not anything but "vanity."[121]

In making these comments, to my mind, the question is not that of evaluating the possibility or impossibility of the famous "amalgam" between Shoah and the slave trade. That's not the question I'm asking. What I want to understand is why Levinas excludes the historical martyrdom of slaves from ethical trauma and constructs a concept of servility that ostracizes the true heteronomy of slavery and voids its meaning. Why does he forge a concept that excludes slaves from slavery since they do not have a substitutable Self inasmuch as their self, which is already dominated, is never theirs.

The construction of slavery or the slave as *philosophical or ethical categories* is clearly impossible. First, because one cannot discuss slavery as if slaves constituted "a community, a group defined solely in terms of economic exploitation."[122] Slavery is always diasporic. We know that Greek slaves came from different lands. Those who suffered the transatlantic slave trade also had no homogenous identity. Glissant "reminds us that the deported Africans came from different regions and cultures and that the slave ship's hold ground all these identities into pieces. The experience of the abyss of the Middle Passage comes of this destruction of all connection and memory."[123] This is also the case of migrants sold as slaves in Libya today.

This historical-geographical reality prohibiting unification presents a philosophical impasse. To repeat, it is impossible to construct a category or concept of slave without immediately perpetuating the act of slavery. Since the "slave" in general does not exist, it threatens the validity of the general idea of a heteronomy of enslavement. Thus, too, the idea of the heteronomy of election, since the heteronomy of enslavement is its purported twin.

*

"Destruction of all connection": contrary to what Levinas claims, slaves do not "remember" having been free, inasmuch as all genealogical understanding of their place of origin is prohibited. They can be resold, dispersed, separated from their companions, parents, and children, and thus structurally stripped of their ancestral lines at any given moment. In this sense, their condition is outside inception. But by the same token, it is also outside command. Slaves are not ruled or governed. Slaves can only be dominated. The master never "governs" his slaves. Slaves are non-governable.

Levinas's ethical anarchy might have taken an entirely different course than the destiny of a future state if the two test cases of the non-governable – ethical responsibility and slavery – had been thought through together *without the misleading mediation of the concept of servility*. Ethical anarchy might have found in this thought of the non-governable the missing anarchist political orientation. Non-governability is not, and never can be, soluble in the state.

Without a total *anarchist* reconsideration of the problem of slavery, ethics runs the risk of being far too well governed.

6

"Responsible Anarchism"
Jacques Derrida's Drive for Power

> *Interviewer*: Could one describe the political equivalent of deconstruction as a disposition, as opposed to a position, of responsible anarchy?
>
> *Derrida*: If I had to describe my political disposition I would probably employ a formula of that kind while stressing, of course, the interminable obligation to work out and to deconstruct these two terms – "responsible" and "anarchy." If taken as assured certainties in themselves, such terms can also become reified and unthinking dogmas. But I also try to re-evaluate the indispensable notion of "responsibility."[1]
>
> Jacques Derrida

> But does one think or not think what one posits in the form of disavowal?[2]
>
> Jacques Derrida

Is deconstruction anarchism?

Make no mistake, says Jacques Derrida, anarchism leaves the question of power intact. To reject power is still to play the power game, whether colonialist, pro-slavery, or censorship. As long as the question of the specific relations between anarchy and power has not been elucidated, the question of power will always come back to haunt anarchism, a nagging voice it can silence only with a terrorist use of force.

To be done with state and government is not to be done with power. What becomes of power when it frees itself of principle? And what does anarchism do with its own power? These questions can only be answered through a deconstruction of anarchism.

But is deconstructing an anarchist gesture? The only answer that satisfies Derrida is "yes and no."

Yes and no: deconstruction and anarchism

In "Force of law" Derrida points out that "Benjamin distinguishes between two sorts of general strikes, some destined to replace the order of one state with another (general *political* strike), the other to abolish the state (general *proletarian* strike)."[3] The first type of strike is reformist, seeking a change of government. The second is revolutionary, aiming for the suspension of all government – which is why "we can ... speak of anarchism"[4] in this instance. Derrida states that these are "the two temptations of deconstruction."[5]

Derrida explains that deconstruction participates in both of these strikes simultaneously, belonging no more to one than to the other. Is deconstruction reformist? Yes and no. Anarchist? Yes and no. "Is that what deconstruction is? Is it a general strike or a strategy of rupture? Yes and no."[6]

"Yes, to the extent that it assumes the right to contest, and not only theoretically, constitutional protocols, the very charter that governs reading in our culture and especially in the academy."[7] Indeed, "there is something of the general strike, and thus of the revolutionary situation in every reading that founds something new and that remains unreadable in regard to established canons and norms of reading, that is to say in the present state of reading or of what figures the State, with a capital S, in the state of possible reading."[8]

And "no," to the extent that "a strategy of rupture is never pure" because it must always deal with the return of that with which it breaks.[9]

"Yes," since deconstruction deposes that which presents itself in texts, talks, and other works, as a center, a guiding theme or position of power. Yes, inasmuch as its strategy is always to identify all the fault lines of institutions. And "no," in so far as there is no rupture without talk and negotiation.

The proliferation of yes and no – from the aporia to autoimmunity to the double bind and all the categories of the virus – confuses the borders between deconstruction and anarchism in Derrida's work. It is apparently impossible, therefore, to catch him in the act of dissociating or disavowing, since that consistent type of flagrant offense is no longer an offense.[10]

The anarchy question

It would be superficial, however, to confine Derrida's "anarchism" to either the nonlogical logic of yes and no, or to the double bind. There definitely exists *a specific problem of anarchy* in his work, a central nerve that, strangely, has remained unnoticed until now.

Texts always contain both a "thematizing" and a "thematized" border.[11] The thematizing border asks the question, while the thematized border is the space where the question is rolled out. More than a relation between form and background, the thematizing and the thematized describe the difference between what might be called the emergence and the identification of the question of the text.

In Derrida's work anarchy-anarchism is "thematized" through the "thematizing" of "yes and no." In addition to his reference to Benjamin's proletarian strike mentioned above, there are four significant occurrences of this thematizing. The first, developed in *Of Grammatology*, concerns the relation between *archē* and writing. The second also appears in *Of Grammatology* in his interpretation of Lévi-Strauss's "anarchism."[12] The third takes shape during his dialogue with Levinas.[13] The last, which is the most significant, supports his reading of *Beyond the Pleasure Principle*, especially in "To speculate – on 'Freud'."[14]

Beyond principle: alternative and its two reasons

Why is the fourth instance the most important? There are at least two reasons.

First, because the ongoing dialogue with Freud is proof that anarchism is definitely not just a question like any other for Derrida. Indeed, more than in any other overtly "political" text, it is in the course of this exchange that Derrida develops his analysis of power in all its complexity.

Second, because behind all the instances of flagrant disavowal and dissociation assumed by Derrida, behind the anarchy of yes and no, on this occasion the discussion reveals the full extent of a non-deconstructed disavowal of anarchism in his thinking.

First reason: Freud presents anarchism with the most serious question of all

We recall that right at the beginning of *Beyond the Pleasure Principle* Freud states that he has long considered the pleasure principle as the *archē* of the psyche, its sovereign authority and government. The pleasure principle, he says, is a law according to which "the course taken by mental events is automatically regulated." "Invariably set in motion by an unpleasant tension ... it takes a direction such that its final outcome coincides with a lowering of tension – that is, with an avoidance of unpleasure or a production of pleasure."[15] Freud adds that up until this point, all psychic events appeared to conform to this law.

He continues: "Nevertheless, the investigation of the mental reaction to external danger" has come to "produce new material and raise fresh questions bearing upon our present problem."[16] In the end, the pleasure principle may not be the only example of governing in the psyche. There are occasions when the homeostatic dike bursts. Under the effect of trauma, when it is no longer maintained at its base level, psychic energy overflows the principle, flooding it, pouring over it. Freud himself does not say "anarchy" – even though it does literally mean "beyond the principle" – Derrida says the word for him.

Derrida engages Freud here because the question of beyond the *archē*, as elaborated by Freud, is, for him, one of the most serious questions ever addressed not only to psychoanalysis but also to anarchism. As if this question found its greatest political radicalness, its blade and fire, in its psychic form.

The question is then: Is beyond the principle beyond power, or is it the essence of power? Not the power of the state-government paradigm, but power freed of the shackles of the law? Not principled power, but the power of drives? Power free of all safeguards. *Pure* power. Isn't it a stroke of genius for Freud to have named it the death drive?

How then should this release of energy be interpreted? Once the principle has been transgressed, the state adjourned, the government overturned – what happens? Again, once the state-governmental dike that guarantees social homeostasis bursts – what happens? Let's translate it radically: *is the death drive anarchic or anarchist?*

There are two possibilities. Either beyond the principle is equated, in its release, with absolute license, political, psychic, and affective. That's anarchy-chaos, the reserve of all forms of domination, the origin of sadism, cruelty, and all the various modes of destruction. Or else, beyond the principle may reveal the existence of a power unbound from domination, uncoupled from itself, in a sense, an energy available for *another* organization, the prelude to an entirely new political and social dynamic, one that is revolutionary and anarchist.

This is where the Derridean yes and no comes into play. Derrida's reading of *Beyond the Pleasure Principle* adopts the middle ground. In the middle of the alternative between the compulsive obsession of power and a nirvana of uncoupling, in the impossibility of a clean break between the two: the boundary separating them is always fragmented and divided. As we read in *Resistances of Psychoanalysis*, "The question of divisibility is one of the most powerful instruments of formalization for what is called deconstruction. If, in an absurd hypothesis, there were one and only one deconstruction, a sole thesis of 'Deconstruction,' it would pose divisibility: difference as divisibility."[17]

In the unresolved tension between the radicalizing of power and the dissolution of power, Derrida defers the answer, plays for time, saves the question of whether beyond the principle is beyond domination, or nothing but the root of domination.

Second reason: Freud requires a special deconstructive reading

Why does this tension reveal simultaneously a non-deconstructed dissociation and a disavowal of anarchism? Because the reading developed in "To speculate – on 'Freud'" is unlike any other. It bears no resemblance to any of the innumerable readings of traditional authors deployed by Derrida elsewhere. Deconstructive reading – its "anarchism" and "revolutionary situation" – usually isolates a "defective cornerstone" in a text in order to insert its lever and show that the text denies itself, that its "truth" lies in its "neglected corners."[18]

But it's not at all clear what this "defective cornerstone" might be in Derrida's reading of *Beyond the Pleasure Principle*. Nor is it evident what is actually deconstructed in Freud's text. Indeed, faced with the alternatives of unbinding and terror, the deconstruction and radicalization of power, *Freud already answers yes and no.* To his own question, he offers no response other than "yes and no." Moreover, Derrida recognizes the lack of a thesis in *Beyond the Pleasure Principle*, its "athesis."[19]

Is there a beyond the pleasure principle? Freud has no last word on the question, does not answer whether he thinks that the drive is ultimately more powerful than the principle, whether freed energy is more threatening than bound energy. Nor is it clear which is more repressive: government or absence of government. Or which prevails between anarchy-chaos and anarchism, and whether it is even necessary to have a winner. Between destruction and relinquishing, the status of the death drive remains unresolved. Long before Derrida, Freud is a philosopher of the economy of violence.

Are we witness to a confrontation of a double yes and no with Freud and Derrida? A closer reading of the Derridean interpretation reveals a strange exchange of roles. Contrary to expectations, it is Derrida who calls the shots for Freud. Perhaps this is what explains the use of quotation marks in the title "To speculate – on 'Freud.'" A title that actually means "To speculate – for 'Freud,'" that is, in his place. As Derrida's reading progresses, from the compulsion to repeat to the death drive, it becomes evident that instead of yes and no, a "no" to anarchism is emerging. There is no beyond the principle. Significantly, the term Derrida gives the death drive in *Archive Fever* is already a retrospective indicator of this answer: he calls it the "anarchic drive," or the "anarchy drive"[20] – not the "anarchist drive."

In Derrida's reading of *Beyond the Pleasure Principle*, this "no" to anarchism bears witness to all the special attention, even excessive privilege, that he grants the drive for power – *Bemächtigungstrieb*, "domination, power, possession," or "mastery"[21] – despite the fact that it makes only a brief appearance in Freud's text. Dislodged from its position as intermediary between the compulsion to repeat and death drive, *Bemächtigungstrieb* takes on the prime role for Derrida: the role of principle.

This drive, which Derrida terms indiscriminately the drive for power and the drive for mastery, gradually imposes itself on the reading and becomes (no pun intended) the sole master and commander. Exit anarchism. Even if Derrida introduces to Freud's text the notion that it is impossible to circumscribe power, to assign it to any given role, principle, or drive – the drive for mastery still dominates, causing the thematizing and thematized edges of discourse to coincide. For Derrida, perhaps ultimately more than for Freud, there is only pleasure "dealing with itself,"[22] mastering itself. Hence, no beyond. Thus, no anarchy.

So, is "To speculate – on 'Freud'" a deconstructive reading of Freud? Or is it an admission that it is impossible to deconstruct the drive for power?

Let's keep these questions for the end.

First occurrence of thematizing "anarchy": metaphysics and the value of *archē*

From *Of Grammatology* all the way to *Resistances of Psychoanalysis*, Derrida always asserted the need for "undoing, desedimenting, decomposing, deconstituting sediments, *artefacta*, presuppositions, institutions"[23] according to the "two orders of order"[24] that are beginning and command. The "deconstruction" of metaphysics is first of all a deconstruction of the value of *archē* that not only governs it, but also, in return, makes it an instrument of domination.

> *Archē* ... names at once the *commencement* and *commandment*. This name apparently coordinates two principles in one: the principle according to nature or history, *there where* things *commence* – physical, historical or ontological principle – but also the principle according to the law, *there where* men and gods *command*, *there where* authority, social order are *exercised*, in this place from which *order* is given – nomological principle.[25]

Nevertheless, the archic paradigm has no linear unity: "It was not a question of taking 'metaphysics' [*'la' métaphysique*] as the homogeneous unity of an ensemble." Derrida continues: "I have never believed in the existence or the consistency of something like 'the' metaphysical."[26]

It is therefore not possible to identify with certainty the existence of a beyond or a below tradition – a beyond that would be its absolute outside (Levinas) or a below that would be its before-beginning, its origin (Heidegger's *Ursprung*): "What the work of deconstruction puts into question, is not only the possibility, but also the desire or fantasy of reclaiming the originary, the desire or fantasy too of never reaching the simple, whatever it might be."[27]

Derrida never tires of reiterating his distrust of "archeological" or "genealogical"[28] moves that claim they are desedimenting *archē*, delegitimizing it, while in fact they serve only to produce surplus origins. These moves are found in "classic" political anarchism, as in all the approaches that believe they have found their protest weapon either beyond or within a clearly defined power. Believing that they exceed state-governmental domination or else going back to the primitive existence of societies without a state, anarchism – anarchisms – are blind to their own desires for control.

Second occurrence: Lévi-Strauss the anarchist

Derrida uses the word "anarchism" for the first time in *Of Grammatology*. The deconstruction of traditional anarchism is the oft-overlooked central nerve in his reading of Lévi-Strauss and in the concept of "societies without writing" developed in the second part of the book.

The conclusions of the chapter "Writing Lesson" in *Tristes Tropiques* are well known. The leader of the Nambikwara, who "does not know how to write," is intrigued by the ethnologist's use of a pencil and notepad. He borrows them and pretends that he too is writing when he "traces on his paper some sinuous line or two." Lévi-Strauss comments that "He [the leader] alone … was the one who understood the function of writing. And so he asked me for one of my notepads." The leader then convenes the members of the tribe, feigning to read his lines on the paper, acting as if they listed an account of the gifts the ethnologist was due to give to the villagers: "No sooner was everyone assembled than he drew forth from a basket a piece of paper covered with scribbled lines and pretended to read from it. With a show of hesitation, he looked up and down his 'list' for the objects to be given in exchange for his people's presents."[29]

Lévi-Strauss claims that the change in the leader's attitude – he had never acted this way before – was due to the increased power drawn from his ruse. The symbol of writing "had been borrowed, while its reality remained quite foreign. And the borrowing had been with a view to a sociological, rather than an intellectual end: for it was not a question of knowing, of retaining, or understanding, but enhancing the prestige and authority of one individual – or one function – at the expense of others."[30]

Thanks to the appropriation of the "function" of writing, the leader presents as sovereign. He commands, and thereby discovers the taste of power.[31] With the "invasion" of writing in this "society without a state," the compulsive relation to power appears. The "writing lesson" thematizes the emergence of political domination in a world where it was previously unknown.

Lévi-Strauss then compares the effects of the Nambikwara "writing lesson" with the consequences of obligatory literacy, which he views as one of the most efficient instruments for "man's exploitation by man"[32] in Western societies.

> To bring the matter nearer to our own time: the European-wide movement towards compulsory education in the nineteenth century went hand in hand with the extension of military service and with proletarization. The struggle against illiteracy is thus indistinguishable from the increased powers exerted over the individual citizen by the central authority. For it is only when everyone can read that Authority can decree that "ignorance of law is no defense."[33]

Lévi-Strauss assumes the Marxism of his analysis, which he says is "based upon dialectical materialism."[34] But behind Lévi-Strauss's profession of Marxism, Derrida perceives – and in this lies his original contribution – an *anarchist position*. Lévi-Strauss in fact proves to be less Marxist than "libertarian" in his defense of a vision of the pre-archic "social authenticity," without government, without state, and thus without domination or violence, prior to the appearance of writing.

> Self-presence, transparent proximity in the face to face of countenances and the immediate range of the voice, this determination of social authenticity is therefore classic: … it communicates, we recall, to the Anarchistic and Libertarian protestations against Law, the Powers, and the State in general, and also with the dream of the nineteenth-century Utopian Socialisms, most specifically with the dream of Fourierism.[35]

Derrida goes on to say that this "classic" anarchism would be "perfectly respectable, completely utopian and a-topic as it is ... if it did not live on a lure"[36] – the lure that consists in assimilating the purported space of nonpower to a state of nature. "Lévi-Strauss makes no difference between hierarchization and domination, between political authority and exploitation. The tone that commands these reflections is of an anarchism that deliberately confounds the law and oppression ... Political power can only be the custodian of an unjust power."[37]

Obviously, Derrida does not contest the fact that writing is an instrument of power, but he challenges the notion of a social cohesion foreign to any and all "instruments" of power, including writing: "I do not profess that writing may not and does not in fact play this role [Man's Exploitation by Man], but from that to attribute to writing the specificity of this role and to conclude that speech is exempt from it, is an abyss that one must not leap over ... lightly."[38]

"To leap over lightly" is to leap without looking. Anarchism is "irresponsible" insofar as its apparent pacifism, its dream of innocence, in fact reveals a fantasy of domination, "the lure of presence mastered."[39] The concept of a "society without writing" is the pure product of an ethnocentrism lacking any self-awareness projecting onto a community without any relation to the Western reality, mechanisms that make sense only for this reality.

Derrida does not deny the relation between writing and violence: "It has long been known that the power of writing in the hands of a small number, caste or class, is always contemporaneous with hierarchization, let us say with political *différance*: at the same time distinction into groups, classes, and levels of economico-politico-technical power, and delegation of authority, power deferred and abandoned to an organ of capitalization."[40] This idea also figures in *Archive Fever* in a reminder of the link between writing and the domiciling of power: "the Greek *arkheion*: initially a house, a domicile, an address, the residence of the superior magistrates, the archons, those who commanded ... The *archons* ... have the power to interpret the archives ... they recall the law and call on or impose the law."[41]

However, the power of writing, power as writing, is not initially subordinate to human power. There is human power because writing exists. To understand this point, it is necessary to modify the usual meaning of the word "writing," to distinguish between its narrow technical meaning as a technique for recording speech and its wider sense of "*archē*-writing," at work in all societies, including those described as being "without writing." A silent operation dislocating presence, one that "anarchivizes" the very space where archives are deposited.

Why "*archē*," not "*anarchē*-writing"?

So why is it "*archē*-writing," then, not "*anarchē*-writing"? Derrida does claim that "the problematic of writing is opened by putting into question the value *arkhē*."[42] So why doesn't he speak of "*anarchē*-writing"?

Because political attacks on property have never, up to this point, been attacks on the proper. Instead, whether anarchist or Marxist, all of them have maintained a desire for authenticity – one that is proper to humans, or proper to a nature preceding politico-economic exploitation: "the law of the same and of the proper which always re-forms itself."[43]

In his reading of Artaud in "La parole soufflée," in a thinly veiled allusion to Proudhon, Derrida brings to light another phantasmatic belief of anarchism, namely the belief in the existence of "a place where property would not yet be theft."[44] This place before theft, and prior to private property, is precisely the proper, the assumed authenticity of the self, its treasure. It is what Proudhon, and later Artaud, were afraid of having "soufflé," that is, stolen from them. Prior to any material possession, it is the fear of losing their body, their speech, their genius: "Artaud attempted to forbid that his speech be spirited away [*soufflé*] from his body."[45] Proudhon shares this fear. For him, the revoking of governmental power, the abolition of private property, would be only the first stage in a return to the proper, marking the peaceful reunion of humanity with itself.

Instead of referring to anarchē-writing, which would indicate this same phantasmatic hope of reappropriating the origin, Derrida therefore plays on a single word, writing with and against *archē*. More surely than through the virtue of a negative prefix, the meeting of the "*archē*" and writing explodes in a word – archē-writing – the value of *archē*, whose "trace" is all that remains.

Third occurrence: Levinas risking the transcendental

The dialogue with Levinas begins at this point, with the trace:

> What led us to the choice of this word? ... [W]e relate this concept of trace to what is at the center of the latest work of Emmanuel Levinas and his critique of ontology: relationship ... to the alterity of a past that never was and can never be lived in the originary or modified form of presence.[46]

No sooner as it is named, the trace becomes, in a mere two pages, "archē-trace," "archē-phenomenon," then "archē-writing."[47] By slipping without the slightest transition from trace to archē-trace, Derrida exposes himself to the Levinasian objection. He knows this and is prepared for it. Doesn't the prefix "arche" (archē-writing, archē-trace) surreptitiously, but inevitably, reintroduce the transcendental into the heart of anarchy?

Of course, the concept of *transcendental* anarchy would be quite meaningless for Levinas. The opening to the other, the trace of the other, eludes the diktat of the conditions of possibility, the nomologic overlook that identifies what it holds beneath it in advance. Clearly, for Levinas "the transcendental ... function belongs to the order of power."[48]

Derrida's response is that it is not enough to banish the transcendental to be done with it. Despite itself, doesn't banishing it express the desire to attain an absolute beyond – one more originary than any a priori? More transcendental still than the transcendental? Derrida concedes that there is certainly "a short-of and a beyond the transcendental critique."[49] The challenge is to "see to it that the beyond does not return to the short-of."[50]

Levinas's critique of the transcendental takes aim at both Kant's transcendental – the condition of possibility – and Husserl's transcendental – the condition of intersubjectivity. For both philosophers the transcendental determines the first form of subjectivity and thus establishes its priority over alterity. This is the priority Levinas contests. In particular, he objects to the Husserlian rule stating that the other can appear only as my "alter ego." Derrida comments: "The disagreement [with Husserl] appears definite as concerns others ... To make the other an alter ego, Levinas says frequently, is to neutralize its absolute alterity."[51]

For Levinas, "before the originarity of the *archē*, there is what works always to interrupt it, the pre-original anachrony of an-archy."[52] This anachrony coincides with "heterological purity," that is, the irreducibility of any Other to the "ego-based" approach. But is it possible to posit a non-negotiable "*dream* of a purely heterological thought at its source"?[53]

Derrida demonstrates that "the other cannot be the other – of the same – except by being the same (as itself: ego), and the same cannot be the same (as itself: ego) except by being the other's other: alter ego. That I am also essentially the other's other, and that I know I am, is the evidence of a strange symmetry whose trace appears nowhere in Levinas's descriptions."[54] However, heterology cannot be absolute since "the necessity of speaking of the other as other, or to the other as other, on the basis of its appearing-for-me-as-what-it-is: the other"[55] is inevitable. The Other as other cannot appear, cannot show itself to me. By return, the I cannot think itself as identical to a self, inasmuch as it discovers itself as the other of this other.

A language believing itself to be totally free of this dialectic of self and other would be "a language without phrase, a language which would say nothing"[56] since it would speak to *no one*. The other would be so entirely other that it would become impossible to perceive it as such, and thus to speak to this other. In this silence, this pure light, this absence of expression, "peace itself would no longer have meaning."[57] Anarchy would lose its mind. "A speech produced without the least violence would determine nothing, would say nothing, would offer nothing to the other."[58] Thus, "like pure violence, pure nonviolence is a contradictory concept."[59]

An-archic nonviolence, especially as defined by Levinas, runs the risk of *reducing the Other to slavery*. In fact, "a master who forbids himself the *phrase* would give nothing. He would have no disciples but only slaves."[60] As we have seen, slavery is indeed, here again, the unthought shadow of election.

It is simply impossible to escape the plot of same and other. Neither "pure nonviolence,"[61] nor "absolutely peaceful."[62] There's no choice. "Here as elsewhere, to pose the problem in terms of choice, to oblige or to believe oneself obliged to answer it by a *yes* or *no*" to the transcendental question, leads to an interrogation more powerful still: the question of the silent master. There's no choice here: "In the deconstruction of the *archē, one does not hold an election.*"[63]

The economy of violence therefore calls for negotiation with the transcendental. To say yes or no to it, "the value of the transcendental archē [*archie*] must make its necessity felt before letting itself be erased."[64] To say "yes" first in some sense assumes the transcendental gesture, the opening of articulation. To then say "no" as it is written down. To write the "archē" under erasure "is to recognize in the contortion the necessity of a trail [*parcours*]. That trail must leave a wake in the text. Without that wake, abandoned to the simple content of its conclusions, the ultra-transcendental text will look suspiciously like the precritical text."[65]

But is it certain that the transcendental erases its traces in the deconstructive "trail"? That is what is to be studied in Derrida's dialogue with Freud.

Fourth occurrence: Derrida's reading of *Beyond the Pleasure Principle*

In the course of this dialogue, which continues the engagement with Levinas to some extent, Derrida gets a grip on the question of mastery: "The concept of mastery is an impossible concept to manipulate ... the more there is, the less there is, and vice versa."[66] As if to say, this concept is inevitable, unavoidable. But does that mean it plays a transcendental role?

These are the stakes in the elucidation of what Freud names *Bemächtigungstrieb*, translated variously as drive for mastery, drive for control, or drive for power. This synonymy (mastery = control = power), which allows one term to be used in place of the other, appears to ensure the existence of an untransgressible economy of domination. If all mastery is power, if all power is control, then beyond the pleasure principle transgresses the principle only in order to better reveal the force of this economy. The drive to master (power-control) therefore enjoys a transcendental status that would condemn any anarchist attempt to simply be an expression of it.

In any event, the line of interpretation developed by Derrida is that Freud in fact constitutes mastery (power-control) in a "role of transcendental predicate."[67] It is this constitution that Derrida seeks to trouble, arguing for the need to negotiate with mastery, reducing its hold to a mere "quasi transcendental" status.[68] A form of yes and no. But does he do so successfully? Does he manage to strike through the "transcendental function"[69] of power, to cross it out? The reading is gradually caught in the circle of mastery (power-control) that it is trying to render fluid and differentiate. Prisoner of the trap of his own reading, there's no way out for Derrida.

Freud and the ambiguity of the *Bemächtigungstrieb*

Is there a beyond of the pleasure principle? The title of Freud's work formulates this question elliptically.

Let us recall what is at stake for him. As mentioned earlier, at the beginning Freud recognizes that the pleasure principle is not the only regulating system at work in the psyche. It is possible that other automatisms operate within it. These automatisms have no purpose except their repetition, representing a form of constraint that exceeds the logic of governance. Not knowing satisfaction, or the avoidance of displeasure, or how to compromise with reality, they do not protect their subjects and cause nothing but anxiety and suffering. Severe trauma, the impact of war wounds, and serious accidents haunt the psyche, returning in dreams to reiterate the shock. Repetition, whose compulsive nature Freud was quick to identify, exceeds the pleasure-reality couple. We are now led, he says, to recognize "that there really does exist in the mind a compulsion to repeat which overrides the pleasure principle."[70]

Under the effect of trauma, psychic energy, which is usually "invested," put into circulation, and disciplined by the pleasure principle, loses control. It emancipates itself and remains "free," resisting the conversion of its "change from a freely flowing into a quiescent state."[71] In other words, it resists the "liaison (*Bindung*)" which ordinarily allows "for the dominance of the pleasure principle … to proceed unhindered."[72]

This "freedom" is also a "constraint" (*Zwang*). No longer obeying the principle, the traumatic energy has no way out other than to return, repeating the mechanism that triggers its release. It loses control by binding itself to the mechanism of its unchaining. This is why "the patient is, as one might say, fixated to his trauma."[73]

At first glance, this sort of analysis of compulsion appears to oppose a "no" to an anarchist interpretation of the "beyond." Its mechanical, rigid domination is established. It is during his examination of this compulsion, after observing his grandson's *fort-da* game with the spool, that Freud introduces the drive for mastery, power, or control (*Bemächtigungstrieb*).

The repetitive movement with the spool – throwing it away, then reclaiming it, acting as a substitute for the mother's departure and return – undoubtedly gives the child pleasure. But this pleasure is "of another sort"[74] from that which is usually offered by the decrease in tension. Indeed, "the child cannot possibly have felt his mother's departure as something agreeable or even indifferent. How then does his repetition of this distressing experience as a game fit in with the pleasure principle?"[75] Is it because the return of the spool, which mimics the return of the mother, erases the painful sensation, producing satisfaction? "But against this must be counted the observed fact that the first act, that of departure, was staged as a game in itself,"[76] writes Freud. The explanation must lie elsewhere. Up until now, as a helpless witness to his mother's departure, the child "was in a passive situation – he was overpowered by the experience; but, by repeating it, unpleasurable though it was, as a game, he took on an active part. These efforts might be put down to an instinct for mastery [*Bemächtigungstrieb*] that was acting independently of whether the memory was in itself pleasurable or not."[77]

The drive for mastery is the source of a satisfaction indifferent to the pleasure of its object. It is the satisfaction of control, of "power over." In the game, the child acts as the master of the repetition: "Each fresh repetition seems to strengthen the mastery [*Beherrschung*] they [children] are in search of."[78] Freud thereby establishes a structural relation between the pleasure of mastery and the origin of aggressiveness. However, it appears he sees the beyond the principle only as a hyperarchy, the very origin of domination.

But yes and no appear there where they are least expected, with the entry into the scene of the death drive. What is the nature of the relation between the death drive and the compulsion to repeat, asks Freud.[79] In both cases, it is a return. Death, like compulsion, brings about a return. The elasticity of inertia, death is the return to the inorganic, the repetition of the eve of life. Freud goes on to say that we must formulate the hypothesis "that an instinct is an urge inherent in organic life to restore an earlier state of things."[80] This is the expression of the "conservative nature of living substance,"[81] which "would from its very beginning have had no wish to change."[82] Thus, Freud concludes, "if we are to take it as a truth that knows no exception that everything living dies for internal reasons – becomes inorganic once again – then we shall be compelled to say that '*the aim of all life is death*' and, looking backwards, that '*inanimate things existed before living ones.*'"[83]

Analyzed in this way, death is the yes and no of power. On the one hand, death manifests in life as the sharp edge of the power drive, as shown with sadism and masochism, its aggressive and destructive versions. Freud writes that the "original sadism takes on … the function of overpowering the sexual object." Meanwhile masochism, the "component instinct which is complementary to sadism, must be regarded as sadism that has been turned round upon the subject's own ego."[84] The desire to kill, to suffer, to impose suffering, to hurt (oneself) are all messengers of Thanatos.

On the other hand, while death is murder and violence, it is also repose. The backward return marks the extinction of the compulsion, the "remov[al] of internal tension,"[85] the place without a place in which all principles surrender to principleness. The return of the living to the inorganic state is an undoing in the literal sense. If this return still obeys a principle, it is not the pleasure principle, but rather the "Nirvana principle"[86] – the very opposite of a principle, despite its name. As Laplanche and Pontalis explain: "The term 'Nirvana,' which was given currency in the West by Schopenhauer, is drawn from Buddhism, where it connotes the 'extinction' of human desire, the abolition of individuality when it is fused into the collective soul, a state of quietude and bliss."[87]

The impossibility of clearly establishing the status of a beyond the principle in Freud turns out to offer either murder or relinquishing: hyperpower on one side, relinquishing power on the other. Yes and no.

"What is the difference between a principle and a drive?"[88]

It is striking that, in his reading of Freud's text, Derrida spends more time on chaining[89] than on unleashing, focusing more on binding (*Bindung*) than on unbinding – to the point that it is no longer clear which of them – Freud or Derrida – is the least anarchist. Derrida certainly fully acknowledged the activity of unbinding:

There is trauma when, at the limit, on the frontier post, the protective barrier is broken through. In this case the entire defensive organization is defeated, its entire energetic economy routed ... The PP [pleasure principle] is put out of action (*außer Kraft gesetzt*). It no longer directs the operations, it loses its mastery when faced with submersion, flooding (*Überschwemmung*, the image of a sudden inundation, as at the breaking of a dike): great quantities of excitation whose inrush instantaneously overflows the psychic apparatus.[90]

Nonetheless, Derrida asserts that this transgression of the pleasure principle can never "permit the conclusion of a last step."[91]

Even as he recognizes that Freud's text is going nowhere, "limping along," failing to answer its own question, even as he takes on this unanswered question, leading it to its most extreme aporia, Derrida tightens the vice and does in fact come to a resolution on the question: his answer is no. There is no beyond the principle. The difference between principle and drive – between power and death – comes of their complicity: "It is always a question of knowing who is the 'master,' who 'dominates,' who has 'authority'."[92] Ultimately, Derrida shows that the master is well and truly, always, mastery.

What does "mastery" really mean for Derrida?

We recall that right at the beginning of his text, Freud calls into question the "mastery" (*Herrschaft*) of the pleasure principle. When he studies the possibility of a beyond the pleasure principle by analyzing the compulsion to repeat, as we saw above with the spool game, what he observes is the existence of "mastery." This time it is the mastery of *Bemächtigungstrieb*. If, as Derrida is apparently confident, *Herrschaft*, *Beherrshung*, and *Bemächtigung* are taken to have the same meaning in German, then it is fully legitimate to conclude that beyond mastery lies mastery. But is it the same mastery as the mastery of the pleasure principle? Or another? It's both at once, says Derrida.

While he recognizes that the beyond the pleasure principle can be "something other than mastery, something completely other"[93] than the *Herrschaft* of the principle, Derrida also asserts that, despite everything, this completely other remains an effect of the principle, that is, it is only the displaced figure of the same: "The mastery of the PP [pleasure principle] would be none other than mastery in general: there is not a *Herrschaft* of the PP, there is *Herrschaft* which is distanced from itself only in order to reappropriate itself: a tautoteleology which nevertheless makes or lets the other return in its domestic specter."[94] The completely other of mastery is also its identity.

Derrida claims that this "yes and no" of the identity and alterity of mastery (power-control) to itself is the *différance* of mastery: "It is the same *différant*, in *différance* with itself."[95] Between principle, government, control, drive, compulsion, mastery, "there is only *différance* of power."[96] The power (mastery, control), is power difference, power as it is distributed among its many different instances, its numerous synonyms. This is how Derrida fluidifies the transcendental function of power, showing how it circulates between its "posts,"[97] its positions, without stopping at any of them.

So, is it *différance*, as a metamorphic, plastic instance of power that is beyond the pleasure principle? Is *différance* the anarchist?

Despite everything, the answer is "no." To say that power is nothing but the *différance* of power amounts to recognizing that power can never be exceeded by anything that is not power. Power is differed, but never lost. Its multiple "posts" are but one and the same "dynamics of dynasty."[98]

Derrida would respond that the argument of *différance* of power is also what prevents power from existing as the proper. And he would do so *contra* Freud. Indeed, he considers that, for Freud, "the most driven drive is the drive of the proper, in other words, the one that tends to reappropriate itself. The movement of reappropriation is the most driven drive. The proper of driveness is the movement or the force of reappropriation. The proper is the tendency to appropriate oneself."[99] The death drive does its tour of the property by bringing the organism "back to their primeval, inorganic state."[100] Not only does it bring life back to its proper "goal," it also guarantees each one its own death. Freud does claim that each death is singular, that "the organism wishes to die only in its own fashion."[101] With the introduction of the death drive, Freud finally completes the circle.

> The drive to dominate must also be the drive's *relation to itself*: there is no drive not driven to bind itself to itself and to assure itself of mastery over itself

as a drive. Whence the transcendental tautology of the drive to dominate: it is the drive as drive, the drive of the drive, the drivenness of the drive.[102]

For this reason, "mastery" (power, control) has a transcendental status in Freud's work. To the point that psychic control, both principled and driven, "would be from this ... mastery in its so-called current, usual, or literal, to wit proper, sense would be derived, in the "domains" of technique or expertise, of politics or the struggle between consciousnesses."[103]

If there is anarchy, then according to Freud it would be nothing but this transcendental laid bare. Anarchy would be power a priori.

One of the great advantages of this type of interpretation is that it asks the question of what might become of the drive for power, the desire to harm, to be hurt, the impulse to destroy, and cruelty in an anarchist society. Wouldn't the relation between dominating and submitting replace the relation between commanding and obeying? Wouldn't it be worse than the logic of government?

But we have to ask again whether *différance* would manage to introduce play (the play of "quasi") into the transcendental? Whether *différance* would enable the emergence of a deconstructed and deconstructive anarchism?

The anarchist drive

No, it's by no means certain. Where does Derrida get the idea in Freud of an alterity of the pleasure principle that "overlaps" with it?[104] Where does he draw this identification between mastery and the proper? Where does Freud imply that the compulsion to repeat can only be the postcard of the pleasure principle, the send-off it offers itself from itself through the detour of a momentary deferral? What about trauma, accidents, war wounds, and other shocks? Don't they come from outside, from a place *outside and beyond différance*? Perhaps, too, then from a place outside and beyond mastery? Why do anarchy or the anarchic always have to be the envoys of the prince?

There is absolutely *nothing* confirming categorically that, for Freud, anything beyond the pleasure principle is the proper exiled or momentarily decentered. Nor does anything suggest a drive of the proper – which is a phrase that Freud never uses. By contrast, and contrary to

Derrida's assertion, *there is nothing in Freud that prohibits the possibility of envisaging the death drive as independent from power.*

Derrida would probably say that independence is another power effect. And Freud partially supports this view when he recognizes, for example, the independence of the "sadistic component in the sexual instinct." Freud writes: "From the very first we recognized the presence of a sadistic component in the sexual instinct. As we know, it can make itself independent and can, in the element of a perversion, dominate an individual's entire sexual activity."[105] This component "also emerges as a predominant component instinct"[106] and detaches itself from the libidinal organization in order to behave in an autonomous manner and with compulsive repetition.

Freud acknowledges that "it was not easy ... to demonstrate" the existence of an instinct of death – which operates "silently within the organism towards its dissolution"[107] – except by offering its only visible manifestation as an example, namely the partial drive of aggression and destruction.[108]

At the same time, it is difficult to ignore that the death drive, as conceived by Freud, opens anarchy to *another fate, another différance.* By working to undo the assemblies that Eros constructs, the death drive interrupts its compounding work, the fusional weaving together, sheep-like, of the social bond. Moreover, this dissolution, this unbinding, is not necessarily the effect of a destructive fury. Paradoxically, it can give rise to other types of connection that are different from the social cohesion of government and different from the obedient community. Bonds born of a breaking of bonds. Breaking with the bonds of dependence. Breaking with hierarchical bonds. Breaking with the tendency to gather, the movements of crowds and their correlative, cult leaders and celebrating tyrants. What if – contrary to what Derrida claims – the death drive were a prefiguring of political anarchy as a community *unbound from its bonds to mastery*?

The fact that Freud himself never thematically imagines such a fate does not stop some psychoanalysts, such as Nathalie Zaltzman, from proposing it as a hypothesis.[109] For Zaltzman, the death drive is neither the anarchic drive, nor the anarchy drive; rather, it is the drive that is "anarchist" and "liberating." Moreover, "La pulsion anarchiste" [the anarchist drive] is the title she gives her most important work, in which she claims that there is "another type of death drive,"[110] one that grasps *another form of life from the death drive*. A life that resists the unifying and otherwise destructive grasp of Eros.[111] One that also fundamentally breaks away from mastery. As Dominique Scarfone puts it, "we might then suggest that control is another name for that which the anarchist drive rises up against as Nathalie Zaltzman has drawn to our attention."[112]

I shall return below to Zaltzman's work, since her reflections on the relation between this other death drive and political anarchism are invaluable. For the time being, I want to emphasize that Derrida never imagines that *Beyond the Pleasure Principle* might be read in terms of this kind of anarchism, this *other* anarchism that has the possibility of surviving the absence of a master without being "irresponsible." The possibility of a non-governable — which is not to be confused with the ungovernable of Derrida's *différance*.

Questions for Foucault

In *Resistances of Psychoanalysis* Derrida admits he would have liked to ask Foucault if *Bemächtigungstrieb* had played a role in his thinking: "How would Foucault have situated this drive for mastery in his discourse on power or on irreducibly plural powers?"[113] What would he who never mentions *Beyond the Pleasure Principle* have thought? "Would he have inscribed this problematic matrix *within* the whole whose history he describes? Or would he have put it on the other side, on the side of what allows one, on the contrary, to delimit the whole, indeed, to problematize it?"[114] Would the drive for power occupy the thematizing or the thematized edge of Foucauldian thought on power?

Derrida suggests that, just as for him, Foucault would answer that it's on both edges at once, with both parties participating in the same network, the same *différance*. Derrida imagines Foucault's response in the following words (his own):

> What one must stop believing in is principality or principleness, in the problematic of the principle, in the principled unity of pleasure and power, or of some drive that is thought to be more originary than the other. The theme of the *spiral* would be that of a drive duality (power/pleasure) that is *without principle*.[115]

This means that Foucault would have said exactly what Derrida wanted to hear. What he wanted to hear is what he believed himself to have said in his reading of *Beyond the Pleasure Principle*, namely, that *différance* is the non-principled unity of principle and drive, which prevents us from settling on either one by relating them to each other as a short-of and beyond. Power circulates, transgresses itself, without finding itself stuck in any one of its positions, including transgression itself. The *différance* – rather than the beyond – of power is its constitutive anarchy, which is never fixed or hardened, and which keeps moving among its positions.

But this Foucauldian ventriloquism is not entirely convincing. In fact, Derrida was not able to support this response, or, rather, what he believed to be his response. The pyramid was replaced by a spiral. Despite himself, Derrida recognized the non-derived, originary nature of the drive for mastery (power-control) – and thus, ultimately, its value as principle.

Freud's answers

As we have seen, Derrida would object that it is Freud who grants a "role of transcendental predicate"[116] to this drive. Meanwhile, we have also seen that Derrida himself grants it only a "quasi transcendental" status.

Transcendental or quasi transcendental. In this almost Kantian interpretation of the role of *Bemächtigungstrieb*, Freud might perhaps have seen a sort of masked avowal by Derrida of the inevitably unmovable, untransgressible nature of this drive. At the end of "To speculate – on 'Freud'" an undeconstructed Freud might have undertaken a deconstruction of the *mastery* obsession of his keen reader.

What might Freud have said? That, in the end, Derrida fails to establish the difference between *différance* and the drive for power. Since any beyond the drive for power would be nothing but the play of *différance* with itself, how could they not be identical? Consequently, *différance* remains the drive for power and power the drive for *différance*. Can *différance* be anything except a logic of domination then? In the end, for the sake of his "responsible anarchism," and by paradoxically trying to deconstruct Freud, doesn't Derrida demonstrate that the drive for power ultimately always gets what it wants?

Of course not. He would never accept that. But how then, if not through an *abuse of power*? Clearly, it's not a matter of choice. In order to put a stop to the insane identification of *différance* with power, the only solution is to set up firewalls, dikes in *différance*, since it cannot be distinguished from power, since the control over control appears to be limitless. *Since deconstruction cannot deconstruct the drive for power – starting with its own drive for power.*

How can the intransigent tendency toward mastery, control, domination be brought to an end except by reintroducing the obstacle of the old opposition between violence and nonviolence, even if it was believed to be deconstructed – *thereby acting violently against deconstruction itself*? The disavowal of anarchy and anarchism occurs right there, by restoring the old borders we thought were divisible and divided.

Terrorism, anarchy, and protective barriers

Derrida's late work applies itself precisely to this restoration. Years after *The Post Card*, in *Philosophy in a Time of Terror*,[117] Derrida remarks that the new "world order" makes it no longer possible to distinguish between state terrorism and anarchist terrorism. After the attack on the Twin Towers, the difference "between war and terrorism, national and international terrorism, state and nonstate terrorism"[118] became undecidable. The trauma of September 11 catalyzed the reality of this lack of differentiation between state-governmental power and the power coming from nonstate entities such as Al-Qaeda and Daesh, "anonymous and nonstate organizations, armed and virtually nuclear powers."[119]

By asserting ever more strongly the global, hegemonic, and undifferentiated nature of the drive for power, Derrida well and truly reintroduces a short-of, and a beyond-of, this drive.

Short-of. The drive for power is eventually equated with what can only be called a *state of nature*. Admittedly, it is not the type that Lévi-Strauss projects onto Nambikwara society, but rather a Hobbesian-style state of nature, the nature of wolves. One can't help noticing Derrida's very conventional interpretation of Hobbes. In *Philosophy in a Time of Terror*, he sees this in the notion of "terror," which Hobbes equates with the natural "anarchy" that is the direct ancestor of terrorism.[120] The drive for power is thus absorbed into terror, and terror into anarchy-chaos. When Derrida reads Hobbes, anarchy becomes the state of nature of power.[121]

Beyond. Looking backwards, toward "nature," toward the wolf, also determines the opposite move – a look toward the "beyond" of this generalized terror. Toward the halo of a promise that Derrida calls the "beyond of the beyond." Beyond the Freudian beyond the pleasure principle, since, as we have seen, Freud apparently does not go beyond. In "Psychoanalysis searches the states of its soul," the question is as follows: "Is there, for thought … another beyond, if I can say that, a beyond that would stand beyond these *possibles* that are still *both* the pleasure and reality principles and the death or sovereign mastery drives, which seem to be at work wherever cruelty is on the horizon?"[122]

The beyond of the beyond is invested with a messianic dimension. Without a messiah, without even messianism, of course, but nevertheless available to a redemptive coming. To a "hospitality of visitation."[123] This hospitality has several names: absolute arriving, *khôra*, and the "non-places" that are the island, promised land, and desert – "the most anarchic and anarchival place[s] possible."[124] In this way, "pacifist" nonviolent anarchism stages its (re)entry.

This messianic anarchism does, of course, have a political basis for Derrida. But it is anchored *in the center*, in a very solid conception of parliamentary democracy and the state, as seen when he asks: "What could one do with an irreducible death drive and an invincible drive for power in a politics and a law that would be *progressive*?"[125] To ask this is to call for a conception of democracy that protects messianic anarchism against the natural *anarchy* of revolutionary anarchism.[126]

Although he states that democracy is still to come, and although he engages in a biting critique of representative democracy,[127] Derrida nonetheless considers that for now it offers the only acceptable compromise. This is the case even if the traditional concept of democracy still conforms to his classic definition of "sovereign self-determination," "autonomy," and "one-self that gives itself its own law."[128] Even if it still plays its role of *archē*. This concept may also make a false start in its traditional role to emancipate itself from it. Democracy, which "is never properly what it is, never itself,"[129] may be surprising. For this reason, it is the only political regime "that welcomes the possibility of being contested, of contesting itself, of criticizing and indefinitely improving itself."[130] It is in this sense that democracy is always still to come.

So, Derrida says, let us accept compromise again for the time being:

> In this unleashing of violence without name [September 11], if I had to take one of the two sides and choose in a *binary* situation, well, I would. Despite my very strong reservations about the American, indeed European, political posture ... despite all the de facto betrayals, all the failures to live up to democracy, international law, and the very international institutions [...] I would take the side of the camp that, in *principle* [here it is, the principle], by *right of law*, leaves a perspective open to perfectibility in the name of the "political," democracy, international law, international institutions, and so on.[131]

Deconstruction is saved from evil – and it turns out democracy is "undeconstructible."

Undeniable anarchism, anarchism denied

But this is also to deny deconstruction. The undeconstructible nature of democracy would then simultaneously both mark and mask the undeconstructible nature of the drive for power. Nothing can be done to prevent it except installation of the governmental guard rail.

Of course, Derrida would object that to deny something always amounts also to asserting that it is undeniable. To deny the possibility of anarchism is thus perhaps to declare that it is undeniable. The disavowal of anarchism would then be the condition *sine qua non* of its affirmation. Derrida would most likely say the same thing about anarchism as he did about faith: "One cannot deny it, which means that the most one can do is to deny it."[132] Indeed, "Any discourse that would be opposed to it would, in effect, always succumb to the figure or the logic of disavowal."[133]

Despite everything, Derrida never imagined – even to deny it – the possibility of an anarchism that would be neither a sadomasochistic republic nor a promised land. That's why there's no dismissing the reader who claims that Derrida "ends up reading politics as nothing more than a question of the State."[134] This claim was already made in the GREPH report: "A certain state rationality seems to us to have been granted to the unity of the philosophical. We do not want to abandon that purely and simply, but to represent the most powerful means of struggling against the class forces or interests (for example) that would profit from empiricism or political anarchism."[135] The "freedom in relation to a State" must therefore be only "relative."[136]

How would class interests take advantage of political anarchism? There's no way to know since deconstruction gave political anarchism no chance.

I'd like to close with this idea of "relative freedom." With this distrust of absolute freedom, which Derrida never gave up – whether it be the freedom of unconscious energy unleashed or the rational autonomy of the subject. In a conversation with Jean-Luc Nancy, Derrida admits: "I ... have been led ... to treat this word [*à mettre le mot de liberté en veilleuse*] with some caution, to use it guardedly, indeed sparingly, in a reserved, parsimonious, and circumspect manner. I've always done so with some concern, in bad conscience."[137] How can we not underline every word in this confession? Use the word freedom with caution! Put freedom on hold! Put it on the back burner![138]

With no ill-intent and the best will in the world, philosopher Charles Ramond goes so far as to claim that "Jacques Derrida was never a philosopher of freedom."[139] Is he right? At this point, I no longer know whether to say "yes and no" ... But what a claim!

Ultimately, the anarchist, like the rogue [*voyou*], finds their place only in the street or in prison.

> The *voyou* is at once unoccupied, if not unemployed, and actively occupied with occupying the streets, either by "roaming the streets" doing nothing loitering, or by doing what is not supposed to be done, that is, according to established norms, laws, and the police. The *voyou* does what is not supposed to be done in the streets and on all the other byways.[140]

So the unemployed, the crooks, and the revolutionaries are all mixed up together. Is that fair? Again, at this point, I no longer know whether to answer "yes and no" ...

One thing is sure: by situating "voyoucracy" somewhere between "anarchic chaos" and "structured disorder,"[141] Derrida seems to have forgotten a third way – the possibility of an anarchist order. The very possibility of the non-governable.

By the same token, he occludes the possibility that perhaps anarchists are not, in fact, rogues.

7

Anarcheology
Michel Foucault's Last Government

> One day, Plato would have seen Diogenes the Cynic washing his salad. Plato sees him washing his salad and, recalling that Dionysius had appealed to Diogenes and that Diogenes had rejected his appeal, he says to him: If you had been more polite to Dionysius you would not have to wash your salad. To which Dionysius replies: If you had acquired the habit of washing your salad, you would not have been the slave of Dionysius.[1]
>
> Michel Foucault

For Foucault, there's no drive for power. He says it's impossible to ascribe an origin, root, or provenance to power, even one "deferred" (*différante*) or diffracted on the edges of a play of masks. Contrary to widespread assumptions, there's no instinctual origin of power such as a violence or death instinct. If there's no power without manifestations of truth and if the relation between power and truth is the political question – the most obscure and difficult to think through – it is because, paradoxically, power has no truth. There's no pure state of power. Hence Foucault's striking statement:

> It is often said that, in the final analysis, there is something like a kernel of violence behind all relations of power and that if one were to strip power of its showy garb one would find the naked game of life and death. Maybe. But can there be power without showy garb? In other words, can there really be a power that would do without the play of light and shadow, truth and error, true and false, hidden and manifest, visible and invisible?[2]

Even if power relations can become fixed as relations of domination, and even if domination can become fixed as Terror, there is still no universal destructive "tendency" revealed in these fossilizations that transcends each and every historical occurrence of aggressiveness. It is tempting to strip down the drive for power, but this nakedness only reveals another layer. Power does not exist in its own right and has no "relation to itself." There is no drive for power. No power principle. Not even a "postal" one.

The definition of anarchy is therefore not to be sought short-of or beyond, and still less in beyond the beyond or in the *archē*. Foucault situates anarchy elsewhere – in the place where it resists – and so perhaps also in a place where it resists anarchism.

Anarchism rethought

It is extremely difficult to pinpoint Foucault's disavowal of anarchism. An obvious first reason is that the dissociation between anarchy and anarchism is not as clear and frank in his work as in the work of other philosophers.

Foucault does distance himself from traditional anarchism. He says, "I am not anarchist in that I do not accept this entirely negative conception of power."[3] And he does not accept "the idea that there exists a human nature or base that, as a consequence of certain historical, economic, and social processes, has been concealed, alienated, or imprisoned in and by mechanisms of repression."[4]

To accept the anarchist hypothesis that human nature is oppressed by the state would be to believe that "all that is required is to break these repressive deadlocks and man will be reconciled with himself, rediscover his nature or regain contact with his origin, and reestablish a full and positive relationship with himself."[5] Given that nineteenth-century anarchists share in the political racism "inscribed in the workings of the modern State,"[6] this conclusion is all the more contradictory.

It is evident that these critiques of traditional anarchism cannot be viewed as formal rejections, however. Foucault himself considers them to be off-the-cuff, sweeping comments, and sometimes tempers them.[7] For example, in *On the Government of the Living*, he exclaims:

> You will tell me: there you are, this is anarchy; it's anarchism. To which I shall reply: I don't quite see why the words "anarchy" or "anarchism" are so pejorative that the mere fact of employing them counts as a triumphant critical discourse. ... The position I adopt does not absolutely exclude anarchy – and after all, once again, why would anarchy be so condemnable?[8]

Generally, Foucault's wariness amounts to rethinking and reorienting political anarchism – never to discounting or dismissing it.

The concept of "anarcheology" that appears in *On the Government of the Living* reveals all that Foucault excludes, and what he retains, from classical anarchism: "Instead of employing the word 'anarchy' or 'anarchism,' which would not be appropriate, I shall make a play on words … So I will say that what I am proposing is rather a sort of anarcheology."[9]

Anarcheology is a critical attitude positing "that no power goes without saying, that no power, of whatever kind, is obvious or inevitable,"[10] and which undertakes a contradictory genesis of hierarchies without a founding term and without teleology.

It is difficult to thematize a disavowal of anarchism in the work of one of the only twentieth-century philosophers who takes it seriously in the realm of politics – to the point that, with his concept of anarcheology, Foucault has become the main philosopher of "post-anarchism." All contemporary theorizations of anarchy inevitably relate, one way or another, to Foucault. "Post-anarchists" read a deep redeployment of historical anarchism in his work, one that rids itself of teleology, making it available to ideas of transversality, multiplicity, and the intersection of different battles. Todd May, for instance, claims that Foucault "offer[s] a compelling anarchist vision that at once emerges from and continues the anarchist tradition"[11] by displacing it toward a new theory of practice. Saul Newman goes further, suggesting that Foucault opened up a perspective that "one can theorize the possibility of political resistance without essentialist guarantees."[12]

Resistance and transformation

Increasing numbers of scholars are making the argument that a Foucauldian anarchism exists. Post-anarchists, such as Derek Barnett, and before them Gilles Deleuze, highlight two of its salient features, which are inseparable from one another: *resistance* and *transformation*.

Resistance

To claim there is no "kernel of violence" hiding "behind" power relations is to question the existence of a state of nature, whatever form it takes:

traditional, updated, or even deconstructed. The origin of power is resistance to power, thus still another power.

As we have seen, the Foucauldian reading of Hobbes tends to demonstrate that what Hobbes describes as a state of permanent war is in fact society, rather than the state of nature.

> The social body is not made up of a pyramid of orders or of a hierarchy, and it does not constitute a coherent and unitary organism. It is composed of two groups, and they are not only quite distinct, but also in conflict. And the conflictual relationship that exists between the two groups that constitute the social body and shapes the State is in fact one of war, of permanent warfare. The State is nothing more than the way that the war between the two groups in question continues to be waged in apparently peaceful forms.[13]

One might leap to the conclusion that, for Hobbes, sovereignty acts as a force with which to eradicate "anarchy," and, indeed, it is true that "basically, Hobbes's discourse is a certain 'no' to war."[14]

But if "anarchy" can nevertheless be interpreted as the "permanent grounds" for civil war, it is because Hobbes is thinking about the emergence of rebel groups that formed during the English civil war of 1642–51 – specifically the *Levellers* and the *Diggers* who claimed equality before the law against the sovereign. Their rebellions are often related to anarchism as examples of historical battles. For the Levellers (thus named as a criticism that they sought to flatten social hierarchy), "the relationship between the nobles and the king, and the people, is not one of protection, but simply one of plunder and theft."[15] It is not royal protection that is extended to the people; rather, it is the exaction of the nobility from which the king benefits and that the king guarantees. Foucault later explains:

> The people have in a sense never ceased to denounce property as pillage, laws as exactions, and governments as domination. The proof is that they have never stopped rebelling – and for the Diggers, rebellion is nothing but the obverse of the permanent war. Laws, power, and government are the obverse of war ... Rebellion is a response to a war that the government never stops waging. Government means their war against us; rebellion is our war against

them. ... [The Levellers and] the Diggers therefore say that a war declared in response to that war must free us from all laws. The civil war against Norman power has to be fought to the end.[16]

Hobbes's apparent revelation of the root of power – man's wolf-like nature – in fact conceals a strategy that consists in stating that there is, on the contrary, no pre-political state of politics. That nature is always already in the political. The reality of the supposed state of nature is the social war that determines that state politics will be nothing but "the continuation of war by other means."[17]

For Foucault, resistance is thus no less than constitutive of power:

> Yes. You see, if there was no resistance, there would be no power relations. Because it would simply be a matter of obedience. You have to use power relations to refer to the situation where you're not doing what you want. *So resistance comes first*, and resistance remains superior to the forces of the process; power relations are obliged to change with the resistance. So I think that resistance is the main word, the key word, in this dynamic.[18]

The claim that resistance comes first implies that it is resistance, rather than state-governmental *archē*, that is the origin of politics. Against official theories that make the institution of state and government a principle-based political act, Foucault asserts the primacy of "agonism," "of a relationship which is at the same time reciprocal incitation and struggle."[19]

> [To start from agonism] consists in taking the forms of resistance against different forms of power as a starting point. To use another metaphor, it consists of using this resistance as a chemical catalyst so as to bring to light power relations, locate their position, and find out their point of application and methods used. Rather than analyzing power from the point of view of its internal rationality, it consists of analyzing power relations through the antagonism of strategies.[20]

Foucault's intervention is unique in that it makes the archic paradigm secondary, both logically and chronologically, to that which resists it. Political thought is based then neither "on legal models, that is: What legitimates power?" nor "on institutional models, that is: What is the state?"[21] in a break from all contract theories. Indeed, "power is not a function of consent" or of "'voluntary servitude.'"[22] Countering "political science" and "the tyranny of overall discourses," Foucault highlights the importance of "subjugated knowledges," "left to lie fallow," those that are dedicated to "a historical knowledge of struggles" and the raw "memory of combats."[23]

Resistance to *archē* is not, however, invested with any transcendental dignity. Nor does it have the status of a drive. Resistance exists because no power is necessary per se: "All power only ever rests on the contingency and fragility of a history, that the social contract is a bluff and civil society a children's story, [and] that there is no universal, immediate, and obvious right that can everywhere and always support any kind of relation of power."[24] Consequently, resistance itself is unpredictable, taking a contingent form, and always specific, engaged in the movement of its transformations. Foucault explains: "The small lateral approach on the opposite track that I am proposing consists in trying to bring into play in a systematic way … the non-necessity of all power of whatever kind."[25] This "small lateral approach" involves equating the transformability of resistance with the "non-necessity of power" and the non-necessity of power with the "principle of intelligibility of [political] knowledge itself."[26]

Transformation

Transformability is also for Foucault a prime political stake. He claims not only that power relations, thought, *praxis*, trajectories, and personal experiences are transformable, but also that power, thought, *praxis*, trajectories, and personal experiences exist – and can only exist – by transforming themselves. Hence his famous statement:

> My problem is to substitute the analysis of *different types of transformation* for the abstract general and wearisome form of "change" in which one so willingly thinks in terms of succession … Replacing, in short, the theme of becoming (general form, abstract element, primary cause and universal effect, a confused mixture of the identical and the new) by the analysis of the *transformations* in their specifics.[27]

Transformability and transformations of power relations. Transformability and transformations of modes of resistance. Transformability and transformations of Foucault himself.

Far from being the neutral spectator of the "modes of objectification" that make up the process of subjectivation, Foucault always included himself in his analysis, putting his own life into play in the compelling economy of an experimental philosophy: "One should be, for oneself and throughout one's existence, one's own object."[28] This is why he also states that "there is no book that I've written without there having been, at least in part, a direct personal experience."[29] And, "I am not interested in the academic status of what I am doing because my problem is my own transformation."[30]

Personal mutations and collective mutations are closely connected. If a book is always the trace of a metamorphosis one way or another, it necessarily engages its readers in the movement of its plasticity:

> Starting from experience, it is necessary to clear the way for a transformation, a metamorphosis which isn't simply individual, but which has a character accessible to others: that is, this experience must be linkable, to a certain extent, to a collective practice and to a way of thinking.[31]

In *L'Anarchisme aujourd'hui*, Vivien García gets it just right: Foucault "dared to apply the anarchist attitude to anarchism itself."[32]

Disavowal: smokescreen readings

It is, however, precisely in this argument about transformability and transformation, ascribed to Foucault's anarchism, that I begin to see something that turns against this supposed anarchism.

I have described how readers are engaged in the plasticity of transformations. But how can we read Foucault if he's never who he is? The metamorphic nature of his trajectories condemn his readers to embark on a periodization of his work, and there's no end of books and articles: the first Foucault, the second Foucault, the third Foucault …[33] *The thing is, there's also a last Foucault.* The last one: the "ethical" Foucault, the Foucault of the final seminars. Is this Foucault in any way a continuation of his previous forms? Or does he change perspective entirely by somehow becoming a lost cause politically?

These are essential questions for establishing anarchism. Does the "last" Foucault develop a form of ethical anarchism that ends the long critique of government and governmentality developed throughout his work without any real break? Or does he limit himself to what Murray Bookchin condescendingly termed a "lifestyle anarchism,"[34] an anarchism that more or less abandons resistance, threatening to destroy all previous developments? An anarchism that prolongs the ambiguity of the relation to neoliberalism developed in *The Birth of Biopolitics* and that presents itself as a deviation of anarcho-capitalism?[35]

Neither of these interpretations is correct to my mind since they both miss Foucault's anarchism right when they think they've got it. In fact, his anarchism lies *neither in immanence, nor in betrayal.*

It's a unique phenomenon: *Foucault's disavowal of anarchism occurs first of all among his readers*, who try to describe this anarchism but fail to see it where it is. Immanence and betrayal are but smokescreens.

To shed light on this complex situation, I'll take a shot at offering my own periodization, tracking the major transformations of the concept of government in Foucault's thought, with particular attention to the last period. The question of government is certainly the one that underwent the greatest changes in this philosophy, and which, consequently, has been subject to the most interpretations. But in my view, all these readings fail to identify the breaking point that completely eludes the continuity–discontinuity and immanence–betrayal pairings and that signals Foucault's radical anarchism. This rupture comes to light in the very last seminar, *The Courage of Truth*,[36] in which the theme of the non-governable finally appears.

Foucault maintains the necessity to be governed for a long time, even when he claims to be challenging it. Clearly, adjourning the logic of government is the most difficult of all questions for him. In "What is critique?" he equates critique with the desire "not to be governed,"[37] but then adds that this "desire" is the will "not to be governed like that, by that, in the name of those principles, with such and such an objective in mind and by means of such procedures, not like that, not for that, not by them."[38] He does not say: "not to be governed at all." Moreover, in the discussion after the lecture, he adds: "I was not referring to something that would be a fundamental anarchism, that would be like an originary freedom, absolutely and wholeheartedly resistant to any governmentalization. I did not say it, but this does not mean that I absolutely exclude it."[39] And yet, he does exclude it, at least "relatively."

Foucault will manage to abandon the necessity to be governed only at the last moment, when the final explosion occurs. But the problem is that this explosion of government *is still concealed by a concept of government*. This is what authorizes, on the part of his readers, a recuperation either through the misinterpretation of immanence, or through a lifestyle cult that is the direct expression of a renouncing of political resistance.

We're faced with a dual difficulty: the opacity of the readings and the dissimulation of the avowal.

Foucault's veritable anarchist explosion, the underground explosion that is a secret even for him, is thus still to be entirely conceptualized.

The "problem of government" and the problem with the problem

There are three stages and major transformations in Foucault's elaboration of the concept of government. First, in his analyses of sovereignty, Foucault conserves the traditional meaning of government as "the supreme instance of executive and administrative decisions in State systems"[40] devoted to the exercise of political sovereignty. Second, in the early 1980s, "government" is replaced by "governmentality." The study of governmentality, especially in his *Security, Territory, Population* seminar (1981), supersedes the study of sovereignty. Governmentality no longer refers to government strictly speaking, but rather to the "*problem* of government." Indeed, Foucault announces: "We are, I believe, at the beginning of a huge crisis of a wide-ranging reevaluation of the problem of 'government.'"[41]

Third, governmentality is transformed with the introduction of *parrēsia* into the very heart of the "problem," so that it becomes the problem of "government of men by the truth."[42] Foucault develops this problem through his exploration of the two directions of government of self and government of others. But at the end of this exploration, in *The Courage of Truth*, a final transformation takes place, one that is rarely noticed: the abandoning of the "political arena."[43] This abandonment is certainly not an abandonment of politics, but rather a pure and simple abandoning of the theme of government – both its concept and institutional necessity.

Why is this anarchism always unavowed? That's what we must try to understand.

Governmentality

Let's start with governmentality, with the "problem of government." This is a twofold problem since it describes the fact that, beginning in the sixteenth century, the emergence of a logic of "governmentalization of the state"[44] gradually replaces the legal model of sovereignty, while at the same time referring to resistance to this same governmentalization.

Governmentalization of the state. Behind all the sixteenth-century treatises on the "art of governing," Foucault discerns the appearance of a new economy of power that must be clearly distinguished from sovereignty.[45] A specific governmental rationality emerges that is still at work today – one that no longer consists simply in "imposing law on men" but rather in developing "multiform tactics," that correspond to a mass of "specific finalities" in order to improve the "welfare of the population."[46] Living conditions and life expectancy, health and hygiene: "the population comes to appear above all else as the ultimate end of the government."[47]

These different "tactics" constitute a new "reason of state":[48] "The state is governed according to rational principles that are so intrinsic to it and cannot be derived solely from divine laws."[49] The fact that this reason of state seeks to establish itself as a new type of sovereignty and that, according to the logic of the archic paradigm, sovereignty and governmentality absolutely cannot exist without one another, does not block the autonomous development of this art of governing. Moreover, Foucault concludes: "Government has a finality of its own and ... I believe that it can be clearly distinguished from sovereignty."[50]

Resistance. New forms of resistance emerge. While sovereignty establishes itself according to a rule of *obedience* organized around an end that is the "common good," governmentality implements a rule of *subjectivation* structured around "modes of objectification," that is, relations between humans and things, "which transform human beings into subjects."[51] This difference covers two types of government logic.

The main feature of sovereignty is "obedience to the laws"[52]: "the common good ... is in sum nothing than submission to sovereignty."[53] The most frequent form of resistance to this form is therefore civil war.

Governmental subjectivation is thus also a logic of submission. But according to its literal meaning – that which constitutes the subject as subject – subjectivation cannot be dissociated from an awakening of consciousness, that is, the subject's consciousness of being a subject; in other words, consciousness of their autonomy. This is why subjectivation is also the paradoxical condition of desubjectivation. Henceforth, "the problems of governmentality and the techniques of government have become the only political issue, the only real space for political struggle and contestation."[54] Subjectivation resists.

Contemporary techniques of government apply "to immediate everyday life which categorizes the individual, marks him by his own individuality, attaches him to his own identity, imposes a law of truth on him which he must recognize, and which others have to recognize in him."[55] Individuals are subjugated and submitted twice over: from outside, "through mechanisms of power that adhere to a truth,"[56] and from inside, insofar as they interiorize these mechanisms. The subject is thus both "divided from others" and "divided inside himself."[57] Foucault describes his observations of these phenomena during research trips to Sweden, Poland, and Tunisia: "What was it that was being questioned everywhere? ... a kind of permanent oppression in daily life."[58]

Resistance takes the form of "'transversal' struggles," "opposition to the power of men over women, of parents over children, of psychiatry over the mentally ill, of medicine over the population, of administration over the ways people live."[59] These contests, which "are not limited to one country," may not be guided by a promise of "liberation, revolutions, end of class struggle" but that does not mean they are any less "anarchistic."[60]

Between "relations of power" and "strategy of struggle," there is therefore a "perpetual linking and a perpetual reversal."[61]

The persistence of commanding and obeying

This is the point where what I call *the problem of the problem of government* emerges: despite his claims, in Foucault's conception, desubjectivation as resistance to government remains subservient to the logic of obedience. Desubjectivation draws its power in effect from the obedience of the subject to their self. The Kantian overtones of the analyses of the relation between desubjectivation and critique bear witness to this. Foucault writes: "Critique will be the art of voluntary insubordination, that of reflected intractability. Critique would essentially insure the desubjugation of the subject."[62] But obedience is swift to return: "Instead of letting someone else say '*obey*,' it is at this point, once one has gotten an adequate idea of one's own knowledge, and its limits, that the principle of autonomy can be discovered. One will then no longer have to hear the *obey*; or rather, the *obey* will be founded on autonomy itself."[63] Despite – or perhaps precisely because of – its "critical" reach, desubjectivation respects the logic of government through the government of the self by the self.

The transformations that Foucault imposes on the concept of government with governmentality do not, therefore, completely supersede its traditional meaning. Despite the attacks on this meaning, it resists: it resists resistance, and resists anarchism.

The last turn: *parrēsia*

Although it is not sufficiently acknowledged, Foucault's last seminars make a decisive break in the approach to the problem of government. Introducing the theme of *parrēsia*, he begins "elaborating ... the notion of the government of men by the truth,"[64] thereby initiating the third metamorphosis of the concept of government.

There is something other in the concept of government than "what is useful and necessary to govern in an effective way."[65] The "alethurgic"[66] examination eventually becomes imperative since to define governmentality through the pragmatic question of the suitable end in the arrangement of things is not, or is no longer, sufficient. It is now a matter of bringing to light this "supplement"[67] or "excess"[68] of government in government. A question of looking for it beyond pragmatic purposes. Returning to a former meaning of the term "government" as a set of "mechanisms and procedures intended to conduct men, to direct their conduct, to conduct their conduct."[69] Naturally, this new examination also involves a reevaluation of resistance.

After the pragmatism of the inquiry into governmentality, why does Foucault engage in this apparently regressive move? Contrary to all expectations, and despite its conventional aspect, the idea of a government of men by the truth is, in fact, the revolutionary ferment that prepares for the mutual destruction of both the concept of truth and the concept of government. Even though many people saw it as his weakest, Foucault's last word is thus his most potent.

The most radical Foucault is not the Foucault of sovereignty, and it is not even the Foucault of biopolitics or apparatuses. The most radical Foucault is the one usually considered least radical, least exposed, most "neoliberal." The Greek Foucault and the classical Foucault. The cynical Foucault. The Foucault to come. The Foucault who *changes subject* – but who does so only at the end, having traversed a complex trajectory that is often misunderstood and that we must now track with utmost patience.

The impossible possibility of the relation between government and truth

Parrēsia, truth-telling or speaking freely, is the name given to a specific type of truth, a truth irreducible to scientific truth. It "manifests itself ... in the form for subjectivity ... beyond ... relations of knowledge."[70] This space in which subjectivity and truth are articulated appears now to Foucault as the very heart of the problem of government. The theme of *parrēsia* is not at all concerned with the search for a truth of power; rather, it signals the existence of another economy of power than the one based on commanding and obeying.

Foucault initially defines this other economy of power, from which the duality between one who commands and another who obeys disappears, as a "partnership with the self." He writes: "*Parrēsia* is a way of binding oneself to oneself in the statement of truth, of freely binding oneself to oneself."[71] It suspends hierarchy, along with the distance between commanding and obeying. This is a freedom different from autonomy. The self is accompanied by the self, moving forward on the same ground as itself. A self that lives with itself. This is why Foucault claims *parrēsia* cannot be separated from "life form." With *parrēsia*, the *bios* is introduced into the problem of government.

First approach: the instrumentalist soul

How can this "free bond" to the self be described? In *The Hermeneutics of the Subject*, Foucault's reading of *Alcibiades* draws on the Platonic metaphor of the instrumentalist soul. When the soul cares for itself, it accompanies itself as a musical instrument accompanies the instrumentalist and the instrumentalist accompanies their instrument. Instrumentalist and instrument thus play each other. The metaphor of the instrument explains why Foucault refers to "technologies of the self." The instrument-soul is not a substance, but rather the subject of a *tekhnē*: "in music, there is the instrument (the cithara), and then there is the musician."[72] This relation is expressed through the verb *khraōmei*, "I use," and the noun *khrēsis*. The soul "uses itself" and the body, but this "using" is not a subjectivation. *Khraōmei* also means "to use" but "does not at all mean utilizing."[73] It is a matter of distinguishing between use and utilization. Use is "a certain attitude," that does not consist in dominating but rather in "giving way" to that which is being used, giving oneself to the instrument, and thereby, in a sense, renouncing oneself, renouncing the self as an instance of commanding. This is why Foucault says that the "using" soul "is not the soul structured according to a hierarchy of levels which must be harmonized, as in *The Republic*."[74]

Use therefore has the effect of unbinding the bonds that link the soul to power.

The concern of justice is the instrument of the soul of those governing: "Taking care of oneself and being concerned with justice amount to the same thing."[75] To be concerned with justice obviously assumes resisting one's own power in a way: "If it is true after all that there is no first or final point of resistance to political power other than in the relationship one has to oneself,"[76] the governing individual must then, paradoxically, themself resist in some sense. To govern oneself in order to resist the desire to govern.

The relations between Plato and Denys and between Aristotle and Alexander prove this partially: "The idea that *parrēsia* is always risky with the Prince ... but not in itself impossible,"[77] even if "the power the Prince exercises is, by definition, unlimited, often without laws, and consequently capable of every violence."[78] Despite everything, "that the sovereign may be open to the truth, and that there was a site, a place, a location for truth-telling in the relationship with the sovereign, is recognized by some authors,"[79] starting, therefore, with Plato.

Is the problem of the problem of government resolved then? Have we really escaped the logic of government with government by the truth, partnership with the self, and the instrumental soul?

In a sense, yes we have. The idea of abandoning the archic paradigm has haunted a certain political modernity for a long time. Eighteenth-century physiocratic theories offer an example. Foucault attributes to François Quesnay the "utopian" thought of a government by truth that would reach such perfection that it would no longer need government.

> If the truth can succeed in constituting the climate and light in common to governors and governed, then you can see that a time must come, a kind of utopian point in history when the empire of the truth will be able to make its order reign without the decisions of an authority or the choices of an administration having to intervene otherwise than as the formulation, obvious to everyone, of what is to be done. The exercise of power will therefore only ever be indicator of the truth. And if this indication of the truth takes place in a sufficiently demonstrative manner, everyone will be in agreement with it and, when it comes, there will no longer be need for a government … Let us call this, if you like, Quesnay's principle, which, despite its abstract and quasi-utopian character, was of great importance in the history of European political thought.[80]

Differences aside, all conceptions of the relation between government and truth that were to follow, from Saint-Simon to Rosa Luxemburg, right up to Solzhenitsyn, are "basically only the development … of this physiocratic idea.[81]

Yet we must ask again: is the problem of the problem of government resolved? Has Foucault radicalized "the physiocratic idea"? For many of his critics, the only answer he offered this fundamental question is that of an "aesthete or … a nihilist."[82] In the end, the very last seminars attested to the fact that the only way to envisage the non-necessity of government is ethical isolation. This is seen already in *The Hermeneutics of the Subject*, where Alcibiades' political interrogations are quickly abandoned in order to explore withdrawal into care of the self as the sole form of resistance.

Foucault asks: "What is the relationship between the fact of being subject in a relation of power and a subject through which, for which, and regarding which the truth is manifested? What is this double sense of the word 'subject,' subject in a relation of power, subject in a manifestation of truth?"[83] Many critics assume he never answered this question.

It is true that no sooner does he raise it than Foucault appears to close off the possibility of an abolition of the logic of government through the political use of truth. The notion of a "free partnership" between self and self, and between the self of governors and the self of the governed, soon reveals its tremendous fragility because a counter-discourse immediately emerges to destabilize it.

Impossible *parrēsia*

Referring to Polybius' *Ion*, Foucault reminds us that there were two concepts of equality in Greece: *isonomia* and *isēgoria*. *Isonomia* refers to "the equality of all before the law" and describes "the equality of speech, that is to say, the possibility for any individual, provided, of course, that he is part of the *dēmos*, to have access to speech,"[84] to defend themselves before the courts and to freely share their opinion. By contrast, *isēgoria* is qualitative, serving to measure equality, and thus, too, inequality and talents.

Foucault notes that in Greece "politics" relates not only to *politeia* but also, and equally, to *dunasteia*. *Politeia* is "the constitution, the framework, which defines the status of citizens, their rights, how decisions are taken, how leaders are chosen, and so on"; meanwhile, *dunasteia* defines "power, the exercise of power."[85] He goes on to say: "The problems of the *politeia* are problems of the constitution. I would say that the problems of *dunasteia* are problems of the political game, that is to say, problems of the formation, exercise, limitation, and also the guarantee given to the ascendancy exercised by some citizens over others."[86] *Dunasteia* requires talent, which is not possessed equally by all parties.

This is why one can be equal before the law (*isonomia*) without being equal in terms of talent (*isēgoria*).

Thus, "the place of *parrēsia* is defined and guaranteed by the *politeia*; but *parrēsia*, the truth-telling of the political man, is what ensures the appropriate game of politics,"[87] *dunasteia*. This "appropriate game" requires a specific talent in rhetoric.

Those with talent hold the keys to the "political game:" "In the democratic game set up by the *politeia*, which gives everyone the right to speak, someone comes on the scene to exercise his ascendency, which the ascendency he exercises in speech and in action."[88] The person who exercises this ascendency is destined by everything to become "archon." The problem then becomes the impossible coexistence of equality and ascendency, which again constructs a gulf of dissymmetry between the governed and the governing.

A successful balancing of *politeia* and *parrēsia* occurred only once in Greece, during the reign of Pericles. In *History of the Peloponnesian War*, "Thucydides says it – it is precisely both the paradox and genius of Pericles to have been at the same time the single most influential man and yet not to have exercised his power through *parrēsia* in a tyrannical or monarchical way but in a truly democratic manner."[89] The Pericles moment is the unique moment in which ascendency is not conferred on the wealthy or on the well-born, but rather on those of merit.[90]

This equilibrium was soon upset: "After the death of Pericles ... the game of democracy and the game of *parrēsia*, of democracy and truth-telling, do not manage to combine and suitably adjust to each other in a way which will enable this democracy to survive."[91] *Parrēsia* becomes flattery, demagogy, "false truth-telling."[92] Anyone can now say anything. Those with ascendency over others are no longer the best according to merit, but rather the strongest, those most apt to convince in order to satisfy their own selfish interests.

Parrēsia, the condition of possibility for democracy, is thus at the same time its condition of impossibility. It introduces something that is "irreducible into the egalitarian structure of democracy."[93] At the end of the chapter, Foucault presents the democratic paradox: "No true discourse without democracy, but true discourse introduces differences into democracy. No democracy without true discourse, but democracy threatens the very existence of true discourse."[94] The crisis of democracy and the crisis of *parrēsia* are one and the same. So, isn't it observing this crisis that leads Foucault to conclude that *parrēsia* is only truly liberating when it is individual, the ascetic transformation of the individual, the shaping of a life into a work of art, an ethical style? Doesn't the stylized *bios* suddenly seem to be the only possible horizon of resistance – one that is in some sense *bio*-apolitical? The Foucault of *parrēsia* would then advocate this "lifestyle anarchism" as the only answer to the crisis. Michael Hardt and Antonio Negri go further: "In fact, at this point, if we were to ask Foucault … who is the *bios*, his response would be ineffable, or nothing at all."[95] He would therefore have failed to demonstrate the political relevance of the *bios*: "What Foucault fails to grasp finally are the real dynamics of production … By contrast, Deleuze and Guattari present us with [an] … understanding [of it] that renews materialist thought and grounds itself solidly in the question of the production of social being."[96]

Foucauldian immanence according to Deleuze

Unlike Hardt and Negri, Deleuze was always convinced by the effective political reach of the Foucauldian *bios*. He is fully aware of an "uncoupling" in Foucault's late thought, but he demonstrates that it in no way interrupts the continuity of his thought. To defend Foucault from the accusations of a neoliberal, individualist drift, Deleuze develops a reading organized around his own concept of immanence.

If uncoupling there is, it comes in the shift from a "heteronomous" subject to a "self-constituted" subject.[97] In the last seminars, the subject Foucault had long described as the norm from the outside gives way to a subjectivity that finds its power of resistance in the relation to the self. Deleuze thinks it important to assert that there is no break.

He asks: "But how was this new dimension present from the beginning?"[98] The "thought [of Foucault] underwent a crisis … but it was a creative crisis, not a recantation."[99] A creative crisis of "modes of subjectification" produced "beyond the confines of power."[100] These modes of subjectivation – born of the "relation to oneself" thought of as "self-constitution"[101] – correspond to "inventing new possibilities of life."[102]

For Deleuze, immanence is not a stubborn insistence on the identical; rather, it reveals that the same is the same only by differing from the self. In Foucault, the subject of the care of self does not break with prior subjects: "It is not a doubling of the One, but a redoubling of the Other. It is not a reproduction of the Same, but a repetition of the Different. It is not the emanation of an 'I', but something that places in immanence an always other or a Non-self."[103]

Like all great work, Foucault's is a cloth that folds in on itself. The *fold* is the other name for immanence, the way that Foucault's work-subject adds to itself constantly through intensive self-differentiation. Its "redistribution or reorganization"[104] are not separate achievements, but rather creases in a single cloth. Foucault always described the relation to the self as a folding.

Deleuze describes Foucault's late work as a "snag"[105] since care of the self introduces a dimension to the subject previously absent. He writes: "This derivative or differentiation must be understood in the sense in which the *relation to oneself* assumes an independent status."[106] However, "the snag is no longer the accident of the tissue but the new rule on the basis of which the external tissue is twisted, invaginated, and doubled."[107] Like Roussel, "Foucault has knitted or sewn together all the meanings of the word *doublure*."[108] And "from snag to snag,"[109] the threads are seen to reinforce themselves while the cloth resists tears. To speak of the fold is to describe the outside as an invagination. The "folding of the outside" appears as the lining of the space of the "inside."[110]

The choice to read Foucault in light of immanence is well established and already developed in Deleuze's seminars. However, Deleuze does briefly acknowledge that "the word 'immanent' is not suitable ... I retract that, since Foucault does not use the word 'immanence,' telling us just that power and knowledge are each in the other." However, he adds, "to translate this in terms of immanence does not seem to me to be exaggerated. Power and knowledge are each in the other, I would say, good ... and I gave the reasons for why I thought that we can say that relations of forces or of power were the immanent cause of forms of knowledge."[111] It is therefore possible to argue that, despite everything and without saying so, Foucault "selected for himself in the writing of his books, the point of view of immanence."[112] Doesn't he say resistance is never exterior to power? And in *The History of Sexuality* isn't "the rule of immanence"[113] one of the five rules for the methods for analyzing power? This is why Deleuze allows himself to see the continuous development of an "immanent cause" in Foucault's work, one "which is realized, integrated and distinguished in its effect. Or rather the immanent cause is realized, integrated and distinguished by its effect. In this way there is a correlation or mutual presupposition between cause and effect."[114]

What is the effect of this immanent cause in the last seminars? What holds my attention here is no less than the fact that the concept of *government* becomes "self-government" without losing its political relevance:

> It is as if the relations of the outside folded back to create a doubling, allow a relation to oneself to emerge, and constitute an inside which is hollowed out and develops its own unique dimension: "*enkrateia*." The relation to oneself that is a self-mastery, "is a power that one brought to bear on oneself in the power that one exercised over others" (how could one claim to govern others if one could not govern oneself?) to the point where the relation to oneself becomes "a principle of internal regulation" in relation to the constituent powers of politics, the family, eloquence, games and even virtue.[115]

Deleuze notes here a similarity between Foucault and Spinoza. Between the relation of constitutive power and constituted power in Foucault's thought, and that of *natura naturans* (substance and cause) and *natura naturata* (mode and effect) in Spinoza. These relations that are, in the work of both philosophers, the two sides – inside and out – of the same cloth.

Auto-affection

We are coming now to the essential point: for Deleuze this fold in the cloth is the concrete image of *auto-affection*. A folded paper touches itself. When Foucault speaks of government of self, he is referring specifically to a folding of self against self. But this re-touching is an act of resistance. A folded paper is thicker. A force gains in power by folding in on itself: "Going beyond power, involves as it were bending force, making it impinge on itself rather than on other forces: a 'fold,' in Foucault's terms, force playing on itself."[116]

Auto-affection is the core of Deleuze's philosophy of immanence. Without concerning himself with all the deconstructions undergone by this term in the second half of the twentieth century, Deleuze maintains that auto-affection is the law of being that: "essence affects itself."[117]

This is the meaning and relevance of Spinoza's third mode of knowing. Deleuze's lecture of March 24, 1981 in fact demonstrates that the three modes of knowledge identified by Spinoza correspond to the three ways of being affected: skin affected by the sun, the painter's canvas touched by the light it reflects, and the affection of God through his own essence. Deleuze sees a real proximity between this theme of intrinsic differentiation as a fold and the meaning of the government of self in Foucault.

For Deleuze, the dynamic of auto-affection has clear political implications in that it is precisely what determines an *anarchist orientation of ontology*. If even God auto-affects, then auto-affection is the law of all beings. The image of power folded in on itself "expresses" the lack of hierarchy between constituting and constituted, cause has no authority of principle over effect. Consequently, effect is no longer subordinated to cause. Immanence is well and truly the anarchist dissident of ontology.

> What appears to me striking in a pure ontology [such as Spinoza's ontology] is the point at which it repudiates the hierarchies. And in fact, if there is no One superior to Being, if Being is said of everything that is and is said of everything that is in one and the same sense, this is the point that we have reached, this is what appeared to me to be the key ontological proposition: there is no unity superior to Being. And, consequently, Being is said about everything that is spoken of, that is, is said of everything that is, is said of all be-ings [*étant*] in one and the same sense. This is the world of immanence. This world of ontological immanence is an essentially anti-hierarchical world [...] Any be-ing [*étant*] realizes its being as much as there is in it, full stop, that's it. This is anti-hierarchical thought. At the extreme, it's a kind of anarchy. There is an anarchy of be-ings in Being.[118]

In a text entitled "Zones of immanence," written in honor of Maurice de Gandillac, Deleuze claims that in Plotinus too there is an early and striking resemblance with Spinoza, even if they appear to be so very different: "Being is univocal, equal. In other words, every entity is equally being, in the sense that each actualizes its power in immediate vicinity with the first cause. The distant cause is no more: rocks, flowers, animals, and humans equally celebrate the glory of God in a kind of sovereign an-archy."[119]

Opting to read Foucault in terms of immanence, Deleuze finds in him a striking instance of the same ontological anarchism: a fundamental form of auto-affection, government of self, construed as a fold, loses all hierarchical dimensions. There's no more slope. There's no more "originating." The subject is no longer, as in Aristotle, a substance from which accidents derive. No more predicative signal. The government of self, folding self into self, reduces distance, horizontalizes it, if you like. Immanence is an ontological flux that connects Plotinus to Spinoza, Spinoza to Foucault. Every time they are one. Every time different. Anarchist each and every time.

*

If it is true that immanence and anarchy coincide, why does this reading leave me dissatisfied?

Because even Deleuze himself can't help reintroducing the logic of commanding and obeying into the fold of immanence. How exactly does he define government of self? He says that the "relation which force has with itself," is a "power to affect itself, an affect of self on self." And this "affect of self on self" is "a *domination* of oneself."[120] The free individual must know how to dominate the self in order to command others. Deleuze states that "Following the Greek diagram, only free men can dominate others … But how could they dominate others if they could not dominate themselves? The domination of others must be doubled by a domination of oneself. The relation with others must be doubled by a relation with oneself."[121] In the concept of auto-affection, surreptitiously but inevitably, the activity–passivity pair is reintroduced, which is difficult to separate from commanding and obeying. Domination remains in situ. Consequently, due to the supporting concept of auto-affection, the interpretation in terms of immanence misses the truly anarchist dimension of Foucault's thought, that is, his assertion of the non-governable.

Foucault's response

Let's go back to the question asked in *The Hermeneutics of the Subject*: "What, then, is this self with which we must be concerned when we are told that we must care about the self?"[122] Foucault replies: "We must know what is auto *to auto*."[123]

The question is only answered definitively in the last seminar, *The Courage of Truth* – and it's an answer that erects a wall against the thesis of immanence. Foucault starts by cutting through the Platonic corpus, an attack that destabilizes everything else that follows in the lecture. He claims there is the Plato of *Alcibiades* and the Plato of *Laches*. A series of cascading splits provoked by this bring about *the crack in the subject, the rejection of auto-affection and eventually the final farewell to government*.

Two Platonic dialogues, two subjects

Alcibiades and *Laches* both discuss education, but from two opposing perspectives, between which Foucault makes a radical cut.

We recall that Alcibiades intends to govern the city and that Socrates therefore educates him in care of the self, exhorting him to take care of himself first and foremost. *Parrēsia* with the future archon is still possible and the concern for justice remains compatible with the political game. This care appears as the very form of the soul.

The education of the soul for care is analogous to playing an instrument. It is noticeable, however, that in the course of the dialogue Plato moves almost imperceptibly from the image of the using-soul to that of the piloting-soul, from instrument to cybernetics. Partnering with the self is gradually equated with controlling the self. In the end, the psycho-hierarchical structure of commanding and obeying imposes its schema in place of use and free binding to power. Gradually, taking care of oneself comes to mean nothing but governing oneself. Caring for the self means interiorizing the archic paradigm, the logic of commanding and obeying.

Writing about *Alcibiades* in *The Courage of Truth*, Foucault recognizes that,

> basically the philosopher is someone who is able to establish a type of hierarchy and a type of power in his soul and in relation to himself which is of the same order, has the same form, the same structure as the power exercised in a monarchy by a monarch … So, there is in fact an essence, form, or structure which is common to political monarchy and sovereignty of self over self.[124]

This hierarchical structure supplants the partnership economy.

The Courage of Truth develops a critique of this structure explicitly – the same structure that *The Hermeneutics of the Subject* still struggles to give up. For a long time, Foucault continued to define techniques of the self as practices of domination of the self, which would appear to support Deleuze's interpretation. In "Technologies of the self," he wrote:

> This contact between the technologies of domination of others and those of the self I call governmentality. Perhaps I've insisted too much on the technology of domination and power. I am more and more interested in the interaction between oneself and others and in the *technologies of individual domination*, the history of how an individual acts upon himself, in the technology of the self.[125]

Foucault has not yet left the monarch-individual – but this is not his last word on the matter.

In *The Courage of Truth*, the reading of *Laches* begins, shedding new light on the "self." This dialogue is about a failed education: the young Melesias and Lysimachus were poorly raised by their fathers, who did not take care of them because they were too busy with their political careers. The young men explain: "If we really have led such insignificant lives, is this not precisely because our ancestors, our fathers, attended to the affairs of others? They were so absorbed in the city's affairs, so concerned to deal with *ta tôn allôn pragmata* (the affairs of others), that they could not but neglect us."[126] As a result, in conversation with two well-reputed generals, Nicias and Laches, Melesias and Lysimachus discuss their fear of reproducing the same pattern with their own children.

How should children be raised? Should they be entrusted to a master, and, if so, which one? The two generals each present their own vision of education with a view to courage. Socrates intervenes late in this dialogue and, says Foucault, transforms the topic by bringing about "the transition from the political to what could be called the technical model of discussion."[127] When it comes to education, what's best is not a governor but an instrumentalist, "a technician of the care"[128] who learns to sculpt existence, like a statue, or in the same way that an instrument is whittled from a piece of wood. Commanding is erased, and governmental hierarchy along with it. In the process, "soul" becomes "form of life." The instrumental schema finally acquires the power to suspend the logic of government. This time, unlike in *Alcibiades*, it is not contradicted by any theme of control.

The difference between the two dialogues is becoming apparent: it is the difference between the "knowledge of the soul" by itself and "test of life,"[129] between "the soul's ontological mode of being" and "the style of life, the way of living, the very form that one gives to life."[130] Two contrasting conceptions of care. *Laches* is a text "in which *bios*, much more than the soul, appears very clearly as the object of care."[131]

Between these two dialogues, what is at stake is no less than the emergence of an *entirely other subject*: "How do things stand with *you* [emphasis mine] and *logos* ... can you give the *logos* of yourself?"[132] asks Socrates in *Laches*. To give the *logos* of the self is to show how the *logos* is inscribed in "the way in which one lives."[133] From this point on, the seminar concentrates on this bifurcation that leads to the topic of "mode of life."[134]

The interpretation of *Laches* is only the beginning, however.[135] It is the beginning of a total change of trajectory that becomes more pronounced after the seminar. Indeed, during the same lecture of February 29, 1984, there is a shift without any transition from reading *Laches* to reading the Cynics. Care as "formative ... of one's mode of life"[136] assumes its radical political dimension. Admittedly, in *Laches*, the closing words of Socrates' lecture are: "Bid farewell to the political arena and its procedures,"[137] exhorting the young people abandoned by their fathers to withdraw for this very reason from that which caused their abandonment.

Cynicism appears to be the most radical form of taking leave. A departure that – I'll say it again – is not a departing from politics, but from its "arena." A farewell to dynasty, a farewell to *archē*, to microcosm, caste, oligarchy – in a word, as we shall see, it is a *farewell to government*.[138] Far from being the cemetery of politics, the *bios* is its rebirth.

Cynicism and anarchism

How should we understand this? Foucault emphasizes the familial relation connecting Cynicism and anarchism. Indeed, in *The Courage of Truth* cynicism appears as the first expression of the anarchism to come.¹³⁹ Foucault writes: "Cynicism, the idea of a mode of life as the irruptive, violent, scandalous manifestation of the truth is and was part of the revolutionary practice and of the forms taken by revolutionary movements in the nineteenth century."¹⁴⁰ The *bios* of the Cynics announces "revolutionary life."

Why? Is it just because of the "scandalous" behavior of the Cynic who attacks "conventions, laws, and institutions?¹⁴¹ No doubt, but that's only a first level of explanation. The second, where a veritable breach occurs, concerns the definitive separation of *form of life* and *auto-affection*. This is a separation that initially appears to be impossible in so far as auto-affection is usually presented in both biology and philosophy as the phenomenon of life itself. Yet, it is indeed just such a separation that characterizes the Cynics' life and, beyond this, provokes the split of the Foucauldian subject. The anarchism outlined in *The Courage of Truth* actually comes from a *break with the schema of auto-affection*.

Let's return to the government of the soul in *Alcibiades*. The hierarchical relation that structures it is rooted in the soul's possibility of self-reflection: "If we want to know how the soul can know itself, since we know now that the soul must know itself, then we take the example of the eye. Under what conditions and how can the eye see itself? Well, when it sees the image of itself sent back to it by a mirror."¹⁴² Auto-affection is therefore the belated naming of reflexivity of the soul.

The mirror of the soul signals the presence of the divine within it: "So it is by turning round towards the divine that the soul will be able to grasp itself."¹⁴³ In an economy not so far removed from the one Deleuze described as affection of essence, the soul reflects on itself by illuminating its divine part, as if folding itself in order to better capture the light.

But this "fold" must also be understood as a "giving in to," an obeying. Indeed, the soul turns first to look upward to see in the mirror: auto-affection initially assumes an interior "ascent," a gesture of obedience toward "the divine, when it has grasped it and is able to think and know the divine." Strong in this knowledge, the soul is now ready to "come back down" again.¹⁴⁴ The angle of the slope in this ascension and descent, this internal hierarchy from high to low, reveals the archic structure of government of self.

Is it auto-affection (the fold mirroring self to self) that determines the political logic of commanding and obeying, or is it the political logic of commanding and obeying that determines the auto-affection of the psyche? Impossible to know. What's sure is that, in any event, in all these instances, auto-affection implies the "monarchic structure" that assumes passivity and activity, the distance between top and bottom.

Now, the "*gnôthi seauton*, this self-knowledge, which applies in the *Laches* as well as in the *Alcibiades*, which is valid both for the discovery of the soul and for bringing the problem of the *bios* to light, obviously has a very different form when giving an account of oneself is indexed to the problem of the *bios* (life) rather than to the discovery of the soul as an ontologically distinct reality."[145] This "difference" derives from the fact that the "self" of the Cynic does not reflect itself, breaks mirrors, and, along with them, the pairing of activity and passivity.

Schürmann saw clearly in Foucault's late texts, "the dispersal of inward-directed reflection into as many outward-directed reflexes."[146] Asserting the difference between the "two strategies, analytical and strategic,"[147] he understood that in the last Foucault there was no "topical withdrawal to the inner life" at all.[148] He saw that Foucault's thought remained political right to the end. Nonetheless, as he too sought a means of suturing "the snag," he imposed on the Foucauldian text a schema that was no fairer to it than the immanence schema since it is far too reminiscent of his own thought: the schema of self-constitution, which is none other than another name for auto-affection.

It is striking that, like Deleuze, Schürmann ultimately finds the wrong anarchism in Foucault. "What can I do …?"[149] asks Schürmann, giving the Foucauldian subject a chance to speak. "Constitute myself as an anarchist subject."[150] The title of his fine article – "On constituting oneself as an anarchist subject" – designates the switch back that moves from a subject governed "by discursive formations and … power effects" to a "practical" subject in the process of "self-constitution."[151]

The problem is that the idea of a constitution of the self still relates to the logic of government and somehow still assumes authority.

The point is that the Cynics' self does not self-constitute. In this sense, the asceticism of the Cynic is different from care. Of course, there are two "halves" in this self, but they do not reflect one another, since one is a dog. There's no mirroring possible between the two faces of this strange couple. The Cynics' life – *bios kunikos* – is "without modesty, shame, and human respect"[152] precisely because the Cynic stops looking at himself in the mirror. Foucault reminds us that the Cynic masturbated in public. So, he did touch himself, but, by exposing himself in this manner, he ridiculed self-touching, profaning auto-affection, substituting it with indifference:

The Cynic life is a dog's life because, like the latter, it is indifferent. It is indifferent to whatever may occur, is not attached to anything.[153]

It is said that there is no life without auto-affection and homeostasis. True. But they do not, for all that, necessarily imply specular contact with the self. Today, we know that auto-affection is, first and foremost, a cerebral mechanism and that on this count it eludes the grasp of reflexivity. Diogenes, who spent a long time watching animals, seemingly foresaw this. Foucault writes: "There is a whole series of anecdotes on this: Diogenes observing how mice live, and Diogenes seeing a snail carrying its house on its back and deciding to live the same way."[154] Later he writes: "Animality is an exercise … The *bios philosophikos* … is the human being's animality taken up as a challenge, practiced as an exercise, and thrown in the face of others as a scandal."[155] Animals do not go through the mirror stage – but that's a resource, not a failing.

The coin's currency

The Cynics' motto was "*parakharaxon to nomisma*," translated as "change the value of your currency," or "alter your currency."[156] The motto illuminates the direct connection between currency (*numismos*) and the law (*nomos*): "To change the value of the currency is also to adopt a certain standpoint towards convention, rule, or law."[157]

The metaphor of the coin is usually employed in philosophy to evoke wearing, the devaluation of truth that results from being in circulation for too long. By circulating, the coin is worn down, its effigy erased, the metal rubbed thin. To revalue currency therefore involves issuing new coins. The meaning of this metaphor designates the loss followed by its regeneration of truth. Foucault insists on the fact that, by contrast, in the Cynics' motto, the coin is not worn out and is not devalued. It loses none of its material.[158] It is not therefore a question of changing or altering its value, of reissuing it or replacing it. It is a question of changing its effigy.

This metaphor is far less intelligible than the metaphor of wearing down. We have all seen worn coins, rusty coins, dirty, dull coins – but never a coin changing its effigy. When a coin changes its effigy, it's another coin. A new currency.

In this instance, the metal of the coin remains what it is and only the effigy changes. The metal symbolizes "its true value," the set of "principles of the true life" (*alêthês bios*), which the Cynics share with Plato and which they want to take "back as close as possible to its traditional meaning."[159] "From this perspective, the Cynics do not ... change the metal itself of this coin."[160] *But the effigy is no longer the soul.* The coin is no longer marked with the psychic seal. The principles lose the stamp of their pilot, their government. At that point, the change of effigy pushes "these themes to their extreme consequence," to the point that they no longer mean anything: "Taking up the coin again, changing its effigy, and, as it were, making the theme of the true life grimace."[161]

Ordinarily, the coin of the soul is the shining surface on which the soul sees itself in perfect conformity with the principles, the *arkhai* of true life. Yet here, through a change on the surface, the coin becomes the other of the mirror. Cynicism is "the broken mirror" of philosophy.[162]

On the Cynics' coin there's a dog in place of the soul. Foucault says that the Cynics' dog is diacritical, incarnating the difference between two effigies, the difference that cannot be seen and that is not reflected. It incorporates it: the soul of the dog is its body. The animal effigy of life incorporates the limit of what can be governed, barks out, if you like, the non-governable. That which never looks at itself. That which can only be dominated or subordinated to domination. An animal is never governed, whatever method is employed. An animal is dominated. Even the most gentle, loving taming is domination. As I said from the outset, like the animal, the non-governable is that which can only be dominated, never governed. A dog only obeys through training, and in this sense the dog remains non-governable. The non-governable is what the Cynic raises against hegemony. Through his mode of life, his *bios*, Diogenes exposes himself absolutely to domination, to murder. He can be crushed like a snail is crushed underfoot. He can be broken, reduced to pieces. He can be exiled and tortured. But he cannot be governed. He is *other* to government. It is not that the Cynic is disobedient. Rather, there is something within that is an absolute stranger to hierarchical order. This "something" within is life – nothing less than life itself.

Far from being self-identical, Foucault's subject is split in two, torn asunder between the monarchic government of the soul and the anarchist organization of the non-governable soul. In the end, the subject, who has become weary of self-reflection, abandons the political arena, quits government. And yet Foucault continues to call this farewell "government." Government of the self. This is why we should read *The Courage of Truth* as a covert anarchist legacy.

Conclusion

What then should we say in the end about the "neoliberal" Foucault? It is true that in *The Birth of Biopolitics* he claims that neoliberalism offers a kind of emancipation since, as a result of its "state phobia," the question "Why, after all, is it necessary to govern?" is its clear motto.[163] Many people thought Foucault had failed in his task when he presented this conclusion, given that a commonly agreed critical vocation of philosophy is precisely to counter and refuse neoliberal order. Yet, at the same time, clearly, this kind of critique is organized by principles that Foucault was always the first to challenge: the celebration of obedience, submission, the figure of the subject of law, or the citizen who respects government. As Geoffroy de Lagasnerie quite rightly put it: "If it is true that political power functions via obedience, resignation, negativity, then getting out of this context is an urgent task [for Foucault]."[164] Remember that for Foucault, "where there is obedience, there cannot be *parrēsia*."[165]

The Cynic in *The Courage of Truth* is radically different from the capitalist anarchist inasmuch as this anarchist remains vassal in all circumstances to what can be called an anti-governmental governmentality: the governmentality of the company, interest, and transactions.[166] By contrast, the Cynics' coin has no currency in market circulation. It buys nothing.

The anarchist *bios* of the Cynic remains extra-economic, outside of it. But does it incarnate, as has so often been argued, a narcissistic individualism, detached from all political concerns and busy only resisting that which threatens it? Obviously not. *The Courage of Truth* implies that the withdrawal from the political scene, made necessary by corruption and the devaluing of *parrēsia*, is but the prelude to a rebound, an awakening that announces a new category of action.

Cynical anarchism prefigures proof via life – what contemporary activists call *prefigurative action*. Prefigurative action asserts that things can be changed without any need for government – through lifestyle in the here and now and through transformations in ways of living. The Cynic is a "militancy" king, says Foucault. Now, "it is therefore a militancy which aspires to change the world, much more than a militancy which would seek merely to provide its followers with the means for achieving a happy life."[167]

Political "prefiguration" is an experimental mode of action. It does not depend on principles, it confuses the lines between means and ends and concentrates on the present, on the possibility of transforming it.[168] Through his reading of the Cynics, the "present" – so finely analyzed in "What is Enlightenment?"[169] – became the present of direct action for Foucault. It is no longer "the other world" to be attained, but rather the "world other," that is, "another life."[170] Between another life and a different life, between another world and an other, different world, the splitting apart of the two fates of subjectivity emerges. Consequently, too, the two fates of philosophy and politics: "the other world and other life have basically been the two great themes, the two great forms, the great limits within which Western philosophy has constantly developed,"[171] even if the second "limit" here is constantly concealed and hidden by the first.

*

The two most widespread interpretations of Foucault's apparent anarchism – immanence and betrayal, the first of which is clearly the deepest and most interesting, which is why I have given it such a lengthy discussion here – fail to illuminate it as what it is: a breach of the subject, a failure in command–obey, a critique of auto-affection.

Doubts about the relevance of the immanentist reading also enable a reconsideration of the Deleuzean assertion of the link between politics and affect and a reassessment of the suspicion of the now well-established habit of thinking the political game from these same affects. On the one hand, because any affect theory, whatever it is, is *necessarily* rooted in auto-affection, and this assumption imprisons political thinking, even when it calls itself "revolutionary," within the logic of government. And consequently, on the other hand, because the political theory of affects usually concludes that the unchained multitude, with its passions overflowing, needs a master.

After many different attempts, it is this inevitability of government that Foucault contests and dismisses. There is the governing subject, there is the governed subject, there is the subject "not governed like that,"[172] and – in the end – there is the non-governable subject. There is governmental politics. Political governmentality. Then, too, the assertion of the non-governable and an other politics.

*

The non-governable is a concept I must articulate on my own, however, since Foucault stops on its threshold. For Foucault, as we have seen, the disavowal of anarchism is revealed through the paradoxical persistence of the theme of government – even where it no longer governs.

Let's return to the famous passage from "What is critique?" – the one about "not to be governed thusly, like that, in this way."[173] Judith Butler says that with these words Foucault "does make clear, however, that he is not posting the possibility of radical anarchy, and that the question is not how to become radically ungovernable."[174] This is true in a sense. Foucault's question is not, and never was, the problem of the ungovernable. The problem that is Foucault's is the non-governable, which found the space to unfurl right at the end. A space that is finally the space of anarchism, whatever Butler might say. Anarchism draws its resource from difference, a difference that initially appears to be miniscule, but that is, in fact, a gaping chasm: the difference between the ungovernable and the non-governable.

The difference between ungovernable and non-governable goes back to the difference between power and domination.

> When one defines the exercise of power as a mode of action upon the actions of others, when one characterizes these actions by the government of men by other men – in the broadest sense of the term – one includes an important element: freedom. Power is exercised only over free subjects, and only insofar as they are free. By this we mean individual or collective subjects who are faced with a field of possibilities in which several ways of behaving, several reactions and diverse comportments may be realized.[175]

Meanwhile, states of domination appear when different elements "succeed[s] in blocking a field of power relations, immobilizing them and preventing any reversibility of movement."[176]

The relation between the governing and the governed is a power relation, a coercion that assumes the "freedom" of subjects, their resistance, their capacity for disobedience, and, through this, admittedly, their potential ungovernability – the refusal to submit, acts of rebellion, civil wars. We have seen that the capacity to govern oneself and autonomy are the positive sides of the governed being. For Foucault, power involves an undeniable creative dimension. Between freedom and government, there is both opposition and circularity. The government can be contested, or even overthrown. The country can be ungovernable for a time. But the power–freedom circle, the reversibility of the power relation, are not suspended. Self-government, like subject autonomy, authorizes the ungovernable as one of its essential manifestations.

By contrast, domination takes the concept of government to the limit inasmuch as it blocks – that is, actually annuls – the power relation. It is not exactly, as one might think, the freedom of subjects that is the target or game of domination. What it seeks to crush, or destroy, is something that, unlike freedom, is not part of the power relation: it is indifference to power, indifference to the logic of command and obey, a foreignness to freedom itself. That's what domination dominates. That's what can't be governed. This indifference to government is the *bios*, the life that Foucault finds in the ethic of the Cynics – an ethic that offers an encrypted anarchist message whose political meaning is being revealed today.

*

Foucault did not believe there was a drive for power. He didn't even believe that S&M reveals the existence "of S&M tendencies deep within our unconscious ... S&M is much more than that; it's the real creation of new possibilities of pleasure, which people had no idea about previously. The idea that S&M is related to a deep violence, that S&M practice is a way of liberating this violence, this aggression, is stupid."[177] In this sense, S&M is also of the order of the relation of power, the reversibility that all power relations assume, and freedom too therefore. In the power relation, freedom and constraint mirror one another. Any power relation, of whatever kind, is specular. By contrast, domination is not specular.

Remember the extraordinary radio broadcast entitled "The Utopian Body," given in 1966, in which Foucault claims that a body is "always elsewhere. It is tied to all the elsewheres of the world."[178] Neither obedient, nor disobedient, it is elsewhere. What brings it back to the reality of power is the mirror. The mirror is the thinking cadaver: "It is the mirror and it is the corpse that silence, and appease, and shut into a closure (for us now sealed) that great utopian rage that dilapidates and volatizes our bodies at every instant."[179]

Now, why didn't anarchism, why didn't this "great utopian rage" of a soul-body without archon, irreducible to all principles and all drives, appear more clearly? Why did Foucault conceal the most revolutionary aspect of his philosophy beneath the well-behaved features of an apparently inoffensive ethic?

Here's where the answer may lie, via a partial revelation of the secret:

> The idea of a "limit-experience" that tears the subject from itself is the fundamental lesson that I've learned from these authors [Nietzsche, Blanchot, and Bataille]. And no matter how boring and erudite my resulting books have been, this lesson has always allowed me to conceive them as direct experiences to "tear" me from myself, to prevent me from always being the same.[180]

Far from the polish of immanence, or a full form of life, Foucault's subject, wrenched from itself, reveals a troubling truth despite itself: the limit-experience of politics is anarchism. Here is an experience that brings politics to the brink, an experience of the limits of politics, an experience of beyond politics, an experience of the unlimited as a political experience.

Perhaps that's what is unavowable about anarchism.

8

Profanatory Anarchy
Giorgio Agamben's Zone

> Why, for example, is it difficult to think things such as anarchy (the absence of command and power) or anomy (the absence of law)? Why is it difficult to think this concept, which does appear to contain something within it?[1]

> The ambiguity that consists in conceiving government as executive power is an error with some of the most far-reaching consequences in the history of Western political thought.[2]
>
> Giorgio Agamben

Agamben does not agree with Hardt and Negri, any more than I do, that the Foucauldian *bios* is poorly defined. The long trajectory that is *homo sacer* seeks precisely to highlight the political, more specifically anarchist, significance of "form-of-life." From Deleuze, Agamben retains immanence. Like him, he "immanentizes" Foucault's thought (hence the decision to add hyphens to "form-of-life"). However, unlike Deleuze, Agamben considers there is an ontological determination in immanence that can no longer accommodate the concept of government, whether in the form of self-government or auto-affection. On the strength of this conviction, he sets out to complete Foucault's critique of government, which he sees, quite rightly, as left unfinished in the last seminars.

It is thus through a new use of immanence – in fact via a definition of immanence as use – that Agamben seeks to suture the division between commanding and obeying, which is still present in the Foucauldian concept of self-government, and to be done once and for all with the logic of government.

What is the political gesture of this new orientation of the relation between immanence and anarchy leading to an "ungovernable" position? The answer lies in the trajectory of the philosophical project Agamben names "profanation" (*profanazione*).

The question of profanation and anarchy

Agamben is the only contemporary philosopher who interrogates the relationship between anarchy and sacredness. The only philosopher to remind us that all anarchism is profanation and that all profanation of the sacred bears an anarchist "signature." The challenge is not misinterpreting this relation, since the sacred and the profane are not first and foremost religious categories. In a decisive move, Agamben claims they are political categories whose meaning is established by the law.

According to the Roman jurist Trebatius, "in the strict sense, profane is the term for something that was once sacred or religious and is returned to the use and property of men."[3] Profanation is thus firstly the restitution to the sphere of human law of something that was separated from it.

Agamben does not draw on the habitual synonyms of the word "profanation": desacralization, disaffection, execration, violation, or blasphemy. Nor does he deploy common equivalents of the verb to profane: to degrade, to sully, to soil, to violate. He instead deploys terms like "deactivate," "destitute," "neutralize," "render inoperative." These verbs and associated nouns have nothing to do with common associations with the term profanation, whose most extreme meaning is the violation of the sepulcher. Rather, in each case they refer to a suspension of action, a reduction of pressure.

Profaning is firstly a matter of suspending a power, an implementation, an actuality (*energeia*). The issue is, then, of understanding how the suspension of a power to act cannot be an action in itself. How profanation is not an act. How deactivation, destitution, neutralization can remain possible without actualization. For Agamben, authentically profanatory anarchy sits right in between potentiality and actuality.

What does this mean? Agamben's unique audacity is to assign the term *sacer* to something that is not sacred: *homo sacer*. Taken in terms of the Roman *sacratio*, the sacred is originally a political phenomenon.

"Sacred" thus means separated. But what does "separated" mean? Agamben argues that all separation depends on a mechanism – the mechanism of exception. The mechanism of exception – the separation machine – is the originary political fact.

The exception is "the structure of sovereignty"[4] that consists in integrating, encompassing an element within even as it is excluded. A thing is termed sacred on account of its "inclusive exclusion" or "exclusive inclusion" in the political order.[5] Now, the exceptional exception – the one that makes all the other gestures of separation possible, all the gestures of exclusion and hence sacralization possible – is life. The mechanism of exception reveals the "secret tie uniting power and bare life."[6] "Bare life," initially included in the political sphere on account of its very non-belonging to this same order, is thus the privileged exception of power.

The ground for this Western "originary exclusion [of life] through which the political dimension was first constituted,"[7] asserted in Rome, was clearly prepared in the Aristotelian definition of the *polis*. As we have seen, by separating *oikos* from *polis*, Aristotle already defined the space of citizenship by distinguishing it from domestic space. This distinction made it possible to assign to each of the spheres its own "life": life as *zoē* – bare life – in the domestic sphere – and life as *bios* – qualified life – in the political sphere.

It was therefore life itself that served as a criterion in determining the specificity of the political through its division: "It seemed to me that the originary site of the political, in Western politics, is some sort of operation on life, or an operation that involves dividing and capturing life through its very exclusion, in other words, including life in the system through its exclusion."[8]

Ordinarily, the "sacred" refers to that which is prohibited and inviolable as the object of religious veneration. Yet Agamben points out that, contrary to common belief, life was not considered "sacred" in this sense in either Greece or Rome. He writes: "Decisive as it is for the origin of Western politics, the opposition between *zoē* and *bios* ... (that is, between life in general and the qualified way of life proper to men), contains nothing to make one assign a privilege or a sacredness to life as such."[9] Indeed, "life is sacred only insofar as it is taken into the sovereign exception, and to have exchanged a juridico-political phenomenon ... for a genuinely religious phenomenon is the root of the equivocations that have marked studies both of the sacred and of sovereignty in our time."[10] The fact that something is sacred does not mean it is separate. On the contrary: it is separation that makes it sacred. As much as to say that the sacred is not a property existing in the thing. Nothing – not even life – is sacred in and of itself: "We seem to forget that classical Greece, to which we owe most of our ethico-political concepts ... ignored this principle."[11] Exception is what renders sacred.[12]

Analysis of a legal case helps Agamben shed light on the political meaning of the "sacred." This is the now well-known case of *homo sacer*, "the enigma of a figure of the sacred ... before or beyond the religious."[13] The case of an individual who is excluded from the political sphere, who no longer has any civic rights, who can be killed by anyone (*qui occidit parricidi non damnatur*), without the murder being considered a homicide and without the person's execution being the object of a religious sacrifice (*neque fas est eum immolari*). The life of *homo sacer*, discarded with total impunity and available for any kind of murder, is thus both "killable and unsacrificeable"[14] – descriptives which, as we can see, are strangers to common definitions of the sacred as venerable, untouchable, sanctified, and protected by the gods.

Of course, religion itself also has the power to except: "Religion can be defined as that which removes things, places, animals, or people from common use and transfers them to a separate sphere. Not only is there no religion without separation, but every separation also contains or preserves within itself a genuinely religious core."[15]

This conception does not, however, undermine the profound dissociation between *sacer* and sacred, *sacratio* and consecration. Whether or not it is religious, the power to separate is where the arcane lies in political power. Proof of this is, again, that the law effects the first distinction between the sacred and profane – and no religion is independent of the law.

Religion, law, and politics all circulate starting from the structure of exception. This is why profanation does not seek to abolish the sacred in the purely religious meaning of the term, but rather to dim its dazzling light by revealing its political origin.

True anarchy

Let's return to the question of anarchy. How can the mechanism of exception be profaned? How can its power be deactivated? How, at the same time, can the "sacred" be destituted?

One thing is certain: according to Agamben, traditional anarchism failed in this. It failed to disclose the true political meaning of profanation, to identify the mechanism of exception as "the originary structure and limits of the form of the State."[16] Consequently, it was not aiming at the correct target in its desacralizing operation. "True" anarchism must therefore be distinguished from classical anarchism.[17]

The traditional anarchist critique of the state attacked effect more than cause by focusing superficially on the supposedly mystical nature of political authority. For anarchists, "the problem of sovereignty was reduced to the question of who," in state order, "was invested with certain powers."[18] Anarchism shared with Marxism a view of state authority as sacred authority – in the common meaning of the term – surrounded by an aura of religiosity and, in the superstructure, the reflection of the fetishization of commodities. Because they overlooked the true meaning of the sacred, anarchism and Marxism were too quick to equate politics, along with the religion they considered inseparable from it, with a purely ideological construction. "The weakness of anarchist and Marxian critiques of the State was precisely … to have quickly left the *arcanum imperii* [arcane command] aside, as if it had no substance outside of the simulacra and the ideologies invoked to justify it."[19]

Bypassing the true nature of sovereignty, the anarchist critique of the sacred – No Gods, No Masters – is in no way profane and entirely misses its object, namely, "the Ungovernable, which is the beginning and, at the same time, the vanishing point of every politics."[20]

Denouncing semantic inflation, destituting the symbolic

What is the cause of this failure? It comes from the fact that anarchism, again like Marxism, is contemporaneous with a certain semantic blindness. Agamben's initiative goes far further than a mere restitution of the political meaning of the sacred; it also assesses the political consequences of sacralizing meaning. It is a matter of understanding why words like "sacred" or "profane" came to mean more than themselves (and thus also far less), by inflating them to the point of vacuousness. The effort to put the sacred back in its place is always supported in Agamben's work by a wider move, which can be described in terms of the other name for profanation: *a deflation of the symbolic.*

By trying to defuse the mystical aura of the sacred – extinguishing its halo – Agamben denounces a general tendency in Western thought toward semantic inflation, the inseparable companion of the archic paradigm, which began with the birth of revolutionary ideologies and reached its apex with the development of the social sciences. The most striking symptom of this tendency is the mythologeme "of the ambivalence of the sacred ... constituted between the end of the nineteenth century and the first decades of the twentieth."[21] This mythologeme consists in displacing a word from its original semantic register to take it to the point where it loses all meaning and reference and becomes a "floating signifier," an "excessive signifier with no meaning other than that of marking an excess of the signifying function over all signifieds."[22] The political state of exception is thus accompanied by linguistic states of exception.

The "theory of the ambivalence of the sacred" has "consistently led the social sciences astray." Agamben continues: "this mythologeme was first formulated in William Robertson Smith's Lectures on the Religion of the Semites (1889)."[23] It influenced Freud's work deeply, especially *Totem and Taboo*. It can also be found in Hubert and Mauss's *Sacrifice: It's Nature and Function* (1898), which "opens with an evocation of precisely 'the ambiguous character of sacred things.'"[24] Several years later, Wundt formulated the famous concept of "sacred horror."[25] The article on *Sacer* in Ernout-Meillet's etymological Latin dictionary, *Dictionnaire étymologique de la langue latine* (1932), "confirms the 'double meaning' of the term" as both venerated and damned: "*Sacer* designates the person or the thing that one cannot touch without dirtying oneself or without dirtying; hence the double meaning of 'sacred' or 'accursed.'"[26] Emile Benveniste's 1969 *Dictionary of Indo-European Concepts and Society*, "that masterpiece of twentieth-century linguistics,"[27] also served to make these meanings official.

This mythologeme has also weighed heavily on the political critique of the sacred. The theory of a state doctrine, as found in Marxism and anarchism, derives from it. As a result of having associated the political, as an ideology, with a form of magic, this critique has only ever tilted at windmills, never touching the heart of the political problem, which is exception.

How, then, can profanation be wrenched away from the supposedly all-powerful symbolic order born of this tendency for semantic inflation? Agamben's response to this fundamental question consists in marking the irreducible difference between *profanation* and *transgression*. Until now, by assimilating politics to religiosity, anarchism has conceived of profanation as transgression, in other words, as a logic of sacrilege, breaking in, iconoclasm, the death of God. As if it were indispensable to compound the effective destitution of state-governmental power with symbolic murder. As if, in order to go over to the other side of the state, it were also necessary to go over to the other side of meaning. As if to overthrow government were to gouge out an eye.

Transgression profanes nothing, deactivates nothing. It certainly does not affect the symbolic itself. The difference between traditional anarchism and "true anarchism" plays out for Agamben by contrasting symbolic transgression with deactivating profanation. Deactivation is the favored enemy of transgression.

Because transgression is hemmed into the symbolic order, it always leads to a reconstitution of the sacred. This is probably what Foucault saw when he wrote on Bataille in "A preface to transgression":

> Profanation in a world which no longer recognizes any positive meaning in the sacred – is this not more or less what we may call transgression? In that zone which our culture affords for our gestures and speech, transgression prescribes not only the sole manner of discovering the sacred in its unmediated substance, but also a way of recomposing its empty form, its absence, through which it becomes all the more scintillating.[28]

Agamben's most virulent critique of Foucault addresses precisely his fascination for Bataille, who, because he is forever attached to the "logic of transgression,"[29] is politically "unusable" today.[30] Foucault is thus too transgressive to be an anarchist. Too taken with Bataille to be ungovernable.

For Agamben, transgression always plays the game of capitalism, which manipulates the symbolic like none other and always goes further in the creation of new floating signifiers. Capitalism is transgressive inasmuch as it reduces idols to pure empty forms. In so doing, it finds new idolatries, thereby precipitating the real into the theater of its own spectacle: "Capitalism and other modern forms of power seem to generalize and push to the extreme the processes of separation that define religion."[31]

> [Henceforth,] where sacrifice once marked the passage from the profane to the sacred and from the sacred to the profane, there is now a single, multiform, ceaseless process of separation that assails every object, every place, every human activity in order to divide it from itself. This process is entirely indifferent to the caesura between sacred and profane, between divine and human.[32]

The sacred, running on empty, is always already (that is, never) transgressed, making all profanation impossible.[33]

Impossible? Unless the anarchism of transgression, the basic lining of capitalism, is replaced with another anarchism. A profaning anarchism that gives up fetichizing excess, celebrating the mystery of ecstasy, eroticism, and what lies outside itself. "Three decades of non-stop pornographic innovation have exhausted all the allure of transgression and liberation," we read in *The Coming Insurrection*.[34] Instead of transgressing, going beyond, it is necessary to see that "power is constituted through the inclusive exclusion (*ex-ceptio*) of anarchy" and therefore that "the only possibility of thinking a true anarchy coincides with the lucid exposition of the anarchy internal to power."[35]

Lucidity is the antonym of bedazzlement. To deactivate the inner anarchy of power is to dim the brilliance of its transgressions. To see clearly by bringing down the lights. It is not a matter of denying symbolic power, but of challenging the idea that in the end the symbolic is the essence of power. Whether it is the body of the king (as in his discussion of Kantorowicz's theory), liturgical celebrations, glory, or Christ's "sacrifice" itself, in Agamben's work, on every occasion, we find the same critique of symbolic privilege.

The challenge is to speak about power, potentiality, body, murder, religion, glory, sacrifice, life, and form-of-life, without borrowing anything from the signifying supplements conferring the "sacred" dimension on the archic paradigm. To rise to this challenge, it is necessary to reveal the political dimension of God, to recall that "God" is perhaps none other than the mechanism of exception itself, freeing up the absurd and vain desire to kill God.

Paradoxically, "true anarchism" is developed at the cost of giving up this desire. Why? Because anarchy is within God. To understand this difficult point, the problem of government must be addressed. Although it figures in *Homo Sacer I*, at that point this term did not yet entail the defining meaning it acquired in subsequent volumes: the "apparatus" that Agamben borrows from Foucault, to translate the Greek word *oikonomia*. In *The Kingdom and the Glory*, Agamben declares, "[my] study will inquire into the paths by which and the reasons why power in the West has assumed the form of an *oikonomia*, that is, a government of men."[36] In this work, analysis of the theme of government radicalizes the political resituating of the sacred initiated in *Homo Sacer*. The analysis borrows an essential element from Foucault – an element whose consequences Foucault did not, however, fully perceive: the difference between *reigning* and *governing* that characterizes the constitutive anarchy of power.

Foucault's 1977–78 lectures: "The King reigns, but he does not govern"

In his lectures *Security, Territory, Population*, Foucault cites Thiers's famous phrase, "The king reigns, but he does not govern," in the course of explaining the change that led him to shift his attention from the critique of sovereignty to that of governmentality. How should this distinction be understood? With governmentality, he explains:

> I was led to designate or aim at something that again I think is relatively new, not in the word, and not at a certain level of reality, but as a new technique. Or rather, the modern political problem, the privilege that government begins to exercise in relation to rules, to the extent that, to limit the king's power, it will be possible one day to say, "the king reigns, but he does not govern," this inversion of government and the reign or rule and the fact that government is basically much more than the imperium.[37]

To govern is not to reign since, with governmentality, it is no longer a matter of imposing on everyone laws from on high but rather of proliferating rules and norms that are both explicit and vague. Foucault explains the meaning of the concept of "apparatus":[38]

> What I'm trying to pick out with this term [apparatus] is is, firstly, a thoroughly heterogenous ensemble consisting of discourses, institutions,

architectural forms, regulatory decisions, laws, administrative measures, scientific statements, philosophical, moral and philanthropic propositions – in short, the said as much as the unsaid. Such are the elements of the apparatus. The apparatus itself is the system of relations that can be established between these elements.[39]

The apparatus is thus an assemblage without any centralized unity.

In *What is an Apparatus?* Agamben describes what he takes and leaves from the Foucauldian concept.[40] He tries to show that the distinction between reigning and governing is not only historical, but also structural, thereby situating anarchy at the heart of the archic paradigm.

The fracture between beginning and command

The difference between reigning and governing secretly extends the two meanings of *archē*: beginning and commanding. To reign without governing is, in some senses, to begin without commanding. Any "apparatus" stands against this dissociation that Agamben, throughout all his subsequent work, defines as the irreducible anarchic fracture.

To start with, why translate government as "economy" (*oikonomia*)? We recall that economy means "administration of the house"[41] and thus, on the face of it, has nothing to do with government. However, Agamben demonstrates that the governor and the master of the house share the same fate, inhabit the same dwelling. Indeed, to "reign without governing" is the fate of all authority, whether king or master. Master or head of state never reign from anything other than a real, structural impossibility of commanding. Contrary to all expectations, the "ontological position"[42] of government reveals *the inscription in being of an incapacity to command* – the key expression of anarchy in power.

Of course, this type of fracture is denied by the declared unity of the two meanings of *archē*: beginning and commanding: "The Greek term *archē* has two meanings: it means both 'origin, principle' and 'command, order.'"[43] On first glance, Agamben continues, "it is certainly not incomprehensible that from the idea of an origin there would derive that of a command, that from the fact of being the first to do something would result the fact of being the leader. And vice versa: the one who commands is also the first, just as at the origin there is a command."[44]

These two meanings, which are seemingly so well adjusted to one another, are in fact profoundly disconnected. The fissure that runs through them causes a series of "aporias that an archaeology of the command must confront."[45]

Agamben recalls that, although Aristotle ties together the two values of *archē*, in *Poetics* he also takes pains to distinguish the two corresponding grammatical regimes: the constative and the imperative. "This great caesura that, according to Aristotle, divides the field of language"[46] clearly makes the proclaimed unity of *archē* problematic.

Aristotle distinguishes apophantic *logos*, to which the category of beginning belongs, from non-apophantic *logos*, to which the category of command belongs.[47] Apophantic *logos*, which expresses itself in propositions, has the task of making manifest (*apophanein*) the being of things through predication. That which they are truly, as soon as they begin to be. By contrast, there is another *logos*, the proper object of poetics and rhetoric, at work in "prayers, commands, threats, narrations, questions, and responses."[48] It is not the voice of being, but expresses all the modes of address and injunction. Through this distinction between the two types of *logos*, Aristotle appears to have anticipated the theory of speech acts and the difference between constative and performative statements. How then could he have united in the same paradigm the two heterogenous types of enunciation that are beginning and commanding? Apophansis "reigns" over the domain of the truth of being, but is still deprived of interlocution and power, particularly for giving orders. As for command, it touches neither being nor truth, it governs without referring to an existing reality. What it decides may therefore be just as true as false, which also means that government cannot be grounded in being. "Internal" anarchy lodges itself here, in the fracture between the *apraxia* of being and the efficacity of the imperative.

The archic paradigm appears to be a bipolar machine. A machine that, through the mechanism of exception, forces an articulation between an ontology of assertion and a pragmaticism of command. It is necessary therefore to engage in a deep reflection on commanding (about which Agamben notes "the almost complete absence in the philosophical tradition")[49] to understand how exactly it can coexist with beginning. If commanding only finds its foundation in beginning, how can it begin to make itself obeyed?

Agamben thus displaces the center of gravity of his analyses from the concept of power toward that of potentiality. Potentiality is what power can do. But how does power's potentiality begin if, at the beginning, as the beginning, power does not command, *cannot* command?

What we must understand is how an order, an imperative, can be implemented, executed, obeyed, starting from an absence of ontological foundation for this implementation. Where does the necessary energy for effecting a principle, the application of a law, an edict, or quite simply a piece of advice, come from? The main question presented by potentiality is that of the different modalities of its actualization. Agamben is constantly interrogating the ideas of *dynamis* and *energeia* to see how, simultaneously, the bipolarity of beginning and commanding are both resolved and exacerbated within them.[50]

The theological fate of the fracture, or the structure of exception of God

The deconstituting of the archic paradigm consists therefore in demonstrating how apparatuses have ensured the effectiveness of power – the way it "makes itself master" – by simultaneously masking and revealing its bipolarity and anarchic fracture.

The genealogy or archeology of government is developed throughout *Homo Sacer* with the study of Roman, followed by Christian, transformations of *oikonomia*. The first Latin translation of the term *oikonomia* as *dispositio* – ancestor of "apparatus" [*dispositif*] – comes from Cicero, who made it a term of rhetoric. But over the course of the centuries, *oikonomia* became a major theological operator, determining no less than the impossible possibility of government (*dispositio*) of the world by God. From the "ordered arrangement of the material of an oration or a treatise,"[51] it moves to the "'divine plan of salvation.'"[52]

By working his way through the genealogical lineage of government, Agamben pursues his profanation of *sacer*, showing how, in Christianity, the fracture of the archic paradigm lodges itself in the very being of God. How can God be sovereign and governor at one and the same time? How can God be "an" *archē*? Transcendent, outside the world, on the one hand, immanent to the order and arrangement of things, on the other?[53]

The strategy developed by the Church Fathers consisted in declaring that God, as a substance, is ontologically one, but that he acts through the trinity of Father, Son, and Holy Spirit. Agamben claims that *oikonomia* becomes a technical term referring to the trinitarian articulation of divine life in Hippolytus and Tertullian. God is one in terms of being; three in terms of action.[54] Thus, "the *oikonomia* makes possible a reconciliation in which a transcendent God, who is both one and triune at the same time, can – while remaining transcendent – take charge of the world and found an immanent *praxis* of government whose supermundane mystery coincides with the history of humanity."[55]

The trinitarian strategy does not, however, mask the anarchic fracture completely. To start with anarchy of being: being is without power since it does not command: "No figure of being is, as such, in the position of the *archē*."[56] Then comes anarchy of *praxis* since government is not grounded on being.

This is why, from the trinitarian economy to the "invisible hand" of the modern economy,[57] "the fracture between being and *praxis*, and the anarchic character of the divine oikonomia constitute the logical place in which the fundamental nexus that, in our culture, unites government and anarchy becomes comprehensible." Further: "The governmental paradigm, of which we are here reconstructing the genealogy, is actually always already 'anarchic-governmental.'"[58]

The dual anarchy of Father and Son

Analysis of the distribution of power between Father and Son makes manifest the "original 'anarchic' vocation of Christology."[59] God is anarchic since he is unable to govern. According to the "doctrine of divine impotence,"[60] "God's impotence functions to make possible a righteous government of the world."[61] Christ is anarchic because he is unable to be, that is, to be grounded in the Father: "The an-archic character of the Son, who is not founded ontologically in the Father, is essential to the Trinitarian economy."[62] The Son is "without principle, *anarchos*, that is, ungrounded."[63]

In the exchange between Father and Son, two anarchies address each other: "The economy is anarchical and, as such, has no foundation in God's being." It is therefore God who engenders this anarchy – "the original paradox of a generated anarchy."[64] The problem is that "Power – every power, both human and divine – must hold these two poles together, that is, it must be, at the same time, kingdom and government, transcendent norm and immanent order."[65] This is the full mystery contained in the idea of an actualization of divine potentiality. An actualization that is only possible at the price of excluding its impossibility since being does not have the power to act.

We are therefore back at the structure of the exception again. In fact, we never really left it. The anarchy of potentiality only appears to be excluded from the paradigm in which it is actually included. It is included for essential reasons, in the proper sense: lack of ontological foundation of the economy and lack of the practical efficacy of ontology. It is excluded insofar as the fracture between being and action is the object of persistent moves to conceal, forcing potentiality to actualize itself, whether through the intervention of the concept of the "will" of God,[66] which supposedly renders God "operative," or through all the attempts characteristic of medieval ontology to "resolve, or at least to indeterminate, being into acting."[67] Agamben thus writes: "Being is something that must be realized or brought-into-work."[68]

"Politics" and "economy," united and disjointed at once: this is the power machine called God. God is the supreme exception. Although it is impossible to say whether God is the origin of the exception, or whether God is always already subject to it. Whether God begins exceptionally, or whether it is the exception that commands God. What is clear is that "in the sixth or seventh century,"[69] the term *oikonomia* acquired "the meaning of 'exception'."[70]

Return of the "sacred"

Let's consider again the way that Agamben dissociates *sacer* from the "sacred" aura, sacrificial prestige, and symbolic overdetermination. By revealing the theological sources of the concept of government, he achieves an incredible tour de force that consists in situating the profanation of the *sacer* not only in the antique and patristic Christian corpus, but also, therefore, in God.

By highlighting the political dimension of the structure of the divine exception, Agamben prohibits any recourse to symbolic brilliance.

Usually, the sacred and accompanying symbolic dimension are viewed as reducing fracture. What is normally meant by "symbolic power" other than this mysterious force that enables the full and complete actualization of divine potentiality along with royal potentiality? An emergency energy that replaces ontological impotence? As if, giving being a surplus meaning, the aura, prestige, brilliance of signs, conferred on it the imperative energy it lacks. As if, in the same fell swoop, it grants command a "sacred" bedrock, a throne.

It is commonly thought, as Louis Marin puts it, that "signs of power need only be seen for their force to be believed" and that "representations are delegations of powers in signs."[71] Symbolic power is generally conceived as an inductive power, a power to transfer, one that consists in pretending that meaning makes it possible to "intensify a presence."[72] Agamben's critique singles out this belief in the *sui generis* power of the sacred when it is nothing but a cog in the machine of sovereignty, destined to make it work – that is, first and foremost, to mask the anarchic fracture that constitutes it. This criticism has nothing to do with a defense of secularization. Indeed, secularization "is a form of repression. It leaves intact the forces it deals with by simply moving them from one place to another. Thus, the political secularization of theological concepts (the transcendence of God as a paradigm of sovereign power) does nothing but displace the heavenly monarchy onto an earthly monarchy, leaving its power intact."[73]

But how can profanation occur without sacrilege and without secularization? What is the "sacred" reduced to? Agamben answers in three steps that correspond to three key moments in his enterprise of profanation through symbolic deflation: the "archeology of glory" (*The Kingdom and the Glory*); an analysis of the sacerdotal function of Jesus Christ (*The Kingdom and the Glory* and *Opus Dei*); and, most sensitive of all, the interpretation of Christ's sacrifice (*Opus Dei* and *Pilate and Jesus*).[74]

Glory

"Glory" (*doxa*) is a translation of the Hebrew *kâbôd*, which means importance, weight, power. It usually refers to shining, the brilliance of royal or divine force to which homage is proffered through celebration (glorification, *doxazesthai*). The "glory" of Christ often refers also to his aura or halo.

But in Agamben's analysis it is never a question of the ring of light surrounding the head of Christ. The word "aura" appears just once in *The Kingdom and the Glory* and is not related to Jesus. Rather, it is a matter of separating that which appears to be indivisible: glory and "spectacle," glory and "mise-en-scène,"[75] glory and excess of meaning. "If the governmental machine is twofold (Kingdom and Government), what function does glory play within it?"[76] In answering this question, Agamben rejects several theses, all of which claim that glory is essentially, and specifically, a symbolic energy: the theses of a magical function of glory, an aesthetic function of glory, and a Machiavellian function of glory.

The first thesis is proposed primarily by anthropologists and sociologists. Referring to the work of Marcel Mauss, Agamben states that, for them,

> it always remains possible to turn to magic as the sphere that, bordering upon rationality and immediately preceding it, allows one to explain that which we do not understand about the society in which we live as ultimately a magical survival. [Yet] we do not believe in the magical power of acclamations and of liturgy, and we are convinced that not even theologians or emperors really believed in it.[77]

Glory does not suture fracture "through magic."

The thesis of an aesthetic function of glory is presented by Urs von Balthasar in *The Glory of the Lord: A Theological Aesthetics* (*Herrlichkeit, Eine Theologische Aesthetik*).[78] This is another "false lead" that displaces sovereignty and lordship (the German term for glory) "into the sphere of beauty."[79] "But in the Bible neither *kabod* nor *doxa* are understood to have an aesthetic meaning: they are concerned with the terrible appearance of YHVH with Reign, Judgement, throne, all things which can only be taken as 'beautiful' from a perspective that it is hard not to describe as aestheticizing."[80]

The Machiavellian function of glory corresponds to the hypothesis whereby glory enables the sovereign to induce fear among his subjects, thereby forcing their submission. Glory is not the theater of constraint.

> The simple instrumental explanation that states that this is a stratagem of the powerful to justify their ambition or a mise-en-scène to produce reverential

fear and obedience in the subjects, while it can occasionally get somewhere near the truth, is certainly not able to account for the deep and original connection that involves not only the political sphere but also the religious one.[81]

It has become necessary to develop an "archeology of glory" because the glorious dimension of power has not been the object of sufficient studies to define its specific political value – a value not based on magic, beauty, or spectacle, or all the forces of symbolic coercion. We return here to the structure of exception. Glory finds its true space in the juncture of the being of God and the salvation practice of the Son in the "process of [their] reciprocal glorification."[82] The handover of power is to be found between the two of them. Agamben cites John (17: 1–5): "Father, the hour is come; glorify [*doxason*] thy Son, that thy Son also may glorify [*doxasei*] thee"; he comments: "The economy glorifies being, as being glorifies the economy ... Kingdom and Government appear to coincide for an instant."[83] Glory is fully operative in that it is dative (the inter-glorification is a mutual *gift*) and it therefore enables the transfer of potentiality from one side of the fracture to the other. But in doing so (in the literal meaning), it also reveals the anarchic extent of the fracture itself. Glory operates only by revealing the inoperativeness of God.

"The apparatus of glory finds its perfect cipher in the majesty of the empty throne. Its purpose is to capture within the governmental machine that unthinkable inoperativity – making it its internal motor – that constitutes the ultimate mystery of divinity."[84] The power of God coincides strangely with ontological "inoperativeness" [*désœuvrement*] in Agamben: "we can make use of it [the theological apparatus of glory] as the epistemological paradigm that will enable us to penetrate the central mystery of power."[85] The central mystery of power, illuminated in its true meaning by glory, is the fundamental incapacity of being to do work. Such inoperativeness is thus "the political substance of the Occident, the glorious nutrient of all power."[86]

This is how Agamben answers his own question: why does power "need to receive ritual acclamations and hymns of praise, to wear cumbersome crowns and tiaras, to submit itself to an inaccessible ceremony and an immutable protocol – in a word, why does something that is essentially operativity and *oikonomia* need to become solemnly immobilized in glory?"[87] Power "needs" glory not to draw a supplement of being in pomp and circumstance, but, rather, to celebrate with pomp and circumstance the fact that no supplement is capable of suturing the fracture that guts it from the start, "that fracture between theology and economy that the doctrine of the trinity has never been able to completely resolve."[88] The mystery of operativity is thus that being on vacation puts the government to work.

The "symbols of power"

What is the purpose of the "signs" and "insignia" of power? Usually they are held to be "symbols." "We already see this in the way Mommsen observes that, from the third century onward, 'the purple clothing of war becomes the symbol of monarchy' … But what does 'symbol' mean here?" This is Agamben's question again as he asserts that the "symbol" is initially a legal-political notion and that "a juridical theory able to precisely define their sphere and value is still lacking."[89]

The inquiry into the "ceremony" and "signs" of power by which the majesty of both God and emperor or king are manifested begins with "acclamations," or "doxological-acclamatory element."[90] Obviously, there is continuity between the phenomenon of imperial power and phenomenalizing the glory of God, to the extent that there is a confusing interaction of "imperial cult and ecclesiastical liturgy."[91]

So, what then exactly is an acclamation? It is "an exclamation of praise, of triumph ("*Io triumphe!*"), of laudation or of disapproval (*acclamatio adversa*) yelled by a crowd in determinate circumstances." Acclamations are also present in the Christian context: "*A populo acclamatum est* [the people acclaim]: *Deo gratias, Christo laudes* [grace to God, praise Christ]."[92] Agamben explains that, in both instances, Peterson insists on the legal dimension of acclamation, which has the value of a "popular decision" and bears witness to the constitutive power of consensus. By celebrating power, consensus constitutes the people as subjects or of the faithful as people.[93]

This then is the "performative force" of the symbol.[94] The symbol is not a symbol of power, blood, or hierarchy; rather, it performs – that is, constitutes – power, blood, or hierarchy. With regard to the positions of the emperor, either standing or seated during public appearances, Agamben states: "In this case as well, rather than see in the posture merely the symbolic expression of rank, it is necessary to understand that it is the posture that immediately establishes the hierarchy."[95] Symbols are "immediately efficacious,"[96] and for this very reason have very little symbolism. This is the case, for example, with the "*fasces lictoriae* ... elm or birch rods about 130 centimeters in length, bound together with a red strap into which an axe was inserted laterally."[97] Thus, to "to define the fasces as the 'symbol of *imperium*,' as has sometimes been the case, tells us nothing about their nature or their specific function. So *little does the word 'symbol' characterize them* that they in fact served to actually inflict capital punishment in its two forms: flogging (the rods) and decapitation (the axe)."[98]

There is no need for the symbol to refer to anything except itself, and so no need to use this force of transferal to explain how power functions. It is important to understand that "the fasces do not symbolize the *imperium*, they execute and determine it."[99] Indeed, when fasces are raised, the court is in session; when they are lowered, the court is in recess. An "effective" symbol is no longer a symbol; rather, it is a power. And symbolic power is a power like any other.

Christ's sacrifice

What is the role of sacrifice in this desymbolic economy? And what, specifically, is the role of Christ's sacrifice? This vast question immediately prompts another, which, strangely, Agamben never asks in this form, but which is an implicit thread running throughout works such as *Opus Dei*, *The Highest Poverty*,[100] and even *The Use of Bodies*. If, as we saw earlier, life were not "sacred" in itself in either Greece or Rome, doesn't it become so with the Incarnation? Isn't the life of Christ sacred according to a necessarily extra-political and extra-juridical meaning? And isn't this the case precisely because of its sacrificial vocation?

The answer is complex, but it's always a rejection, articulated as it is around a double status of Christ as *priest* and as *accused*. This answer prepares for the conclusion by which Christ is his own structure of exception. He, too, is both sacrificeable and unsacrificeable, sovereign and *homo sacer*.

While, through its supreme performative efficacy, Christ's sacrifice sutures the anarchic fracture between being and acting, it also exacerbates this irreparable yawning gap.

In his extensive inquiry into liturgy in *Opus Dei*, Agamben explores the category of priesthood. Who are the subjects for whom the "ministry of the mystery,"[101] the operativity, is incumbent? In a manner that is initially surprising, Agamben does not look for an answer in worship, officiating, or the faithful, but instead in Christ himself. The text opens with a reading of the Epistle to the Hebrews in which Paul presents Jesus as the first minister of his own religion, the first priest. This is the irreducible singularity that distinguishes Christianity from Judaism: "The theological nucleus of the letter plays on the opposition between the Levitical priesthood ... corresponding to the old Mosaic covenant and encompassing the descendants of Aaron and the new covenant, in which the one who assumes the 'liturgy' of the high priest ... is Christ himself."[102]

The fact that Christ is the first priest, the Grand Priest – an unheard-of descriptor in the history of monotheisms – means that his action is immediately and performatively liturgical. There is not first Incarnation and salvational Sacrifice, then service and worship by ministers of the Church. Jesus is all at once his religion, object, and first officiate. And the proof is the exhibition of his own sacrifice: Christ is "the high priest of a sacrifice in which the officiator sacrifices himself."[103]

With sacrificial efficacy, Christ "accomplishes a liturgical action that is, so to speak, absolute and perfect."[104] Later, Agamben writes that he "coincides without remainder with his liturgy – he is essentially liturgy – and precisely this coincidence confers on his liturgy its incomparable efficacy."[105] His conclusion is striking: the Pauline interpretation of the liturgical dimension of the action of Christ (Christ "the *leitourgos* and high priest"[106]) "has an obvious polemical meaning and *does not intend to confer [upon it] a sacrificial aura.*"[107]

Inclusion through exclusion: in many respects Christ's sacrifice banishes the originary anarchy of a being without acting and an acting without being. By adorning Christ as the figure of the Grand Priest, the Epistle to the Hebrews simultaneously grants him sovereignty in being. The action of Christ is not only an "economic," or governmental, action, it is also an ontological completion. By officiating his own sacrifice, he comes into being: his "being coincides without remainder with effectiveness."[108] The term "effectiveness," which appears in Thomas, brings together efficacy (*effectus*) and essence ("ite"). Insofar as "the Church has founded its liturgical *praxis* on the Letter to the Hebrews,"[109] it produces an ontological transformation that, for a time, sutures the breaking of potentiality. As a result of the "performativity of Christ's words"[110] being and acting coincide.

Ecce homo sacer

In *Pilate and Jesus*, Agamben adds to the study of the sacrificial effectiveness of Christ an analysis of his trial that shifts perspective. In this remarkable text, he shows that the anarchic fracture reappears, or, rather, that it never disappeared.

"Why must the decisive event of history – the passion of Christ and the redemption of humanity – take the form of a trial?" he asks.[111]

Once again, Christ is not only a priest; he's also the accused. According to the texts, it is a matter of determining whether his trial is truly legal. Agamben says it is not: while there is indeed a trial of Christ, there is no judgment. Although John declares: "Pilate led Jesus outside and sat on the judge's bench [*bēma*]"[112] it is still the case that,

> an exegetical tradition that draws its authority from Justin (Apology 1, XXXV: 6) and, among modern authors, from Harnack and Dibelius, understands *ekathisen* in a transitive sense. ... That Jesus [rather than Pilate] was made to sit on the *bēma* accords with the narratives of Mark and Matthew, according to which, immediately before the crucifixion Jesus was dressed in a purple robe and, holding a reed for a scepter, is hailed as king of the Jews. In Justin as well, the Jews, after having made Jesus sit on the *bēma*, scornfully invite him to exercise the function of judge that belongs to a king: "Judge!"[113]

This reading, which reverses roles by making Jesus the judge, also explains why, in the gospel of Mark and Matthew, Pilate never actually hands down a judgment. All he does is "deliver" Christ to the Jews: "He handed over (*paredoken*) Jesus to their will."[114] He himself did not have had the intention to sentence him ("'I find no case against him'"[115]). He therefore "delivers" him under the pressure of the Jews without pronouncing a sentence: "The judge has not handed down a sentence." A trial without a sentence, without a judgment, is "a contradiction in terms,"[116] "the most severe objection that can be raised."[117]

This enigma extends right up to the crucifixion, which, without a judgment, cannot be considered a legal punishment either. Hence, Jesus' crucifixion is nothing but an execution ("From the point of view of law, 'Jesus of Nazareth was not condemned, but murdered'").[118] Without a judgment, an execution is not legal. Jesus is therefore killed, not sacrificed. More precisely, he sacrifices himself by consenting to being killed. Through his sacrifice that has a properly legal dimension, Jesus becomes *homo sacer*.

Through his twofold analysis of the priesthood and the execution of Jesus, Agamben completes his demonstration according to which Jesus is the exception to his own exception. He occupies the dual place of sovereign and *homo sacer*. Supreme power and bare life – and between the two, the anarchic fracture remains.

On Foucault's immanent use

The circle is closing. From the analysis of the "ban" of the sovereign (*Homo Sacer I*, Part Two, section 6) to the governmental archeology, the entire investigation is organized around the structure of exception. The overlap between the logic of inclusive exclusion (sovereignty) and the logic of commanding and obeying now appears clearly: both derive from a single mechanism, which is the partial filling of a fissure.

How should we now dive into this fissure to deactivate the mechanism? The anarchy internal to power eventually reveals another instance, one that is included and excluded by the mechanism of exception. This is another range of meaning than being and practice, one that secretly competes with power: use.

Again, Agamben finds the rudiments of his conceptualization of use in Foucault. As we recall, *The Hermeneutics of the Subject* distinguishes the soul as an instance of commanding from the soul as a subject of use on the model of playing an instrument – the instrumental soul. Yet Agamben argues that, in Foucault, use "is almost never thematized as such."[119] Consequently, anarchy is poorly situated. Foucault's thought moved forward "tangling himself in ever more difficult aporias,"[120] as shown by "the last course at the Collège de France, *Le Courage de la vérité* [*The Courage of Truth*], concluded a few months before his death."[121]

According to Agamben, these aporias derive from the fact that Foucault never clearly distinguished between the free subject and the instrumentalist soul of life. Right to the end, Foucault remained attached to autonomy, to the idea of a subject who "'freely' conducts and governs itself," thus a subject fractured between their own beginning (autonomy) and their own command (imperative). A subject constituted by the logic of exception and consequently destined to "inevitably enter into power relations."[122]

Since he did not assess the significance of the anarchic fracture between reigning and governing, Foucault sought only to illuminate an *other* form of government with the category of use. He was too quick to equate use with care, and in *The Hermeneutics of the Subject* moved too rapidly over "the Platonic gesture in which *chresis* [use] was resolved into care (*epimeleia*) and command (*archē*)." This is why "the theme of care-of-oneself in this way risks resolving itself entirely into that of the governance of the self."[123] The "active subject" of care absorbs the instrumentalist soul. The explanation Agamben offers to the problem I raised in the last chapter is that "the theme of the use of the body on the part of the soul is resolved at a certain point into that of the command (*archē*) of the soul over the body."[124] Foucault termed "ungovernable" that which is – let me be clear – nothing but a form of government.[125]

Just when he believes he is extending Deleuze's approach, Agamben in fact makes immanence Foucault's unthought in a very different way. An unthought that supposedly prevents him from bringing to light that which is not governable in and of life: the absence of all hierarchy, the absence of any difference between that which commands and that which obeys in life.

Yet the structure of use that is both syntactic and ontological, glimmering through the Greek verb *chrestai*, clearly showed that such an absence was possible. In English we say, "to make use of something," but the Greek term does not endorse this understanding at all. Indeed, *chrestai* is "neither active nor passive"; its form consists of the "diathesis that ancient grammarians called 'middle.'" "The subject who achieves the action, by the very fact of achieving it, does not act transitively on an object but first of all implies and affects himself in the process." *Chrestai* is among the verbs that "effect while being affected."[126] This grammatical overlap of the indicative and the gerundive already signals an interruption of the logic of commanding and obeying. If Agamben accepts the Foucauldian metaphor of life as an "art object," it's on condition that it is understood as "a life that can never be separated from its form ... a life for which, in its mode of life, its very living is at stake, and, in its living, what is at stake is first of all its mode of life."[127]

In many respects, this description of the syntactic and ontological process of use corresponds to Deleuze's analysis of the fold. However, as we have seen, in Deleuze, immanence implies auto-affection, which is still attached to government taken as "domination of the self" (one cannot govern others if one cannot govern oneself first). In Agamben, use is subtracted from all logic of domination, including domination of the self by the self: "The subject does not stand over the action but is himself the place of its occurring."[128] The distance that could be established not only between subject and object, but also between subject and self, is thus reduced to the minimum. There is not even room anymore for affection of the self by the self. In *The Use of Bodies*, we also find reference to Spinoza and the question of immanent cause: "the immanent cause is ... an action in which agent and patient coincide, which is to say, fall together." Immanent cause is the "key" concept for a modal ontology in which the "substance ... 'constitutes itself as existing.'"[129] Agamben continues, "In the twentieth chapter of the *Compendium grammatices linguae hebraeae*, he [Spinoza] introduced an ontological meditation in the form of an analysis of the meaning of a Hebrew verbal form ... [which] expresses an action in which agent and patient, active and passive are identified."[130] Take, for example, the Spanish verb *pasearse*, "to 'walk-oneself,'" whose form is "as an expression of an action of the self on the self, in which agent and patient enter into a threshold of absolute indistinction." Agent and patient are "thus deactivated" and "rendered inoperative" by becoming one with each other.[131]

Critique of transgression

Understood in this manner, immanence is linked to the "capacity to deactivate something and render it inoperative – a power, a function, a human operation – without simply destroying it but by liberating the potentials that have remained inactive in it in order to allow a different use of them."[132] This is the difference between anarchy as destituent power and anarchy as transgression.

Foucault remains attached to the question of the free subject who governs themselves precisely because he continues to associate freedom with transgression. His concept of *bios* retains the trace of the definition of "critical ontology of ourselves" proposed in "What is Enlightenment?", a text in which he equates "philosophical life" directly with transgression, taken as a crossing of limits.

> The critical ontology of ourselves has to be considered not, certainly as a theory, a doctrine, nor even as a permanent body of knowledge that is accumulating; it has to be conceived as an attitude, an ethos, a philosophical life in which the critique of what we are is at one and the same time the historical analysis of the limits that are imposed on us and an experiment with the possibility of going beyond them.[133]

And also: "The point, in brief, is to transform the critique conducted in the form of necessary limitation into a practical critique that takes the form of a possible transgression."[134]

In Foucault, the themes of "exit" (let's not forget that he describes *Aufklärung* in terms of an exit), of going beyond and "outside" are numerous and varied. Now, according to Agamben, transgression makes that which it transgresses exist, namely, the traditional structure of subjectivity as an instance that always exceeds and overtakes itself. One that commands and obeys itself. This is especially the case when it is a matter of breaching its own command in the *sacrifice* of the self.

Foucault could not give up the "sacrificial ideology" weighing on his category of desubjectivation. Sacrifice is omnipresent in his work, whether in his analysis of the Passion of Christ in *History of Madness*,[135] the spectacular description of Damiens' torture in *Discipline and Punish*,[136] his reading of *Phaedo* and the sacrifice of a cock to Esculape demanded by Socrates,[137] or the analysis of the Cynic *bios* as a sacrificial life in *The Courage of Truth*. He writes "The dedication of the Cynic king, of that real and derisory king," has as its mission to "take care of others," "a hard mission, and one which might be inclined to call sacrificial, if the Cynics did not say at the same time that the philosopher really finds his joy and the fulfillment of his existence in this sacrifice of oneself."[138] If the anarchism of the Cynic is sacrificial engagement, to Agamben's mind it remains a *sovereign* engagement.

One might object, however, that, ordinarily, sovereignty refers not only to the absolute power of the monarch but also to detachment, power's extravagant scorn and the ecstasy of transgression. As we know, Bataille, names sovereignty the unrecoverable, unproductive expense that includes the playoff of life and asserts itself as the aristocratic gesture in the antonym of the petty sovereignty of the king.

The real originality of Bataille's notion of transgression lies in the fact that it calls sovereignty the execution of the sovereign. The decapitation of the sovereign gives birth to sovereign acephaly. Bataille brings to light the paradox of an anarchist sovereignty. As Foucault puts it, in Bataille

> [sovereignty] explodes and radically challenges itself in laughter, tears, the overturned eyes of ecstasy, the mute and exorbitated horror of sacrifice, and it remains fixed in this way at the limit of its void, speaking of itself in a second language in which the absence of a sovereign subject outlines its essential emptiness and incessantly fractures the unity of its discourse.[139]

Agamben certainly acknowledges that Bataille succeeded in "attempting to think ... the very bare life (or sacred life) that, in the relation of ban, constitutes the immediate referent of sovereignty."[140] But what compromised his inquiries[141] is the fact that he erroneously interprets the sacred as "originarily ambivalent: pure and filthy, regnant and fascinating," and that he does so "according to the dominant themes of the anthropology of his day taken up by Caillois."[142] This erroneous interpretation, based on the supposed ambivalence of sovereignty, helps explain his fascination with sacrifice. In Bataille, "the prestige of the sacrificial body ... is defined ... by the logic of transgression."[143] This is why, at the end of *The Use of Bodies*, Agamben writes: "Having mistaken this bare life separated from its form, in its abjection, for a superior principle – sovereignty or the sacred – is the limit of Bataille's thought, which renders it useless to us."[144] Excess, eroticism, luxury, propping up the prestige accorded to sacrifice, are therefore criticized as being slightly outdated and misplaced. This is due to the political fault of having named sovereignty: "The sovereignty ... has little to do with that of states."[145]

Echoing the discussion initiated by Jean-Luc Nancy in "The unsacrificeable,"[146] Agamben highlights the danger of this "definition of sovereignty with reference to transgression [which] is inadequate with respect to the life in the sovereign ban that may be killed."[147] Moreover, it can lead to an interpretation of Shoah as a sacrifice, but "the wish to lend a sacrificial aura to the extermination of the Jews by means of the term 'Holocaust' was, from this perspective, an irresponsible historiographical blindness. The Jew living under Nazism is the privileged negative referent of the new biopolitical sovereignty and is, as such, a flagrant case of a *homo sacer* in the sense of a life that may be killed but not sacrificed."[148]

Bataille never did equate Shoah with sacrifice, as Agamben recognized: "Not that Bataille does not discern that sacrifice is insufficient and that it is, in the last analysis, a 'comedy,'"[149] but the author of *Homo Sacer* continues to think, with Nancy, that "Bataille didn't just want to think sacrifice; he wanted to think according to sacrifice, and he actually wanted sacrifice itself. At the very least, he never stopped presenting his own thought as a necessary sacrifice of thought."[150]

The critique of Bataille's view of transgression hones in on the true problem in misconceptions of the sacred: the *paradoxical sacralization of the logic of government*. Let me repeat: all transgression maintains the distance, the separation, the "outside the self" that inevitably involves a sharing of commanding and obeying.

Hence, Agamben argues that "the problem of the coming philosophy is that of thinking an ontology beyond operativity and command.'"[151]

Questions and challenges

It's time now to ask: *how can we think of anarchy without transgression?* It's time to ask this question because transgression keeps knocking at the door and it would take deep disavowal not to hear it. The idea of an anarchism without transgression is immediately faced with obvious contradictions.

The four knocks of transgression

The first knock concerns the fact that the critique of separation is expressed systematically by Agamben through verbs of separation.

"Torn away" (form-of-life is "what must unceasingly be torn away from the separation"),[152] "neutralize," "destitute," "render inoperative" (the etymology of "*rendre*" [to render] connects it to "*prendre*" [to take] in French), and "deactivate" – which strictly speaking means to decontaminate a substance: all these verbs are action words. So how could they "go beyond" "operativity"? Isn't "going beyond" transgressing?

The second knock is linked to the ambiguity of the symbolic deflation of the sacred and its political re-situating. To have tried to break with the idea that the sacred is a signifier without a signified, delivered to the drift of semantic inflation, camouflaged under the general category of floating signifier, is no doubt a significant move. Yet how can the opposite trap be avoided – the one that involves re-anchoring the sacred in the hyper-signifier of the mechanism of exception – precisely in reaction to this hyper-signifying? It might be objected that a mechanism is not a signifier, nor really a concept. Fair enough. But the mechanism of exception is nonetheless defined by Agamben as the mark of the "politicity [*politicità*]"[153] of politics itself. How, then, can we avoid viewing this decision as a move from the mechanical to the essential that betrays the search for a founding meaning? A meaning based on principle, an archic meaning?

The third knock of contradiction: according to the definition he had already given it, Agamben says that to deactivate signifies first to bring together, to make touch. Hence the description of anarchy proposed at the end of *The Use of Bodies* as an anarchy of contact: "Anarchy can never be in the position of a principle: it can only be liberated as a contact."[154] Later, he writes: "Just as thought at its greatest summit does not represent but 'touches' the intelligible, in the same way, in the life of thought as form-of-life, *bios* and *zoē*, form and life are in contact, which is to say, they are in a non-relation." Touch and overlap are the response to separation and distance: "like living and life, so also being and form here coincide without remainder."[155]

The prohibition on touching, which is usually associated with the sacred, is thus well and truly profaned here. The problem is that the ordinary meaning of the sacred is also associated with touching. To touch the sacred is not always to profane it; instead it is to confirm it, to consecrate it a second time. To touch the king, to touch the body of Christ, to touch one's idol: isn't that to celebrate and reinforce their sacredness? An anarchy of contact would therefore share the same haptic passion with sacralizing contact. It then becomes impossible to differentiate them rigorously.

The fourth knock. According to Agamben, the anarchic dimension of potentiality is that which, within it, refuses to act. Paradoxically, Aristotle would perhaps be the first philosopher of anarchy since, in his theory of *dynamis* and *energeia*, he reserves a place for disposition of the *dynamis*, which "can ... endure and have mastery over itself, without always already losing itself in action."[156] This disposition is *hexis* or habit, the acquisition of a talent or ability. To have a *hexis* (*hekhein* means to have), is to sculpt one's being, to add to one's essence a potentiality that was not initially possessed and that nevertheless now defines it entirely. This would be true for "philosopher" in the case of Socrates, for example, as an aptitude that was not given at the start, but which then became as important as the "man" gender to which he belongs. To be a man is an ontological fact, to be a philosopher is a use. One is not a philosopher; one makes "use of philosophy," through experience and repetition. Let's also take the example of Glenn Gould, Agamben suggests,

> to whom we attribute the habit of playing the piano, [and who] does nothing but make use-of-himself insofar as he plays and knows habitually how to play the piano. He is not the title holder and master of the potentiality to play, which he can put to work or not, but constitutes-himself as having use of the piano, independently of his playing it or not playing it in actuality.[157]

Likewise for the poet, who "is not someone who has the potentiality or faculty to create that, one fine day, by an act of will (the will is, in Western culture, the apparatus that allows one to attribute the ownership of actions and techniques to a subject) he decides ... to put to work."[158] With *hexis* Agamben mobilizes a meaning of *dynamis* that is not necessarily related to *energeia*. A sort of *dynamis* to the potential of two (forgive the pun). Indifferent to the potentiality–actuality duo. An anarchist potentiality that self-disciplines but remains ungovernable, without any link to the diktat of actualization or the weakness of virtuality's pre-obedience.

Aristotle "thinks potential as existing in itself, in the form of a potential-not-to or impotential (*adynamia*)."[159] Impotentiality would then be the most intimate dimension of potentiality. As if the destitution of potentiality inhabited its very heart. This, then, is the meaning of *hexis*, a potentiality that cannot pass over into the act and that bears within it its own privation (*steresis*). "This relation with privation (or, as he can also say, with *adynamia*, impotentiality or potential not to) is essential for Aristotle because it is only through it that potential can exist as such, independently of its passing into action."[160] And later he explains: "Having a potential in reality means: being at the mercy of one's own impotential."[161] Agamben thus seeks to return impotentiality to form-of-life. Once deactivated, that is, literally cut off from the act, "potential becomes a form-of-life and a form-of-life is constitutively destituent."[162] The problem is that, for Aristotle, the act is always, in every instance, ontologically prior and superior to potentiality. According to him, a potentiality that never actualizes itself and becomes delayed in privation would not be impotent: it would be non-being. The contradiction (and error) that haunts Agamben's lively praise of impotence throughout *Homo Sacer* is that "privation," which can never be a constant state, is defined by Aristotle in *Book Two of Physics* as "privation of form."[163] Yet how could a privation of form (Aristotle would call it matter) become a form-of-life? How could it do so without annihilating life itself?

Of course, as an empty form is eventually filled with this very emptiness ("a law that has lost its content ceases to exist and becomes indistinguishable from life,")[164] a content deprived of form can receive its form from this very deprivation. The form-of-life would then be exactly the same as the way in which it shapes its emptiness: "'My' form-of-life relates not to what I am, but to how I am what I am."[165] But if this is the case, how can this form-of-life not be taken as mere private life? How can we imagine that the way of living can "delineate the contours … of a common use of bodies," allowing politics to "escape from its muteness and individual biography from its idiocy"[166]? Isn't private life idiotic, and, in this sense, aren't we all idiots? Idiots who share nothing? How can this idiocy organize itself in common?

The zone

This is where the disavowal begins. Agamben raises all these contradictions by calling now on his own magic argument: *the "zone" argument*.

Mysteriously and constantly (there are no fewer than twenty-three instances in *Homo Sacer I*): the "zones of indifference" or "indistinction" erase paradoxes, deactivate deactivation, suspend the aggressiveness of neutralization, prevent the re-signified from solidifying into a foundation, retain contact at the edge of the fusional hold, and protect form-of-life from an impotent, formless, idiotic becoming. Both pre- and post-archic, the "zone of indifference" is this placeless place where opposites disappear into one another, and differentiating is miraculously annulled.

I say pre- and post-archic since the "zone" is both beginning and end. As beginning, the zone firstly "is located ... prior to the distinction between sacred and profane, religious and juridical."[167] As end, the zone ultimately appears as the space of deactivation "where both *archē* as origin and *archē* as command are exposed in their non-relation and neutralized."[168] All the scaffolding of sovereignty and governmentality end up by entering "a zone of indifference" (*zona d'indifferenza*) – to the point that, due to its proliferation, the zone of indifference becomes the unidimensional space of contemporary politics.

> Together with the process by which the exception everywhere becomes the rule, the realm of bare life – which is originally situated at the margins of the political order – gradually begins to coincide with the political realm, and exclusion and inclusion, outside and inside, *bios* and *zoē*, right and fact, enter into a zone of irreducible indistinction.[169]

All opposition comes from a seizing operation that forms prisons in thought: the terms in opposition are "distinguished and kept united by the relation of ban,"[170] but the prisons eventually collapse insofar as they are, from the start, wide open, empty. Returning freely to the zone, the opposing terms "abolish each other and enter into a new dimension."[171] Oppositions, dualities – political, logical, conceptual – reveal the lack of differentiation between their terms. Indeed, "we must learn to see these oppositions not as 'di-chotomies' but as 'di-polarities,' not substantial, but tensional. I mean that we need a logic of the field, as in physics, where it is impossible to draw a line clearly and separate two different substances."[172] Separation is abolished in the zone. No more contradiction, therefore, between verbs of action and deactivation, verbs of separation and destitution. In the zone, from the zone, thanks to the zone, there's no danger that the mechanism of exception will freeze into a transcendental signified. In the zone, from the zone, thanks to it, the very politicity of politics reveals nothing but the vacuity of which it is made.[173] The mechanism of exception – itself born of an exception to indifference – returns in the end, exhibiting its originary vacuousness. In the zone, from the zone, thanks to it, contact touches without touching. Agamben says: "Giorgio Colli defines as 'contact' the 'metaphysical interstice' or the moment in which two entities are separated only by a void of representation."[174] The "contact zone" does not confuse the terms touching within it. They maintain between themselves an intimacy without relation. If "Western politics … always already has to reformulate contact into the form of a relation [then] it will therefore be necessary to think politics as an intimacy unmediated by any articulation or representation: human beings, forms-of-life are in contact, but this is unrepresentable because it consists precisely in a representative void, that is, in the deactivation and inoperativity of every representation."[175] The anarchic contact is a touch freed of the fear of contamination, situating it by the same token between sacred and profane, liberating it from the weight of their duality. In the zone, from the zone, thanks to the zone, form-of-life escapes idiocy and maintains itself in the space that separates form as manner and form as *eidos*. It "cannot be brought back to either law or morals, to a precept or advice, to labor or contemplation."[176] In the zone, from the zone, thanks to the zone, anarchy finds its place.

*

I could list so many other instances of the "zone." The signs and emblems of power, for example, refer to "something like a threshold of indistinction that is always operative, where the juridical and the religious become truly indistinguishable."[177] Or "ontology and *praxis*, being and having-to-be enter into an enduring threshold of indifference."[178] I could continue this list without the concept of "zone" ever losing its mystery.[179] Agamben never thought it necessary to say anything more about this word choice. We are led to understand that the zone is a field of disappropriation and that life "dwells in the no-man's-land between the home and the city,"[180] which refuses to be defined.[181]

The problem is that Agamben's persistent recourse to "zone" as the sole and systematic response to any of the logical difficulties that arise en route eventually presents an insurmountable challenge. He writes: "Archaeological regression must neither express nor negate, neither say nor un-say: rather, it reaches a threshold of indiscernibility, in which the dichotomy diminishes and the opposites coincide – which is to say, fall together."[182] Neither expressed, nor denied, neither said nor unsaid: *the problem is that the "zone" becomes a floating signifier*. A hyper-signifier that displaces the immediate topical meaning of the term (defined as a space in the shape of a belt or band, circumscribed on a spherical surface), separating it from its geographical signifier to the point that it says everything – and nothing. To the point that it becomes symbolically sacred. Profanation also occurs at the expense of a sacralization of the zone. Disavowal caught in the act. The restitution of the political meaning of the sacred leads to the precise recomposition of what it sought to dismiss.

Derrida would say "Making explicit the evaded *question* always and necessarily keeps to the *system* of what is evaded."[183]

A symbolic zone – ZAD or zone to defend [*zone à défendre*] – has just encircled the semantic uncertainties deployed in *Homo Sacer* with its halo of deactivation – and has thereby transgressed the rules of profanation.

Incontestably, the desacralization move whose breadth I have sought at length to restitute is fundamentally important for our time inasmuch as it avoids the traps of naive atheism, brutal iconoclasm, and carnivalesque sacrilege. No one has taken on the task of exposing the profanatory potentiality of anarchism today as seriously and as profoundly as Agamben. Without this profanatory potentiality, anarchy does not exist. But to repeat one last time: anarchy cannot be reduced to a summary execution of God.

Despite everything, to do without the symbolic murder of God perhaps always amounts to paradoxically deifying this economy of saving, subtracting it from the possibility of a non-governable. Apart from a few "exceptions," God is omnipresent in *Homo Sacer*. The most convincing examples of "forms-of life" are almost always borrowed from monastic rules.[184]

Without transgression or revolution, interminably stuck in an irreducible sacred zone, "lucid" anarchy, cut off from all anarchism, is only a version of the "unprofanable absolute." And its signifier above all: God.

9

Staging Anarchy
Jacques Rancière without Witnesses

> We do not live in democracies. Neither, as certain authors assert – because they think we are all subjected to a biopolitical government law of exception – do we live in camps. We live in States of oligarchic law.[1]
>
> The sudden revelation of the ultimate anarchy on which any hierarchy rests.[2]
>
> Politics has no *archē*, it is anarchical.[3]
>
> Jacques Rancière

Jacques Rancière is one of the great thinkers of anarchy. There's no need to specify "political anarchy" since, for him, politics and anarchy are synonymous. But why will he never declare himself an anarchist?

False leads

Rancière's hesitation is not fueled by suspicion of the connivance between anarchism and the metaphysical tradition. His is a different path; he tries to demonstrate instead how the traditional anarchist vision of social and political emancipation no longer corresponds to contemporary reality. As he explains: "The tables have clearly been turned vis-à-vis the historical approach espoused by the anarchist movement … The bankruptcy of state Marxism precipitated a rethinking of the notion of the power of immanent liberation in the worlds of production and exchange."[4]

Traditionally, anarchism and Marxism had a shared confidence in the notion that the contradictions of capitalism would eventually lead to its downfall. The anarchist critique of domination shared the Marxist vision of politics as nothing but an ideological servant to the economy, viewing state sovereignty and the logic of government as only instances of the legitimation of capital. "[Anarchism] agreed with Marxism at least on this point: both conceived of democracy as a political lie masking the reality of economic exploitation. Both sought within society – that is, in its core – forms of production and exchange, the principle of a shared suppression of economic exploitation and state oppression."[5] Anarchist workers movements were thus bound together by the idea that anarchy was synonymous with "suppressing political parasitism."[6]

Of course, the connections between domination and property, domination and poverty, domination and exclusion, are not to be underestimated at this point. But it is precisely in order to analyze them that politics must be redefined after its excessive reduction to ideology. This is not, however, to adopt Agamben's apparently similar gesture. Indeed, for Rancière, rethinking politics involves identifying politics with the "democratic principle" from the outset via a radically new understanding of the concepts of politics and democracy themselves.

It would be wrong to read such a claim as the theoretical gesture of a repentant revolutionary converted to liberal democracy. That's not it at all. For Rancière, "the democratic principle" bears no relation to the parliamentary democracies that exist. "Democracy" is not the name of a political regime or a type of government. Indeed, it is a matter of "always further separating democratic radicalness from the consensual idea of democracy as the form of government of free market societies." Contrary to all expectations, democratic radicalness is defined as the "self-negation of the legitimacy of power."[7]

Traditional anarchism apparently overlooked the fundamentally anarchic structure of democracy. By resisting the descriptor "anarchist," Rancière does not, therefore, disqualify anarchism; rather, he radicalizes it. For him, anarchy is as old as politics since it emerged simultaneously with the emergence of the demos for the early Greeks.

Anarchy is, then, the expression of radical equality, as seen with Cleisthenes of Athens. In an interview with Rancière, Miguel Abensour writes: "If we start from Cleisthenes' reform … it is the people who institute an egalitarian city-state, created by privileging a common center, equality, symmetry and reversibility."[8] To understand what at first sight might appear to be a surprising equating of radical equality and anarchy, it is important to understand that equality is not only the possibility for all to take turns in the position of commanding and obeying; it also implies that theoretically no particular quality is required to govern. As Rancière puts it: "The only entitlement left [to govern] is the anarchic entitlement, the entitlement appropriate to those who have no more entitlement to govern than to be governed."[9]

Radical equality thus appears as this first dimension of politics uniting the early spirit of *politeia* to later political anarchism. Indeed, if politics refers to "the egalitarian power concealed in the democratic principle," "then today a rapprochement is possible between anarchism and democracy understood in all its radicality."[10] Rancière concludes:

> I proposed a definition of the democratic signifier that is anarchic in the strong sense: no force exists that is authorized and has the legitimacy to exert power. In the end, democracy is only a reminder of the anarchic signifier. Moreover, I have worked extensively on the anarchist tradition and revolutionary trade unionism: the communist idea makes sense if it refers to the power of anyone – and that's anarchist.[11]

So why is Rancière unwilling to declare himself an anarchist? One answer might lie in his attacks on a particular type of revolutionary anarchism. In an interview in 2017, he criticized the authoritarian and violent tendencies of the anarchist movements from the time they appeared at the end of the nineteenth century up to the present day.

> The libertarian movement has a great historical force and a very strong, diverse heritage. But it must also be said that historically anarchism has too often meant the constitution of a doctrinaire sect: there is dogmatism and political compromise in anarchism as in communism. In my research I found that a certain number of libertarian syndicalists placed themselves in the service of Vichy, taking the place of communists who had been eliminated ... I have a profoundly anarchist sensibility but I separate it from small anarchist groups. And I insist on dissociating the principle from the confusion that reigns today: one calls "anarchists" people who, with or without a black flag, smash ATMs at the end of demonstrations.[12]

Much could be said here (especially about the anarchists' very strange eviction of communists), but I'll focus on equating anarchists with "rogues." It is important to remember that not all rogues are anarchists, just as not all anarchists are rogues. When they are, they don't stop at breaking into ATMs. The Black Blocs – which immediately come to mind and are so often associated with terrorists in the media – have other goals. The Black Bloc phenomenon, which formed in Berlin in 1980 and became more visible in the late 1990s with the emergence of anti-globalization movements (Seattle), is commonly viewed as the expression of an anarchism reduced to the irrational drive that leads "young rogues to violence and chaos."[13] Yet, according to François Dupui-Déri, Black Bloc do not always have recourse to violence:

> They respect diverse tactics and consider it appropriate that, according to preferences and for individual reasons, some demonstrate peacefully while others express themselves through signs of power (some Black Bloc members even refuse to have recourse to violence and organize themselves, for instance, within groups aligned with volunteer medics).[14]

Although, unfortunately, Rancière does not expand on the relation between his "profoundly anarchist sensibility" and some expressions of revolutionary anarchism, I do not think that this statement amounts to a rejection of anarchism. Certainly, all anarchists would share his view that "anarchism is first autonomy. It is cooperatives of production and consumption, autonomous forms of transmission of knowledge and information in relation to the reigning dominant logic. It is independence with respect to the governmental sphere."[15] Despite his reservations, Rancière is still the only contemporary philosopher who has clearly reformulated the core idea of anarchism.

Is it police?

So what's the problem?

Some readers will immediately answer: the "police." Certainly, the "police" is a major concept in Rancière's thought. It does not refer to the "petty" police, "the truncheon blows of the forces of law and order and the inquisitions of the secret police,"[16] that is, the repressive apparatus to which the term usually refers. For Rancière, police is the other name of "politics," understood in the usual sense – the quote marks here distinguish it from the meaning of radical equality. "Politics" determines "the organization of powers, the distribution of places and roles and the system for legitimizing this distribution."[17] Police is politics amputated from its anarchist dimension, the "political" amnesia of politics, the forgetting of its origins. What is commonly called "politics" (which usually include democracy understood as a "regime") results from the substitution of hegemonic inequality for radical equality. In this sense, "politics" is the repression (police) of politics. In this "politics," the equality of citizens claimed by parliamentary democracies becomes an abstract equality, a cover for governmental "oligarchies."

The problem is that although Rancière asserts the heterogenous nature of politics (in the originary sense) and the police, he argues that police is nonetheless necessary. If "politics is specifically opposed to the police,"[18] police is nevertheless not viewed as the evil that a radical politics should seek to overthrow.

Why? Because if politics is originally anarchist, that means it has no given order. The democratic principle has no principle, no pre-constituted form or place to which it is assigned. Radical equality is not a property; it is not, and cannot be, an *archē*. Because it is without a "place," without any given field of existence, politics can only exist *from time to time*: "politics doesn't always happen – it actually happens very little or rarely."[19]

Politics is exactly that which disturbs police distribution, that is, the party political distribution of "politics." But it manifests as an "unpredictable subject," "in eclipses," "intermittently," sometimes it "occupies the streets" and it is "born of nothing but democracy itself."[20] The confrontation between politics and police is always unexpected, emerging momentarily, temporarily. Therefore, "if politics implements a logic entirely heterogenous to that of the police, it is always bound up with the latter. The reason for this is simple: politics has no objects or issues of its own. Its sole principle, equality, is not peculiar to it and is in no way in itself political."[21]

Understandably, these statements might cause some readers to doubt Rancière's "anarchism." Clearly, the assertion that police is necessary is a way of protecting democratic anarchy from becoming archic, dogmatic, principle-based, even if it is paradoxical. If politics were installed, it would become … police. But it is still difficult to accept the idea of the inevitability of police – and what a strange word it is for Rancière, who never uses it pejoratively. It's hard to accept that some police are simply less bad than others: "One kind of police may be infinitely preferable to another,"[22] depending on whether the police leave more or less room for democracy to breathe and live.

These strange relations between politics and police are evidently an obscure area in Rancière's thought and have given rise to two different reactions amongst his readers, particularly in the English-speaking world.

For some anarchist theorists, to achieve true post-anarchism, Rancière's thought must be radicalized by divorcing politics from police. This is the point of view that Todd May, for example, presents in *The Political Thought of Jacques Rancière*.[23] May argues that Rancière's achievement is to propose an "active," rather than simply formal, abstract, or "passive" concept of equality. The problem is that this equality cannot take institutional form without immediately becoming an expression of police: "Rancière claims that the politics of active equality cannot be institutionalized, which denies all permanency to democratic expression. I would like to question this conclusion, on the basis of some of Rancière's own concepts."[24] May goes on to explore whether it is possible to imagine a democratic politics that would free itself from policing, "creating its own space, a space where there is no police order."[25]

Other readers interpret the intimate pairing of politics and police as a direct admission that anarchism is impossible. This is Simon Chambers's view.[26] According to Chambers, in the end Rancière proposes just a kind of compromise: the existing order can be improved, but not radically transformed. The only option is "developing better … forms of police." Chambers goes on: "Obviously, I read Rancière very differently [to May] … we do not live in democracies, and we never will. We never will, not because we will never achieve what we ought to achieve, not because of failures on our part, but because that is not what democracy is about."[27] Democracy, without being a utopia, is also not a real living space: "'To understand what democracy means is to hear the struggle that is at stake in the word.'"[28]

So, is anarchism still inhibited, or is it impossible forever?

Explanatory detour: Granting a leave of absence to the unrepresentable

I would like to go beyond this overly simplistic alternative, apparently taking the question on a detour, by rephrasing it as follows: if politics "has no 'proper' place," no "locale," if "political demonstrations are thus always of the moment and their subjects are always provisional" and it is "always on the shore of its own disappearance,"[29] moreover, if radical democracy also bears no relation to the representative democracies that exist, then why does Rancière so consistently, so vehemently reject the category of the "unrepresentable"?

For Rancière, although it is fleeting, anarchy is not unrepresentable. His critique of parliamentary representation is coupled with a defense of the aesthetic representation of politics.[30] *Why would democracy be irreducible to parliamentary representation but remain absolutely open to artistic representation?*

These lines of interrogation, which take aim at the relation between politics and visibility, anarchy and manifestation, are articulated in Rancière's systematic critique of Jean-François Lyotard's philosophy. Rancière constantly attacks the categories of the "unrepresentable" and the "unpresentable," which play such a critical role in Lyotard's thinking. Treating them as synonymous, Rancière removes all political or ethical potentiality from them.

To my mind, the disavowal of anarchism is right here, in this conception of the *phoronomic* conception of aesthetics. By displacing the relationship between politics and police, Rancière claims to separate politics from police, granting expression to radical equality. My goal is to demonstrate how this conception of the representability of anarchy betrays it.

This detour is only apparent and, in fact, brings us back to police. By claiming that anarchy can elude police only by making itself presentable in the aesthetic order, Rancière is led to police, in the most basic sense of the term, an entire swath of contemporary philosophy that has absolutely no faith in the possibility of a transfer of the politics question to aesthetics.

On the difference between dissensus and differend

At first glance, Rancière's repeated attacks on Lyotard are surprising given that the two thinkers appear to agree on a fundamental point: there's no politics without dissensus. "Disagreement" in Rancière and "differend" in Lyotard both seem to imply the impossibility of representation, even if Rancière claims that "disagreement differs from what Jean-François Lyotard has conceptualized as a differend."³¹

Lyotard defines the differend as follows: "As distinguished from a litigation, a differend [*différend*] would be a case of conflict, between (at least) two parties, that cannot be equitably resolved for lack of a rule of judgement applicable to both arguments ... a universal rule of judgement between heterogenous genres is lacking in general."³²

Rancière's disagreement [*mésentente*] characterizes "a determined kind of speech situation: one in which one of the interlocutors at once understands and does not understand what the other is saying."³³ Clearly, politics puts into play various discursive regimes that remain as foreign to each other for Lyotard as they are for Rancière. Lyotard would probably concur that differend, like disagreement, "is not to do with words alone. It generally bears on the very situation in which the speaking parties find themselves."³⁴ Moreover, both occur when

> X cannot see the common object Y is presenting because X cannot comprehend that the sounds uttered by Y form words and chains of words similar to X's own ... The structures proper to disagreement are those in which discussion of an argument comes down to a dispute over the object of the discussion and over the capacity of those who are making an object of it.³⁵

Disagreement and differend derive from the impossibility of speaking in the same way (and) about the same thing – the lack of argument that renders all discussion pointless.

While it is true that the difference between animals and humans coincides with the difference between cry and *logos*, it is also the case that some subjects who have *logos* are still excluded from the circle of those who have the right to speak because their language is heard as either noise or cry. Both Rancière and Lyotard make this claim. Rancière writes:

> The social order is symbolized by dooming the majority of speaking beings to the night of silence or to the animal noise of voices expressing pleasure or pain ... Politics exists because the *logos* is never simply speech because it is always indissolubly the account that is made of this speech: the account by which a sonorous emission is understood as speech, capable of enunciating what

is just, whereas some other emission is merely perceived as a noise signaling pleasure or pain, consent or revolt.[36]

Lyotard describes "affect phrase"[37] not as the absence of phrase, but as a cry-phrase. On this theme, he too refers to the famous passage in *Politics* in which Aristotle distinguishes between the "articulated voice" (*phônè enarthros*) of human beings required to belong to the political community and the "mixed (or confused) voice" (*phônè sunkekhumenè*), of animals in general.[38] Politics is the domain *par excellence* of expressive language, to the inevitable detriment of cry-phrases, which it passes over without making a connection. As Lyotard writes, "Politics consists in the fact that language is not a language, but phrases, or that Being is not Being, but *There is*."[39] Therein lies all of politics, if by politics we understand "the threat of the differend."[40]

Is litigation the root of the dispute between the two philosophers, then? No, it is not, since even though Rancière discusses litigation, he is careful to distinguish it from what he calls "objectifiable" litigation, that is, legal litigation. He explains: "The wrong ... cannot be regulated by way of some accord between the parties ... through the objectivity of the lawsuit as a compromise between the parties."[41] The wrong cannot be settled through litigation in Rancière any more than in Lyotard. This is precisely why the wrong endures, like the differend, *infinitely*: "The persistence of the wrong is infinite because verification of equality is infinite and the resistance of any police order to such verification is a matter of principle."[42]

Wrong persists because it is structurally linked to the question of *understanding*. The passages on the topic of understanding are amongst the finest in *Disagreement*,[43] seemingly confirming the proximity of Rancière's thought to Lyotard.

When scolding a child or threatening a punishment, what is meant by adding, "Do you understand?" or "Is that clear?" Expressed by an authority figure, "Do you understand?" or "Is that clear?" obviously do not refer to understanding an idea (of the sort "Do you understand this mathematical reasoning?"). Here "It's clear" means "And that's an order." An order that means in fact there is nothing to understand: the only thing to do is obey. If the injunction related to understanding an idea, there would be the possibility of discussion, but since it does not, there's nothing to do but submit.

Aren't we close to Lyotard again, then, with his statement that a differend exists "when no presentation is possible of the wrong he or she [the plaintiff] says he or she has suffered,"[44] when the plaintiff cannot make themselves understood and understands that their only recourse is to say nothing?

Of course, we could discuss the meaning of the terms wrong, litigation, discourse, and even language for these two philosophers, but it wouldn't change the fact that disagreement and differend are born of the same ground: the being in common, defined as absence of community.

Politics, distributions, representations

There is, however, a profound, irreconcilable point of divergence between disagreement and differend. This divergence can derive only from the following: while disagreement and differend both refer to a lack of presentation, disagreement, unlike the differend, can be *staged*. Hence the highly paradoxical nature of the leave of absence Rancière grants the "unrepresentable" and the "unpresentable." To understand, we must study the category of disagreement more patiently, along with the relation Rancière posits between this category and the anarchic structure of politics.

Distribution of the sensible

Disagreement is neither damage nor a specific harm affecting a prior equilibrium or integrity. It is an originary "wrong," one that might be called logical: "Politics begins with a major wrong."[45] According to Rancière, this wrong is linked to what he terms the "distribution of the sensible." The distribution of the sensible produces the layering of politics. There are several distributions in this distribution, organized according to a dual articulation: *having a part* and *apportioning parts*.

Having a part

There are "two modes of access to sense experience: that of pleasure and suffering, common to all animals endowed with a voice and that of good and evil, exclusive to human beings."[46] Access, or having a part, is based on the line between pain and the accompanying sentiment of justice and injustice, "between the unpleasant feeling of having received a blow and the feeling of having suffered an 'injury' through this same blow … the difference is marked … in the *logos* that separates the discursive articulation of a grievance from the phonic articulation of a groan."[47]

The possibility of this discursive articulation, "exclusive to human beings,"[48] marks the opening of politics. Politics is the sphere in which wrongs can be formulated, expressed, judged. Citizenship is therefore defined by "having access (*metexis*)" to *politeia*, an access equal for all. Rancière reminds us that, in Book I of *Politics*, Aristotle "distinguishes between political rule (as the ruling of equals) from all other kinds of rule" and, as we have seen, "in Book III, he defines the citizen as 'he who partakes in the fact of ruling and the fact of being ruled.'"[49]

The reversibility between commanding and obeying for the citizen finds collective manifestation in the people. The people is a subject that acts on itself and suffers from itself. However, this acting-suffering is not auto-affection inasmuch as "it contradicts the conventional 'cause-and-effect' model of action that has it that an agent endowed with a specific capacity produces an effect upon an object that is, in turn, characterized by its aptitude for receiving that effect."[50] Here there is "a rupture … in the correlation between a capacity for rule and a capacity for being ruled."[51] There is no special or qualifying capacity for commanding or for obeying. Politics "does not simply presuppose the rupture of the 'normal' distribution of positions between the one who exercises power and the one subject to it. It also requires a rupture in the idea that there are dispositions 'proper' to such classifications."[52]

The reversibility between commanding and obeying, taken radically, also annuls the distinction between superiority and inferiority. So where does disagreement come from?

Apportioning parts

Disagreement arises from the fact that there can be no community without a distribution of parts. Indeed, political justice is "the order that determines the partition of what is common."[53] Yet this apportionment is inevitably based on a "miscount" that introduces inequality into the equality of having a part. Misunderstanding is the democratic damage that the community inflicts on itself as a result of the disequilibrium between the radical equality of citizens and the impossibility of equally distributing the parts of the common good. The term "miscount" combines the idea of mistaken predictions and miscalculation: "What the 'classics' teach us first and foremost is that politics is not a matter of ties between individuals or of relationships between individuals and the community. Politics arises from a count of community 'parts,' which is always a false count, a double count, or a miscount."[54]

Political equality can never translate into arithmetic equality. Arithmetic equality – to each the same quantity – works only for market exchange. In order for the political community not to be based on "a contract between those exchanging goods and services, the reigning equality needs to be radically different from that according to which merchandise is exchanged and wrongs redressed."[55] The specificity of the political sphere, which distinguishes it from domesticity, also differentiates it from the economy and trade. Political equality is not a countable equilibrium between profit and loss, nor an equation between product and price. It is the "submission of arithmetical equality ... to that geometric equality responsible for proportion, for common harmony, submission of the shares of the common held by each party in the community to the share that party brings to the common good."[56]

Politics thus necessarily assumes the shift from quantity to quality, from linear equivalence to proportional allocation. The harmony of the city can hold only on the basis of the ratio, the proportional relation between the parts of what is held in common by each part of the community and the part each brings to the common good. The parts of the community must be strictly proportioned according to what each part of the community brings and that give them the right "to hold a share in of the common power."[57]

The problem is that some bring nothing, that is, nothing except their lack of contribution. The people have nothing but their freedom to share, but there is nothing properly theirs about this freedom, which "is not proper ... at all ... The people who make up the people are in fact simply free like the rest."[58] The people have nothing to bring the city, no "value part" (*axia*) aside from their status as humans free in their bodies. Insofar as freedom is owned by all citizens, it cannot constitute a specific *axia*. The freedom of the people thus appears as this "part of no part," which cannot be counted and which is therefore excluded from the distribution. The distribution of places in politics occurs therefore without the people, based on qualities rather than a lack of qualities. Thus, wealth and birth become entitlements to govern and legitimate the fact that those who have them are in command.

Geometric equality thus becomes hierarchical, switching from the cardinal (1, 2, 3) to the ordinal (1st, 2nd, 3rd) and henceforth operating according to a logic of more or less. The political imperative is then formulated such that it "places those who count for more above those who count for less."[59] Those with nothing come last. The people become indistinguishable from the "masses," no longer the common, but an indistinct lump that has nothing left to offer except its quantity.

Rancière explains: "I call the distribution of the sensible the system of self-evident facts of sense perception that simultaneously discloses the existence of something in common and the delimitations that define the respective parts and positions within it."[60] This second distribution of the sensible is superimposed on the first, on having access, or parts, as if to eliminate or conceal the miscalculation, even as it serves only to inscribe it all the more deeply within the social body. Thus commences "politics" understood as the distribution of entitlements to exercise power and the required qualifications for the exercising of governmental functions. Thus commences the equating of "politics" with police: "The police is a 'partition of the sensible' ... whose principle is the absence of a void and of a supplement."[61] Thus commences a distribution that feigns that all parties have, or can have, their part.

Philosophy as "archipolitics"

Philosophy plays a leading role in legitimizing and normalizing the miscount. As Rancière demonstrates, building on his compelling readings of Plato and Aristotle, political philosophy presents itself from the start as both "archipolitics" and "parapolitics."[62]

Let's start with Aristotle, by returning to the three great aporias of *Politics*: (1) the introduction of the "principle of the best" to justify the choice of governors, breaking the reversibility of commanding and obeying among citizens; (2) the establishment of synonymy between *politeia* and *politeuma*, state sovereignty and government, even though

Aristotle had reserved only the exercise of power – not its distribution – for the government; (3) the differentiation between democracy taken as the very essence of *politeia* and democracy as mere "regime." All of which gives us pause to think about the subject of the work: is it a philosophy on politics in general, or is it about the determination of which is the best regime via comparisons of different types of government?

Returning to his argument with renewed vigor, Rancière posits that these aporias, far from being accidental, are the very object of Aristotle's work.

First aporia. In Book III of *Politics*, Aristotle introduces the "principle of the best" to justify why not everyone can govern. The fact that the "excellent man," who has no specific talent, but who has virtue, is able, legitimately, to govern, for he alone is able to perceive the "common good." Aristotle tries his best to justify the right of the "minority of men of 'merit'" to govern and thus to command "the majority of ordinary men."[63]

However, virtue is not the only *axia* (value) that confers the entitlement to govern. Aristotle actually "sees three" *axiaï*: "the wealth of the smallest number (*oligoi*), the virtue or excellence (*arété*) from which the best (*aristoi*) derive their name and the freedom (*eleutheria*) that belongs to the people."[64] Admittedly, Aristotle accords no immediate privilege to the "wealthy." For him the primordial *axia* is "virtue." But he is led to acknowledge that the only immediately convincing "value" is, in fact, wealth: "Within the beautiful harmony of the *axiaï*, one single, easily recognizable quality stands out: the wealth of the *oligoi*."[65] As for freedom, we have seen it has no special value: "The people are nothing more than the undifferentiated mass of those who have no positive qualification – no wealth, no virtue."[66] The people possess only this freedom, which does not constitute their privilege at all, since it is held in common with those who also possess wealth and virtue.

The aporias are thus deeper than initially thought. It is not only a matter of contradicting the reversibility of commanding and obeying among citizens through the hegemonic superiority of the virtuous man; it is also a question of acknowledging that, in reality, virtue bows to wealth: "Even Aristotle, who is at pains in *The Nicomachean Ethics* and book III of *Politics* to give substance to the three parts and the three ranks, freely admits in book IV and also in *The Athenian Constitution* that the city actually has only two parties, the rich and the poor."[67] In Aristotle's words: "almost everywhere the well-born and the well-off are coextensive."[68] Even if he seems to deplore it, Aristotle confirms the inevitability of the supremacy of the value of "wealth." The excellent (*aristoi*) can always fail to prove their superiority, whereas the rich have no difficulty in proving the reality of their wealth.

The division between rich and poor, which reintroduces *oikonomia* into politics, thereby transforms all government into oligarchy since, as soon as there is a hierarchy – a dissymmetry between those who command and those who obey – the oligarchic principle is at work. "Political philosophy" will only ever have served to establish and justify it.

Second aporia: the synonyms of constitution and government. The second aporia of *Politics* ensues from the first: ultimately the fate of *politeia* depends on the government, not vice versa. Governors, who draw their authorization from their *axiaï* (values or entitlements to govern), determine the management of "politics" that has become police: "the organization of powers, the distribution of places and roles and the systems for legitimizing this distribution."[69]

The division of labor accompanies the policing distribution of shared parts. Rancière explains that this is already present in Plato, who argues:

> Artisans do not have time to devote to anything other than their work. They cannot be elsewhere because their work cannot wait. The distribution of the sensible reveals who can take part in the common as a function of occupation or situation. To have a given occupation defines competencies or incompetencies in regard to the common. It defines the fact of being visible or not in the shared space, endowed with common speech, etc."[70]

There is a division corresponding to geometrical equality between those citizens who are visible and those who are invisible, occupied by their task and with no quality other than the force of their work, without the time to do anything except try to sell it.

Those at the top of the original list therefore have free reign to devote all their energy to competing with rivals: "parties struggling to occupy the *arkhaï* and to conquer the *kurion* of the city."[71]

The second aporia thus ensues from the fact that "the government of the city, the authority that directs and maintains it, is always government by one of the 'parties,' one of the factions that, by imposing its law on the other, imposes on the city the law of division."[72] The internal contradiction of *politeia* is that sovereignty is the domain of the strongest.

This internal contradiction can be expressed as a kind of return to the arithmetic equality within geometric equality: quantity becomes a hegemonic quality per se.

> The law of oligarchy is effectively that "arithmetical" equality should command without hindrance, that wealth should be immediately identical with domination. One might think that the poor of Athens were subject to the power of the nobles rather than that of the merchants, but the point is that the liberty of the people of Athens reduced the natural domination of the nobility, based on the illustrious and ancient nature of their lineage, to their simple domination as wealthy property owners and monopolizers of the common property. It reduced the nobility to their condition as the rich and transformed their absolute right, reduced to the power of the rich, into a particular *axia*.[73]

There's that haunting *oikonomia*, always impossible to banish!

Third aporia: the status of democracy. What happens, then, to the first democracy when it is divided up, shared, redistributed, miscalculated? Philosophers reduce it to a type of government or regime. The worst – or sometimes the least bad – of bad regimes. Democracy is not the government of *demos* but of *ochlos*, not of the people, but of the populace, the masses, or crowd. Consequently:

> Democracy, Plato tells us in Chapter VIII of the *Republic*, is a political regime that is not one. It does not have a constitution because it has all of them. It is a constitutional bazaar, a harlequin's outfit ... It is properly the regime that overturns all the relations that structure human society: its governors have the demeanor of the governed and the governed the demeanor of the governors; women are the equals of men; fathers accustom themselves to treating their sons as equals; the foreigner and the immigrants are the equals of citizens; the schoolmaster fears and flatters the pupils who, in turn, make fun of him; the young are the equals of the old and the old imitate the young; even the beasts are free and the horses and asses, conscious of their liberty and dignity, knock over anyone who does not yield to them in the street.[74]

Democracy is anarchy. From one distribution of the sensible to the other, we see this phrase take on two entirely opposite meanings.

Plato deems it necessary to limit the equality of anyone to anyone: he reinstates order by carefully enumerating all the elements, functions, and professions of the community in order to assign each member their true role, according to the idea of the Republic. This is the project Rancière names "archipolitics": "Archipolitics, whose model is supplied by Plato, reveals in all its radicality the project of a community based on the complete realization of the *archē* of community, total awareness, replacing the democratic configuration of politics with nothing left over."[75] Archi-politics thus seeks to correct the original wrong, to put an end to dissensus, to settle accounts.

In Aristotle, the shift from democracy as the foundation of *politeia* to democracy as "governing body" marks the transition from the political to the "parapolitical."

Unlike Plato, Aristotle does not substitute the existing order with an ideal order, rather he tries to reconcile the unreconcilable – originary equality and its oligarchical becoming, as Rancière puts it: "The problem for parapolitics will be to reconcile the two concepts of nature and their opposing logics."[76] It is therefore a matter of asserting the originary legitimacy of *demos* while also making it disappear by sending the people off to work in the fields, promoting a sort of agricultural democracy in which peasants are too busy working to participate effectively in government. The integration of the people into the "*telos* of the community" is only possible, in fact, "in the form of a *mise en absence*, a withdrawal of presence."[77]

> This is what is expressed in the famous hierarchy of types of democracy presented in books IV and VI of *Politics*. The best democracy is a peasant democracy, for it is precisely the one in which the demos is missing from its place. The dispersal of peasants – "the farming element" – in distant fields and the constraint of labor prevent them from going and occupying their place of power.[78]

As I have argued, the central aporias of *Politics* are not accidents. They express and justify – without fully admitting it, since that's exactly what an aporia does – the misunderstanding that originally structures politics.

The uneven text expresses the leaning structure of *archē*. The archic paradigm is nothing but "the lie that invents some kind of social nature in order to provide the community with an *archē*."[79]

By never contesting the exorbitant privilege granted to government over state sovereignty, Aristotle's *Politics* is only an archi-police.[80] Consequently, "to put it simply: the *politeia* of the philosophers is the exact identity of politics and the police."[81]

The drawing of lots

If Aristotle's *Politics* had respected his first intentions, it would have stated strongly that the reversibility of commanding and obeying was founded only on "egalitarian contingence," that is, on nothing. But that would have led him to admit that the only acceptable government is that of "anyone," based on a drawing of lots – the only possible legitimacy.

Rancière never abandoned the idea of drawing lots:

> My fundamental idea is that I don't see why a representation by lots would be worse than a representation under the current conditions. Already, representation by lots would eliminate those who want to govern. Secondly, it eliminates clientelism. Thirdly, it eliminates the development of disturbing sentiments that are connected with the electoral relation itself. Evidently, one can always say: "I can't see my family, my concierge or my plumber run the State." One can. But why does one see this task in particular members of a school of administration or business lawyers? Should the State be steered by representatives of well determined particular interests? By those obsessed with power? For that is very much the combination that we have today: the State is governed by addicts of power and representatives of financial interests.[82]

The drawing of lots is justified because "there is, strictly speaking, no such thing as democratic government."[83] Democracy is fundamentally "ungovernable" since no member has any more ability to govern than any other: "It is specifically this ungovernable on which every government must ultimately find out it is based."[84] Paradoxically, if an aptitude to govern did exist, it could only be "the anarchic title, the title specific to those who have no more title for governing than they have for being governed,"[85] and who are therefore indifferent about being either one. The drawing of lots would also assume short, non-renewable mandates that could not be combined – quite the opposite of police and archi-politics.

Staging reconfiguration

The drawing of lots is, thus, the only just form of political representation, and, at the same time, since it depends solely on chance, brands the concept of representation as futile.

Rancière does not conclude from this that democracy is unrepresentable, however. This is where the true difficulty in the heart of his concept of anarchy appears. The whole question is determining just what "representation" means.

Unlike Lyotard, Rancière asserts that, strictly speaking, the originary political wrong has *no victim*: "The concept of wrong is ... not linked to any theater of 'victimization.'"[86] The chain of synonyms – "misunderstanding," "dissensus," "wrong" (*blabē* in Greek), "litigation," "miscounting" – does not refer to any catastrophe or tragedy.

The miscalculation does not signify an annihilation and derives from no sacrifice.[87] True, the originary anarchy has no proper place and, in that sense, cannot assume power. But that does not mean that a different political topology from "politics" – police – is not possible. It is possible to displace the miscount, making it visible. This new topology is achieved through a "change of scene," settling the regime of visibility of the misunderstanding. This time Rancière calls this regime "metapolitics."[88] Workers' movements in the first half of the nineteenth century, the forming of the Commune, the 1968 revolution, the recent Occupy movements: it's not enough for any of these events to take place for them to appear; they only become truly visible at the expense of their aesthetic reconfiguration. Metapolitics therefore refers not only to that which is happening, but also causes what is happening in the *staged metamorphosis*, or *staged distribution of politics*.

As the name metapolitics already suggests, politics is "beyond" "politics" in the current meaning of the term. Metapolitics "shifts a body from the place assigned to it or changes a place's destination. It makes visible what had no business being seen and makes heard a discourse where once there was only place for noise, it makes understood as discourse what was once only heard as noise."[89]

This new distribution of the sensible, this redistribution, "breaks with the tangible configuration whereby parties and parts or lack of them are defined by a presupposition that, by definition, has no place in that configuration – that of the part of those who have no part. This break is manifest in a series of actions that reconfigure the space where parties, parts, or lack of parts have been defined."[90]

There are essentially two types of these closely associated displacements, or translations, if you like: *subjectivations* and *representations*.

"Any subjectivation is a disidentification, removal from the naturalness of a place, the opening up of a subject space where anyone can be counted since it is the space where those of no account are counted, where a connection is made between having a part and having no part."[91] Rancière offers two examples of this process, namely women and proletarians:

> In politics "woman" is the subject of experience – the denatured, defeminized subject – that measures the gap between an acknowledged part (that of sexual complementarity) and a having no part. "Worker" or better still "proletarian" is … the subject that measures the gap between the part of work as social function and the having no part of those who carry it out within the definition of the common of the community.[92]

Subjectivation is the intensification of singularities, which achieve their materialization in "speech events." The upheaval in the order of bodies and existences – "disidentification" – is the prelude to representative processes.

"Representations" describes the transfers through which politics stages itself aesthetically. For Rancière, aesthetics is neither discipline nor discourse on beauty, but rather the metamorphic vehicle through which the miscount is recounted in art.

The staged distribution that presides over the new distribution of the sensible is not, however, a salvaging act. Art does not repair politics. Art itself is political through and through in that it enables the displacement of politics toward its form. Consequently, all form has its own specific political expression. Form is an entrance into the real, a realization, in the literal meaning of the term: "Art does not have to become a form of life. On the contrary, it is in art that life takes its form."[93]

Here, the extent of Rancière's divergence from Lyotard is clear: unlike Lyotard's differend, for Rancière, *even an infinite wrong can be processed*. This processing occurs in and through aesthetic displacement. He writes:

> The wrong cannot be regulated, but this does not mean that it cannot be processed ... Political wrong cannot be settled – through the objectivity of the lawsuit as a compromise between the parties. But it can be processed – through the mechanisms of subjectivation that give it substance as an alterable relationship between the parties, indeed as a shift in the playing field.[94]

Or: "Between legal settlement and inexpiable debt, the political dispute reveals an incompatibility that can nonetheless be processed."[95] Art is thus a major player in this "processing."

Contra Lyotard

Let's return to the question of understanding. "Do you understand?" leaves nothing to be understood. At the same time, Rancière argues that if the person giving the order and the person receiving it did not speak the same language, *if they did not understand each other* somehow, it would be impossible for the person receiving the order to execute it: "The inferior has understood the superior's order because the inferior takes part in the same community of speaking beings and so is, in this sense, their equal. In short, we can deduce that the inequality of social ranks works only because of the very equality of speaking beings."[96] Furthermore:

> This initial *logos* is tainted with a primary contradiction. There is order in society because some people command and others obey, but in order to obey an order at least two things are required: you must understand the order and you must understand that you must obey it. And to do that, you must already be the equal of the person who is ordering you. It is this equality that gnaws away at any natural order.[97]

Even slaves, "non-citizens," understand they must obey. If, for Aristotle, the slave is "the one who participates in the linguistic community so far as to recognize it (*aisthesis*) but not so as to possess it (*hexis*),"[98] this does not prevent the slave from understanding. Governability, which is based on the dissymmetry between those who command and those who obey, is the negative manifestation of the paradox according to which no one is fundamentally governable. *Paradoxically, "to understand" the language of commanding and obeying is, thereby, to immediately posit oneself as equal to the person giving orders and governing.*

But art reminds us that everyone speaks the same language precisely because they understand that they don't speak the same language. Art reveals the poietic-political force of the sensible, the place where cries and words are also *equal*.

> The modern political animal is first a literary animal, caught in the cycle of a literarity that undoes the relations between the order of words and the order of bodies that define each person's place. A political subjectivation is the product of these multiple facture lines through which individuals and individual networks subjectivize the gap between their condition as animals endowed with a voice and the violent encounter with the equality of *logos*.[99]

We are therefore at the farthest remove from the economy of the differend that belongs to the "modern age of litigation,"[100] the age of Shoah, whose cry – all the affect-phrases of the victims – remain definitively unpresentable, and therefore untreatable, according to Lyotard.

Unrepresentable and unpresentable

We know that Lyotard discerns the outline of the differend in the Kantian sublime, challenging the imagination to configure the infinite crossing of thresholds of the sensible. It is an impossible challenge whose crushing weight ultimately inscribes the unpresentable into the heart of contemporary art.

What exactly is the difference between "unpresentable" and "unrepresentable"? Lyotard says we must return to the Kantian distinction between the beautiful and the sublime, which coincides with the distinction between representation (*Vorstellung*) and presentation (*Darstellung*). For Kant, representation is always linked to form. That which is beautiful and pleasing has contour, limitation, aspect. By contrast, the sentiment of the sublime is linked to that which is "formless (*formlos*)." Since it cannot represent it, the imagination, seeking to play its usual role of mediator, attempts to present this defeat of form to reason, but fails to do so. The sublime emerges from the shock of this failure, of this encounter with the infinite of the formless for which *Darstellung* can only be negative.

Lyotard observes that the Kantian sublime already has the structure of a differend via a differend between the faculties. Citing Kant, he argues that the conflict between reason and imagination "is not an ordinary dispute, which a third instance could grasp and put an end to, but a 'differend,' a *Widerstreit*."[101] The "Analytic of the Sublime" updates the heterogeneity of the rules proper to each faculty, which prohibit all transfers, all phoronomy of these rules between the faculties. Through this specific discord, and the problem it presents reason, Lyotard seeks to read the differend that prevents victims from ever making themselves heard. The absence of form of what they have lived is precisely what makes their lived experience unpresentable.

Constituted in this manner, as an instrument of ethical and political interpretation of the catastrophes of the twentieth century, Rancière argues that the sublime has become the aesthetic-political experience of postmodernity. For Lyotard, art can only be abstract art – one without figuration, an art of the unpresentable, a trace. Again, Rancière refuses to differentiate between representation and presentation, the unrepresentable and unpresentable. He considers these notions to be more symptoms than concepts. He criticizes

> an inflated use of the notion of the unrepresentable and a constellation of allied notions: the unpresentable, the unthinkable, the untreatable, the irredeemable. This inflated usage subsumes under a single concept all sorts of phenomena, processes, and notions, ranging from Moses's ban on representation, via the Kantian sublime, the Freudian primal scene, Duchamp's *Grand Verre* or Malevitch's *White Square on a White Background*.[102]

Two regimes of art

Faced with this confused situation, Rancière goes on, we are witnessing the emergence of "a new mode of art"[103] – one that does nothing but attest to its "incapacity."[104] Yet this view of art derives from a confusion that is both conceptual and historical. A confusion between two regimes of art that are actually entirely distinct: the "representative regime"[105] and the "aesthetic regime."[106]

The category of the "unrepresentable" makes sense only in the "representative regime" that characterizes classical art. For Rancière, the unrepresentable exists solely in a regime of representation; its meaning is therefore entirely relative. Indeed, the unrepresentable does not refer to that which eludes all representation, but rather to that which, in order to make representation possible, must endure a certain number of adaptations that "adjust the relations between what can be seen and what can be said."[107] For instance, Corneille, writing an *Oedipus* in 1659, is confronted by the fact that the tragedy has become unacceptable for the spectators of his era: the scene with the heroes' gouged-out eyes, blood "spilling over his face," cannot be shown for reasons of decorum, the theatrical rule of *bienséance*. Corneille must find the correct distance and right means with which to represent it. He therefore decides to "place off stage the undue visibility of the blinded eyes."[108] Although this scene is, to all intents and purposes, entirely unrepresentable, this fact does not compromise its representation, which is simply "adjusted" or "adapt[ed]"[109] by playing it off stage.

Yet, "since Romanticism"[110] and the birth of the "aesthetic regime" of art, the situation has become quite different, since the unrepresentable, as defined here, *no longer exists*. The aesthetic regime of art corresponds to the period of Romanesque realism: "But what is novelistic realism? It is the emancipation of resemblance from representation. It is the loss of representative proportions and proprieties."[111] Consequently, everything is now representable. The need for accommodation, adaptation, convention has dissipated. Nineteenth-century Romanesque realism frees up a mode of saying everything by refusing to hierarchize the visible: "Everything is now on the same level, the great and the small, important events and insignificant episodes, human beings and things."[112] Rancière cites Flaubert, for whom "'Yvetot is as good as Constantinople.'"[113]

There is now "a general availability of all subjects for any artistic form whatsoever," an exhibition integral to representation.[114] Rancière goes so far as to claim that this exhibition "knows no objects that infirm it on account of their particular singularity. And it has proved perfectly suited to the representation of phenomena that are said to be unrepresentable – concentration camps and extermination camps."[115]

Exceptional experiences that would challenge the imagination to present them no longer exist. Representation manifests its own opacity by lifting the bar on the invisible. Nothing is unrepresentable anymore because the regime of representation is over: these days no one would be offended by seeing a blinding, by staring at gouged-out eyes.

Lyotard presents the thesis of the failure of the inscription of the sensible shock and the infinite of the unpresentable, while Rancière presents the openness of all experience to naming, shaping, staging.

The words of witnesses

But what has become of anarchism amid all these discussions? Of course, it's not forgotten, but I need to make one last detour, the most important. It might be objected to Rancière that Lyotard also asserts that art, along with philosophy, must invent new ways of saying. In Lyotard, the unpresentable is neither mute nor without phenomenological resources: "What is at stake in a literature, in a philosophy, in a politics perhaps, is to bear witness to differends by finding idioms for them."[116] Lyotard says it: the only way to show and make oneself heard is to *bear witness*.

Witnessing, "the unstable state ... wherein something which must be able to be put into phrases cannot yet be,"[117] is the only chance for the unpresentable, the only way for it to manifest. Where proving, arbitrating, settling, negotiating have all failed, bearing witness is the only possible idiom for speech and invention. It's a fragile idiom that can always be broken but to which we have a duty to listen. The contemporary task of art and philosophy is to bear witness to the differend.

For Rancière, however, the idea of "art as witness to the sublime"[118] proceeds from an untenable and indefensible contemporary conception of art and politics. Commenting scornfully, he writes: "To bear witness to the unpresentable would supposedly be the imperative, dictated by the after-effect of catastrophe and 'disaster,' which demands the 'transforming of the feeling of the sublime into a form of art.'"[119]

Devalorizing the act of witnessing

We are coming to the heart of the problem. Ultimately, the reason for Rancière's attacks on Lyotard is primarily "the valorization of the words of the witness."[120] Rancière denies the idiomatic and political autonomy of the witness's words – and *this is where the attack on anarchy and anarchism is revealed*.

Rancière takes the risk of drawing an implausible parallel between Robert Antelme's *The Human Race* and Gustave Flaubert's *Madame Bovary*, both of which supposedly speak the same "paratactic," egalitarian language typifying the aesthetic regime of art by "merely connecting simple actions and perceptions one after the other."[121] Thus, the "nocturnal silence of the camps," described by Antelme,

> reminds us ... of other silences – those that characterize amatory moments in Flaubert. I propose to hear the echo of one of the moments that mark the meeting of Charles and Emma in *Madame Bovary*: "She sat down again and resumed her work, a white cotton stocking that she was darning. She worked with her head lowered. She did not speak."[122]

Rancière's conclusion is that: "The concentration camp experience as lived by Robert Antelme, and the invented sensory experience of Charles and Emma, are conveyed according to the same logic of minor perceptions added to one another."[123] The most critical moment in this equating appears in the following passage:

> Robert Antelme's experience is not "unrepresentable" in the sense that the language for conveying it does not exist. The language exists and the syntax exists. Not as an exceptional language and syntax, but, on the contrary, as a mode of expression peculiar to the aesthetic regime in the arts in general. The problem is in fact the reverse. The language that conveys this experience is in no way specific to it ... the language [Antelme] selects for its appropriateness to this experience is the common language of literature in which the absolute freedom of art has, for a century, been identified with the absolute passivity of physical matter.

Then comes the shock statement: "*There is no appropriate language for witnessing.*"[124]

Antelme and Flaubert, along with Zola and Camus, all share the same language – the language in which everything can be said. "Paratactic writing is not born out of the camp experience."[125] It's quite the opposite:

the writing describing the experience of the camps draws on paratactic writing.

With a wave of the hand, along with all Lyotard's work, Rancière sweeps away all Blanchot, all Foucault even (think of a text such as *The Thought of the Outside*), and so many others who claim that witnessing marks the birth of a language that disfigures realism. No philosopher or writer has ever denied that this disfigurement can only occur in the discursive form (in philosophy) or in the telling of an account (literature). If witnessing had "its own language," it would no longer be witnessing – it would be proof. Witnessing is precisely the imprinting of the improper into the realism of the said. It's the intervention of the improbable.

Rancière would stop me right here. What if the true witness were the person who says nothing, the person who refuses to witness, knowing that their own language will always be stolen from them and that their impropriety will always be recuperated? He writes, "The true witness is one who does not want to witness. That is the reason for the privilege accorded to his speech. But this privilege is not his. It is the privilege of speech that obliges him to speak despite himself."[126] Thus, in *Shoah*, for example (what an example!) – a film which, according to Rancière, and whatever anyone might say, "is in no way opposed to the logic of the aesthetic regime in the arts"[127] – the hairdresser Abraham Bomba, who was made to shear victims when they entered the gas chamber, cannot speak. "'You must go on, Abe. You have to,'" Lanzmann says to him.[128] According to Rancière, Bomba is forced to speak, ordered to speak. As if Lanzmann were saying to him: "Do you understand?" "Do you understand me, Abe?" Obey, you must. If that's the case, then the witness is always a subject under interrogation – and *the witness exists only for police*.

What can we say to this? What can we say except "No"? No. Abe's difficulty in speaking is not a refusal to witness. His difficulty is bearing witness to the infinite distancing – to what Levinas terms "anarchy" – between an Other who speaks and the absence of the Other to speak to. The person who speaks is "constrained to be the Other [*Autrui*] for themselves,"[129] to cite Blanchot when discussing Antelme. This is what silences Abe.

Antelme's language is not the "same" as Flaubert's language. For Antelme's language causes a strange distance to arise between all the things and beings at the heart of their parataxis. This distance is the mark of the specific inequality that haunts equality and has nothing to do with the arithmetic–geometric pair. This specific inequality is the translation of a hiatus between two forms of inequality, a hiatus signaling inequality's own inequality. Inequality as social miscount and inequality as alterity. To the point that paratactic juxtaposition, the equality "of things and beings," is torn, leaving the Other, the entirely Other to the one who is speaking, the task of witnessing in their place. Levinas writes: "And when the Other … speaks, the word is the relation that remains radically separated, a third kind of relation, one that asserts a relation without unity, without equality."[130] You must, Abe, says the Other, Lanzmann.

Rancière would say it is "an original poverty of mind" that "transforms … [me] into a hostage of the Other."[131] But that's precisely the problem: Rancière's thought is fundamentally lacking in alterity. He never distinguishes "unequal" from "other." Even if they are radically equal, subjects are no less other, all Others to each other, thus unequal in their equality. Difference – from this differend between inequality and alterity, infinitely exceeding the dilemma of quantity and quality, cardinal and ordinal – can only be witnessed. No proof is possible, no representation is possible.

Rancière considers that even though it has adopted a dominant role in contemporary thought, the saturation of the political and aesthetic fields by "the dramaturgy of catastrophe" is illegitimate. He quite rightly wants to free the space of a re-staging of parts, for a speech by those with no-parts, an audible speech, a paratactic speech of equality. An anarchy speech. But what I think Rancière fails to see is that *there's no anarchy without witnessing*.

The questions of witnessing, of the unpresentable, of dissymmetry and alterity cannot be reduced to an ideology of victimization. They sit at the core of what Rancière is trying to exclude from their orb: the anarchic dimension of democracy that is radical equality itself.

Anarchism without a regime of proof

All anarchists are witnesses. All the different forms of resistance to anarchism start from an expression of a lack of trust. No one – apart from anarchists – believes in anarchism. This is because its idea – the non-governable – is unpresentable. The idea does not present itself spontaneously to the mind or imagination. Perhaps it's not even an idea. No one *believes* we humans can live without government. Anarchism has, and will always have, to provide credibility beyond, and despite, the objective existence of its historical forms. The Paris Commune, the Spanish Civil War, workers' councils in Germany and Italy, revolutionary trade unionism, Zapatismo, the political system of Rojava (Western Kurdistan) – all existed and exist. ZADists and Black Blocs exist. That's a fact. Black Lives Matter exists. Fact. Yet, anarchism must constantly bear witness to its reality. It must accept that its implausible dimension – for both popular and philosophical consciousness – is never dismissed by *fact*, by the reality of its occurrences, theorists, and partisans. Faced with the skepticism that greets its validity, anarchists can offer nothing but their word on the reality of anarchism. When no proof is convincing, they can only bear witness, again and again. It is this that seals the complicity – not the equivalence – of anarchism and traumatic experience.

For reasons that perhaps we'll never know, the possibility of a social organization and life without government lacks proof, despite factual, historical occurrences. This is what exposes it directly to disavowal. It is also what reveals its unwavering connection to the unconscious. Indeed, as we know, the "there has been" – factual and timeless – is what Freud names trauma. The experience of anarchism is traumatic because its occurring, its having occurred, has no place. These are the grounds on which I allow myself to define anarchism, with Foucault, as the limit experience of politics. Contrary to what Rancière thinks, this is not a defense of victim ideology; rather, it is an attempt to recognize the simultaneously specific temporal, discursive, and psychic regime of anarchism. Its sublimeness, its political subliminality.

Is this to declare anarchism unthinkable, hence impossible, and so yet another way to deny it? Perhaps. But as Lyotard demonstrated, the unthinkable has never meant it cannot be thought. Lyotard's problem, which runs through all his work and is certainly not limited to accounting for the political catastrophes of the twentieth century, is the problem of *anamnesis*, that is, a type of memory awoken only by the future. A past that has yet to exist, insofar as one must constantly attest to its reality, infinitely bearing witness to it. Pierre Fédida writes: "The paradox of time rules the work of an anamnesis: that which was announced in the past will take the future to attest to it." This is how it is for anarchism: it has "a great future behind it."[132]

More than any other form of political organization, anarchy has an anamnestic structure. Rancière is forced to admit that his thesis of radical equality, especially the radical equality of intelligences, will never be immediately convincingly. Just like the anarchist idea from which it proceeds, its truth has, and will always have, to be attested, verified by a third party, a witness, an Other. This is what always troubled me in Rancière's *The Ignorant Schoolmaster*,[133] where the thesis of the equality of intelligences is presented as a fact, a matter of will or reason. Strangely, Jacottot's tale is not presented as a witnessing but, instead, as a piece of evidence. Behind the assertion that one must do without a master is hidden an elimination of the third party. *The Ignorant Schoolmaster* is memory without *anamnesis*. It is an argument based on authority – and in that sense, it's an archic demonstration.

"This is what I see right here"

In conclusion, I'll say that if the ungovernable can, without a shadow of a doubt, be represented, either on stage or on film, the non-governable remains unpresentable. The idea of the non-governable – the anarchist dimension of politics – eludes the archi-politics of proof, evidence, verifications, and exhibits. It can appear only as memory, that is, in the future. But this does not mean that it is unreal or phantasmatic.

In 1972, in the "Discours de Toul" [the Toul speech], Foucault demonstrates the political significance of witnesses:

> Our institutions pretend to baulk at criticism from inside, but they manage it, they live from it; it is both their petty conceit and their coverup. What they can't stand is for someone to turn their back on them all of a sudden and start screaming to the inside: "This is what I see right here and now, this is what is happening. This is the event."[134]

What they can't stand is the word of the witness. The witness Foucault is referring to here is Dr. Edith Rose, a psychiatrist in Toul central prison. After having experienced mutinies in the prison in 1971, Rose wrote a report deemed "anecdotal" by the penitentiary administration, who, moreover, suspended her. Yet the report was not anecdotal at all. It recounted "men whose feet and wrists were bound for days on end to the bed; almost nightly suicide attempts; regular alternating of punishments and tranquilizers." The report was not written just in the objective language of administrative rationality, with its statistical segmentation of the real and the paratactic style of description, but rather as a "monotonous chant" that, "throughout the text," intoned: "'I see, I hear' ... 'I swear, I attest, I accept critique'." "'I bear witness to this under oath.'"[135]

What this report witnesses, Foucault says, is "the violence of power relations,"[136] a violence about which power knows nothing – the cry of the non-governable.

No, there's not only a witness for police. To claim this is the case is already to police. To say so would already be to take refuge in the archi-politics that philosophy has never stopped being.

Finally: a touch of anarchist painting

The pointillist movement in painting, sometimes termed neo-impressionism, then later divisionism, was an activist movement that considered the pictorial technique of dots to be the plastic equivalent of anarchism in the fine arts. Georges Seurat, Paul Signac, Félix Fénéon, to name just a few, never hid their anarchist commitments. In their view, it is not the subject matter that counts. Even if *L'Île de la Grande Jatte*, *Le Cirque*, *Un Dimanche après-midi*, *Le Port de La Rochelle*, and *Le Portrait de Félix Fénéon* could be considered figurative paintings, their creators always claimed that the true "subject" of painting was not its "subject," but rather its political theme: the radical equality, which they believed to be *unrepresentable*.[137] Signac wrote: "The subject is nothing, or at least is only a part of a work of art."[138] What counts is the evocation of a future in which formalism will no longer be in opposition to popular consciousness:

> With an educated eye, one day people will see something other than the subject in these paintings, one day when the society we dream of exists, one day, freed of the exploiters who run them down, workers have the time to think and to learn, they will appreciate all the different qualities of the work of art.[139]

The evocation of this future, far more than the theme, is related to the pictorial technique that supposedly supports social redistribution through the distribution of dots. All the dots in the painting are the same size, have the same vibrating significance, the same chromatic candor, suggesting, through their very juxtaposition, a world in which all beings, as in an infinite mosaic, are in the same plane, the same relief, the same geography, qualitatively and quantitatively equal.

Why is this type of equality considered unrepresentable? Isn't Signac's large painting, *Au temps d'harmonie (l'âge d'or n'est pas dans le passé, il est dans l'avenir)*, perfectly explicit, with its images of abundance, leisure, happiness, and peace? And yet … when one looks at a pointillist canvas close up, it is clear that each brush stroke, each color is independent of all the others, separated from them by a white space. Seurat called this phenomenon the "divided touch."

Stepping back from the canvas, it is the spectator who mixes the colors, and the further away one stands, the more the white spaces seem to disappear. But even when they are invisible from a distance, they are never erased and are still perceived, unconsciously perhaps. The canvas under a pointillist painting will always be a white blank.

In the gradual shift from politics to aesthetics, from distance to proximity, to the heart of the equality of the dots and brush strokes, lies this alterity that is always a blank, that sees itself without seeing itself, that says everything without saying and without representing anything. The divided touch, equality and inequality's own inequality – luminous witness of the anarchist stage.

Conclusion
Being an Anarchist

Any woman or man who dives into the heart of their unconscious naturally comes out an anarchist.[1]

Jacques Lesage de la Haye

The history of the motto "Long live Death" [*Viva la Muerte*] offers an exemplary metaphor of the two possible destinies of the death drive. "*Viva la Muerte*" was the rallying call of the national uprising of the Spanish against Napoleon in May 1808. Despite the formidable disparity between native insurgents and imperial troops, this movement could not be repressed by the occupier, lasted five years, and ultimately led to the expulsion of the French from Spain. It was already a cry for liberation. Adopted by the Spanish anarchists half a century later, it became a revolutionary call against a life of injustice. Then it was turned back against the anarchists by the Francoists, as the other destiny of the death drive: the deadly drive to destruction.[2]

Nathalie Zaltzman

Fork the government.[3]

"I am an anarchist." For philosophers, this statement seems forever to bear the stamp of impossibility. One cannot *be* an anarchist. In the era of the withering of principles, the phenomenon that is the anarchy of being resists all reduction to ontic determination: being is no longer such and such and therefore can no longer fulfill its function as a transmitter of predicates (Schürmann).

One cannot *be an anarchist*. Anarchy proves to be more originary than ontology, exceeding ontological difference itself. Its "saying" exceeds its "said," overflows the propositional form infinitely by taking the responsibility of obligation beyond essence (Levinas).

One *can* not be an anarchist. As soon as anarchy and power are associated with one another – "*the power to be able* to be an anarchist"

– anarchism clearly participates in some manner in the drive for mastery (Derrida).

One cannot be an anarchist. It's not the predicate "anarchist" that transforms the subject, anarchizing the subject by determining it. It's not that. The subject must first develop their own anarchic dimension, prepare their own transformability, constitute themself as anarchic subject before "being" it and predicating it (Foucault).

One cannot be an *anarchist*. The word is a signifier so inflated with the void of its own signified that it has become a fetish, rendered sacred, prelude to a new idolatry (Agamben).

One can *not* be an anarchist. The negativity at work in politics, the structure of originary misunderstanding and miscounting, cannot be placed. Its political expression is rare and intermittent, only glimpsed. Its expression plays, but never holds a pose (Rancière).

*

"I am an anarchist." Each word in this statement presents an insurmountable obstacle to all the others. Each word, an echo of the politically untenable nature of anarchism.

*

By emphasizing the impossibility of "being an anarchist," philosophy missed its critique of domination. This occurred even as philosophy ceaselessly interrogated its own position as a dominant discourse. Derrida, more than anyone, demonstrated that traditional European philosophy authorized itself to "speak about the whole,"[4] even if this excessive power is accompanied by a certain "non-knowledge," which is not ignorance, but the refusal to see: "One could say that the philosopher authorizes himself to know about everything on the basis of an 'I don't want to know'."[5]

The problem is that the philosophical concepts of anarchy developed to denounce this "not wanting to know" have participated in the same refusal to see. While they have enabled a destabilization of the archic paradigm of Western metaphysics, they have nonetheless erupted into discourse as constructions *ex nihilo*, without a past, mute on the theft by which they are procured. By dissociating anarchy and anarchism, the philosophical critique of domination has involuntarily opened a space of complicity between conceptualization and repression, dismantling metaphysics and colonialism, ethics and defense of the state, difference and mastery, *parrēsia* and (self-)government, "politicity" and semantic repression, politics and police… This complicity reveals too the extent of the philosophical bonds of subordination to the logic of government.

Thinking anarchy philosophically consisted largely in subverting the legitimacy of anarchism, subverting the subversion of power in a gesture that has never perceived itself and has therefore never analyzed itself either. A gesture both hegemonic and subservient that will remain unthought so long as anarchy as a concept is not confronted with the anarchist radicality of that which does not (self-)govern.

The deconstruction of metaphysics was evidently not enough to dismantle the archic paradigm, it was no more effective than the ethical injunction, the critique of subjectivity, the deconstitution of the sacred or the unrepresentable. Even if radical movements today, especially post-anarchist movements, identify with the major figures of poststructuralism, this does not fully mask their lack of a political commitment that doesn't temporize and makes no compromise whatsoever with the governmental prejudice.

The reason for this is that, contrary to all expectations, philosophy has not fully grasped the ontological meaning – that is, the philosophical meaning – of anarchism. By declaring that only anarchy can and must become Ariadne's thread for the deconstructive questioning of ontology, thus, in a sense again, of ontological questioning; by excluding anarchism from this circle of investigation; by detecting the arrival of an ontological anarchy, an ethical anarchy, a critical anarchy, a theological anarchy, a democratic anarchy, in the fabric of the theoretical and political events of the second half of the twentieth century, but only at the expense of a break with all real links with anarchism; by emphasizing over and again that being an anarchist is impossible, philosophers have failed to perceive the anarchist dimension of being.

The question of being is overlooked because its meaning is anarchism. If being has a meaning, it elides with the non-governable, with radical foreignness to domination. *Being could care less about power.* The real anarchist is being itself.

With impressive acuity, Schürmann sensed this and went so far as to claim that the question of being finds in anarchy its transfiguring future, the place of expression, the tattoo of its indifference to power. But by putting up a wall between anarchy and anarchism, by hiding behind ontological difference as if it were a sufficient guarantee against substantialism, he was unable to give sufficient weight to his assertion of the need to rethink practice. He did not cultivate his problematizing of "action." To think the anarchist being – not just (or perhaps not at all) the anarchic being – requires the invention of activist discourse, not just contemplation; it takes a contemplative-activist discourse that opens philosophical action to its alternative commitment on the horizontal plane.

*

Philosophers of anarchy have some excuse. We must concede that all attempts to think being and politics together have been a disaster. From Plato's "communism" to the mathematical totalitarianism of some forms of Maoism, through the Heideggerian night, the elaboration of connections between ontology and politics authorized by the originary bricolage of *archē*, which, as we have seen, extends its reign in both fields, have given rise to nothing but terrifying dead-ends. This is probably why philosophers of anarchy have insisted on making a clear distinction between the "y" and the "ism" and have kept from rushing the ontological content of anarchy into a possible "staging," preferring, as in the case of Agamben, impotence to a forced pragmatism that might be even more sectarian and dominating than all "governmental prejudices." And Rancière is quite right: these prejudices have not all disappeared from historical anarchism.

Why risk a new impediment? Wouldn't it be better, far better, to make a cut between being and anarchism, to stop ontologizing politics and politicizing ontology, to deconstruct the archic paradigm without transforming it into an anarchist paradigm and thereby to respect the varied battles against domination by refraining from unifying them in a shared destiny that also makes domination uniform? Wouldn't it be better also, as Schürmann suggests, to drop the question of being, which seems to have totally disappeared from the philosophical scene since the banishing of Heidegger, as if in the end this question were his alone, and erased along with him? As if philosophical anarchy were not only the mourning, but also the amnesty of this line of investigation?

*

But how can we seriously entertain the thought that we can be done with being? How can we think that life – form of life – has in some sense *replaced* being? That the only politically correct, ethical, presentable, and representable anarchism is, to put it bluntly, the anarchism of way of life, lifestyle, the easy life of what remains of democracy in parliamentary democracies?

For the moment, it must be said, anarchism has not provided an answer to this ontological, practical saccharin version of itself. At least not a satisfactory answer. Anarchism is evidently also a philosophical archipelago that claims it flees all properly conceptual elucidation and is a refusal of responsibility. Vivien García writes: "For a large part, anarchist theories have developed outside of philosophy," since philosophy "is none other than the avoidance of an-archi[sm]."[6] As we have seen, this is true. Yet must we respond to this avoidance with yet another avoidance? Can anarchism really get out of explaining its ontological dimension?

Daniel Colson argues that "anarchy is not a metaphysical concept; it's an empirical and concrete concept."[7] That's all well and good, but, contradictions aside, what does "an empirical and concrete concept" mean exactly? Bakunin sought to resolve the oxymoron by proposing that anarchism be defined as a "veritable plastic force,"[8] in which "no office petrifies, becomes fixed and remains irrevocably attached to a single person; order and hierarchical promotion do not exist, so yesterday's commander can become today's subaltern; no one is above anyone else, or if they rise, it is to fall in the next moment, like waves on the sea."[9] This must be the direction of the analysis, so that to state "I am an anarchist" is no longer a matter of logic. Subject, copula, predicate all lose their function immediately in the statement. If predicative logic, its incline, the governmental diastema can all disappear from "I am an anarchist," it is because the anarchism of being relieves the anarchist from having to become the subject of its anarchy. As the only political form that is always to be invented, to be shaped before it exists, precisely because it depends on no beginning or command, anarchism is never what it is. That's where its being lies. This plasticity is the meaning of its being, the meaning of its question. If we fail to see this meaning, or if we move too quickly over it, we risk reducing its plasticity to the most simple "empirical and concrete" apparatus, no longer able to distinguish it from a sales pitch, a symptom of de facto anarchism and cyber-power – everything's plastic, away we go.

*

A rigorous reading of the remanences of the governmental prejudice in contemporary philosophy has enabled me to negatively outline the space of the non-governable, allowing certain voices stifled within it to speak – the voices of the colonized, the slave, the witness – but it has also led me to address a question to anarchism that it has not yet answered satisfactorily: how should we interpret its plastic ontology? This is the task dawning in anarchism.

*

Traditional critiques of anarchism are based on two contradictory arguments: a benevolent confidence in human nature and a logic of violence and death. But on reflection, there's nothing specific in these two arguments that could not also be ascribed to any radical political movement – communism as much as anarchism, for example. It's a quick fix to the problem to make anarchism the exclusive symptom of this two-headed, pacifist-criminal monster. Far more important is to decide instead how anarchism can deploy, in a way that is entirely its own, an exit strategy from this dual trap.

For lack of sufficient examination, the anarchist meaning of being and its indifference to power have been equated too quickly with virginity, innocence, lack of corruption. For instance, Saul Newman writes: "Anarchism therefore has a logical point of departure, uncontaminated by power, from which power can be condemned as unnatural, irrational, and immoral."[10] But if we don't even try to show that the non-governable has nothing to do with an intact, untouched, and untouchable origin, philosophers will always be right to suspect that behind the plasticity of the anarchist being sits the persistent presupposition of an incorruptible nature and adherence to a metaphysics of purity. They'll be right in their perception that there is an archaic ontology in anarchism.

The anarchist meaning of being – its indifference to power – has also been taken as a terrorist license, a "poetics of the bomb,"[11] or what Mallarmé described as the fury of "devices whose explosion lights up the houses of Parliament with a summary glow, but pitifully disfigures the passers-by."[12] Here, too, if there is no attempt to show that the non-governable is not the forebear of violence, philosophers will always have grounds to denounce a deep complicity between anarchism and the death drive.

*

Situated somewhere between a treatise on ontology and a revolutionary manifesto, the quotation from psychoanalyst Nathalie Zaltzman's text, "La pulsion anarchiste" [the anarchistic drive], heading this chapter helps us perceive the shared source of these two pitfalls.

Violence first. Evidently there are intimate relations between anarchy, anarchism, and death – relations sewn together with the thread of the black flag. The problem is that while control, *Bemächtigungstrieb*, along with all its destructive variations, is certainly the offspring of the death drive, the battle against domination and control must also draw its energy from this drive. To fight domination is to assume that fixed nodes will be dissolved. Now, what Zaltzman claims is that, while a destructive, dominating, and aggressive uncoupling exists, there is also a "liberational" uncoupling that detaches itself from the other – one that unbinds itself.[13] So, there's death drive and then there's death drive, which is why she refers to death drives in the plural. Anarchism "draws its force from the death drive and turns its destruction back against it."[14] Strangely, this turning of destruction back on itself is not a dialectical construction, but is instead an expression of indifference.[15] An unconscious indifference unlike the compulsive love of power, often hidden behind the love of humanity. For Zaltzman, "all libidinal bonds, even the most respectful, include the goal of possession that annuls alterity. The aim of Eros is annexation, up to and including the other's right to live as they wish."[16]

This is why "the revolt against the pressure of civilization, the destruction of an existing social organization that is oppressive and unjust, can be enlisted under the banner of love for humanity, does not draw its force from this ideological love. Its force comes of the unbinding activity of a liberatory death drive."[17] The anarchist drive erects a wall of impassivity against narcissistic petrification and its authoritarian incarnations.

Thus, in the same way that Eros is not *always* in the service of life – as we have already seen, Zaltzman criticizes the compounding tendencies of "ideological love" – Thanatos is not *always* in the service of death. The tendency of calling for freedom experiences "a mental destiny distinct from a direct inclination to death."[18] A destiny "other than deadly."[19]

If there is a tendency within anarchism to undo what Eros binds to excess, then the anarchist drive is, in a sense, "antisocial," if by "social" we understand community fusion. Insofar as it undoes this fusion and is wary of any idea of unified human nature, the anarchist drive makes room for another opening to alterity.

"To be an anarchist" initially implies an experience of unlinking as lifting anchor, enabling absolute resistance to *archē despotikē*, that is, to *domestication*.

Celebrating the memory of anarchist geographers, Zaltzman cites Élisée Reclus writing to his brother Élie Reclus from Louisiana: "I need to die of hunger for a bit, sleep on stones, sell my watch (a souvenir of eternal friendship) for a piece of howler monkey."[20] She also mentions Jean Malaurie's book on the Inuit, *The Last Kings of Thule*.[21] The Inuit live in "hyperborean landscapes of nothing but ice and stone, with a ground that is always frozen and never the tenderness of friable earth or a gentle rain, snow always blown about by the wind that leaves raw edges and crevasses, those mineral landscapes, so austere, arid, and ever cruel to human life."[22] Yet, "there is nothing forcing these nomads to live on the edge of the Arctic. Like the Sami, one of the Arctic peoples who used to be hunters like them, they could undergo a mutation by abandoning the frozen sea to raise domestic reindeer."[23] But it's precisely domestication that the Inuit don't want. They don't want reindeer domesticated any more than they want domestication themselves. Their freedom comes at this price, the price of a battle of death against death – against dependence, subordination, training, against "all relations fixed to a unifying identity."[24]

*

What about the supposed naive goodness of anarchism then? The non-governable – the place without a place where the death drive turns back against itself, the frozen polar rock, the solitary, floating path of the geographers, the jungle of insurgents – can this "a-socialness" be equated with an origin untouched by power, a sheltered isle? Does the uncoupling assume the return to a state preceding hegemony? To childhood?

Freud does indeed describe thanatological unlinking as a return – but a return to the inorganic state. What kind of return is this other than, quite literally, a *return to nothing*? The "there" to which the return comes back *doesn't exist*. The prelude to the origin *doesn't exist*. The prelude to command *doesn't exist*. There's no state of inorganic state.

Anarchism always assumes a retrospective glance. I have sought here to retrace some of the many ramifications for which the dismantling of the archic paradigm is first a "returning back toward." The question of the provenance of origin cannot remain a question unasked. It is inevitable that we search for what precedes principle. This retrospection "does not engender a return to a state prior to evolution, but rather to one that comes after it, a state that was previously inexistent."[25] The return to before *archē* invents that to which it (itself) turns back toward. The anarchist drive is a regressive energy shaped by a future-facing dynamic. It is the withdrawal that makes the non-place exist, not vice versa. To come back amounts to inventing. Not finding anything in the place one comes back to, not taking anything to the place where one is going. This nothing toward which the future turns back before projecting itself forward is anything except a virgin island or a haven of peace – since it is nothing.

The non-governable is revealed after the fact, like the counterproof of this nothing that is the impossibility of all government. As Proudhon put it, the "anarchist being" will forever be a neologism.

*

One of the great philosophical challenges of our time is to put an end to the competition between being and life – and this requires a rethinking of the death drive. Whether it is the Heideggerian alliance between being and death, sealed by the privilege granted to existence over life, or whether it is the sudden revalorizations of life that believed they have finished with Heidegger by (poorly) substituting precarious modes of life on existents, or whether it is a supposed ancestralism of being, its fossil, neither living nor dead, dehumanized and decorrelated, always older and more real than life: it must be said that none of these versions is up to the urgency of the task.

The sore spot in relations between being, life, and death cries out its name every day: ecology. Who's paying attention now to the fact that the word "ecology" also derives from *oikos*, house, even though it also refers to an entirely different thing – something that is the very opposite of the economy – specifically, home economics? Who's paying close attention to the fact that "ecology" is a "discourse of the abode" battling against domestication? The Earth is a habitat without domesticity, without master or center, absolutely non-governable, yet devasted by power games.

Many critics have attacked traditional anarchism for being a vitalism or a biologism, which is an absurd accusation. The question of anarchist being is the question of life as survival. Survival on Earth, even inscribed in the biological memory of individuals, is political from the start. In the solitude of vast Siberian steppes, under the pale gleam of the winter sun, watching animals help each other, Kropotkin concluded that mutual aid deposes natural selection from its status as principle. Mutual aid is the social response of nature, and is thus a key example of the death drive turning back on itself.

*

Anarchism – so diverse, so difficult to reduce to one authority, including its own – is the privileged theoretical and practical constellation of a situation in which the non-governable bears witness everywhere in idioms unknown to the language of principles. Everywhere, from the massed populace to the individual, people bewail their lassitude, their weariness, their anger in the face of ecological and social devastation of the world by governments that offer them no support. But they also speak, without contradiction, of their lassitude, their weariness, their anger in the face of the absence of any effective governmental regulation of the uberized jungle in which they have to orient themselves alone as they look for support.

Faced with this lassitude, weariness, and anger, many theorists and political activists propose "solutions." It strikes me as more useful to try to give shape to the problem by raising the question. Relating the remains of white, male domination of philosophy to a thieving disavowal of anarchism, I am not undertaking to restore to anarchism what the philosophers stole – it's impossible, anyway, to return the broken bit, to glue it back onto an improbable origin. My approach evidently obeys no proprietary instinct. In any case, anarchism wouldn't take being

CONCLUSION

restored to itself, since its past exists only in the future. So, it's none of that. The question I have raised is the following: if the anarchist problem since Proudhon is precisely to think about politics without the aid of hegemony, in any form whatsoever,[26] it is also now a question of doing so when a certain anarchism has itself become hegemonic.

*

Would you believe it? Today, there are anarchists holding governmental positions. Audrey Tang, Minister of Digital Affairs in Taiwan, the first transgender minister in history, a genius cybernetician and free software creator, defines themself openly as a "conservative anarchist."[27] This pleonasm should not be misconstrued. What Tang means is that they want to work on the conservation of the anarchist utopia experimented by Net programmers who, over the past twenty years, have been suggesting that a virtual participative democracy be substituted for classical political decision-making.[28]

Back in Spring 2014, Audrey Tang participated in the emergent Sunflower Movement, in which young activists, most of whom were students, occupied the Taiwanese parliament to protest a new trade pact with China. They founded g0v (pronounced "gov-zero"), a collective of *civic hackers*. Shortly thereafter, the ex-Minister of Digital Affairs Jaclyn Tsai was looking for a way to bolster trust between citizens and the government. She came across a g0v "hackathon" and, soon after attending, put together a plan for collaboration by proposing the launch of a neutral citizen platform and naming Audrey Tang as her assistant. Tang became Minister in turn in 2016.

Tang's strategy consists in using open source coding tools "to radically redesign and rebuild an existing government process or service – and from this create new tools to show citizens how the state operates,"[29] in other words, to reveal government information to the wider public. In "Hack the pandemic," Tang declared:

> By simply replacing the "o" with a zero in your search bar, you enter a "parallel" government site that might function better and where you will find viable alternatives. In the g0v initiative framework, there are currently some 9,000 citizen-hackers participating in what we call "forking" the government. In open source coding culture, to "fork" is to take something that already

exists in a different direction. Citizens accept digital surveillance, but the state also accepts a transparency, an opening of its data and codes, and integrates the criticism that will inevitably emerge.[30]

*

Is Audrey Tang a symptom of domination or of emancipation? A reinforcement of the logic of government or its defeat? Tang said: "Civic hackers often produce work that threatens the existing institutional structures. In Taiwan, institutions have always adopted an approach along the lines of 'if you can't beat them, join them,' which is rare in Asian jurisdiction. This is definitely why I'm staying here in Taiwan."[31]

Join institutions, all the better to subvert them. Many critics will say that those are the words of the dominant. And yet ... China is dangerously frustrated by these bold words that threaten its omnipotence and trouble its hegemony.

*

So again, we ask: how do we orient ourselves in this new geography whose pathways not only tangle the clear distinction between de facto anarchism and dawning anarchism, but also reveal the rhizomatic, variable topography of cyber-anarchism? How do we orient ourselves in the ontological indifference of differences?

*

How do we orient ourselves when it is as urgent as it is difficult to discern and point to these differences, to distinguish between horizontality and deregulation, liberation and uberization, ecology and economy ...? When it becomes as urgent as it is difficult to assign the non-governable to its place even as it is knocking ever more loudly at the door of consciousness, unconsciousness, bodies ...? That's when we understand that these uncertainties are already openings toward other ways of sharing, acting, thinking. Of being an anarchist.

Let's say it again: there's absolutely nothing more to expect from on high.

Notes

Epigraph

1 Graeber, David, *Fragments of an Anarchist Anthropology* (Chicago, IL: Prickly Paradigm Press, 2004), p. 34.

Chapter 1: Surveying the Horizon

1 Lacoste, Yves, "Élisée Reclus, une très large conception de la géographicité et une bienveillante géopolitique," *Hérodote*, 2/117 (2005), pp. 29–52: p. 30. [CS translation]
2 Reclus, Élisée, *Nouvelle Géographie universelle. La Terre et les hommes* (Paris: Hachette et Cie Libraires-Éditeurs), 19 vols., 1876–94. *The Earth and Its Inhabitants: The Universal Geography*, trans. and ed. E. G. Ravenstein and A. H. Keene (London: J. S. Virtue and Co, 1876–94). See Philippe Pelletier "Élisée Reclus: théorie géographique et théorie anarchiste," *Terra Brasilis* (Nova Série), 7 (2016).
3 Reclus, Élisée, *The Earth: A Descriptive History of the Phenomena of the Life of the Globe*, trans. B. B. Woodward (London: Bickers and Son, 1876).
4 Reclus, *The Earth*, in Béatrice Giblin, "Élisée Reclus, un géographe d'exception," *Hérodote*, 2/117 (2005), pp. 11–28: p. 24. [CS translation]
5 Reclus, Élisée, *L'Homme et la terre* (Paris: Librairie universelle, 1905), 6 vols., quoted by Lacoste, "Élisée Reclus, une très large conception de la géographicité et une bienveillante géopolitique," p. 39. [CS translation]
6 Kropotkin, Peter, *Mutual Aid: A Factor of Evolution* (London: Freedom, 1987). The friendship between Reclus and Kropotkin began when they met in 1877.
7 See Renaud Garcia's excellent thesis on Kropotkin, "Nature humaine et anarchie: la pensée de Pierre Kropotkine," defended on December 7, 2012 at the École normale supérieure de Lyon; École doctorale de philosophie: histoire, représentation, création, ED 487, p. 32.
8 Reclus, Élisée, *Développement de la liberté dans le monde*. Discovered posthumously and published in 1928 in *Le Libertaire*; quoted in Giblin, "Élisée Reclus, un géographe d'exception," p. 14.
9 In France this desertion by the state manifests in the closure of hospitals, police stations, and schools, the privatization and subcontracting of mail services, the spread of "flexible" work, the cancelation of "statutes," the increase in temporary work contracts for public office, especially in higher education, ministry staff cuts, ever-increasing inequality in access to healthcare, legal protection, and education – to name just some of the symptoms.
10 After the riots that followed the murder of George Floyd in the United States, an anarchist collective wrote: "Today, Black Lives Matter activists are also employing a decentralized approach, permitting the movement to spread organically and ensuring that it cannot be contained or coopted." "This *is* Anarchy. Eight ways the Black Lives Matter and Justice for George Floyd uprisings reflect anarchist ideas in action," Crimethlnc, June 9, 2020.
11 Yon, Karel, "Les grèves et la contestation syndicale sont de plus en plus politiques," interview with Marina Garrisi, *RP Dimanche*, February 9, 2020. [CS translation]

12 See, for example, the interesting article by Melissa Lane, "Why Donald Trump was the ultimate anarchist," *New Statesman*, February 8, 2021, in which she writes: "The former president is being tried for his role in inciting anarchy but *anarchia*, in the Greek sense of 'vacant office,' characterized his entire term": p. 3.

13 See my articles, "Cryptomonnaie: Le capitalisme amorce aujourd'hui son tournant anarchiste," *Le Monde*, June 14, 2018, p. 13; "Les cryptomonnaies remettent en cause l'idée même d'État," interview with Octave Larmagnac-Matheron, *Philosophie Magazine*, October 6, 2020; "L'Entre-iconomie: la monnaie à l'horizon," in Peter Szendy, *Le Supermarché des images* (Paris: Gallimard/Jeu de Paume, 2019), pp. 255–60. In these texts, I acknowledge social uses of blockchain organizing around mutual aid, cooperation, and solidarity.

14 Damasio, Alain, "Internet est tellement vaste et polymorphe que l'anarchisme y reste possible," interview with Mathieu Dejean, *Les Inrockuptibles*, June 22, 2015. [CS translation]

15 "Is 'anarcho'-capitalism a type of anarchism?" *An Anarchist FAQ*, section F, version 15.4, March 17, 2020. https://theanarchistlibrary.org/library/the-anarchist-faq-editorial-collective-an-anarchist-faq-full.

16 Paepe, César de, "On the organization of public services in the society of the future," in Daniel Guérin, ed., *No Gods, No Masters: An Anthology of Anarchism*, trans. Paul Sharkey (Edinburgh: AK Press, 2005), p. 227.

17 Rifkin, Jeremy, *The Zero Marginal Cost Society: The Internet of Things, The Collaborative Commons, and the Eclipse of Capitalism* (New York: Palgrave Macmillan, 2014).

18 Derrida, Jacques, *Resistances of Psychoanalysis*, trans. Peggy Kamuf, Pascale-Anne Brault, and Michael Naas (Stanford, CA: Stanford University Press, 1998), p. 25.

19 "Anarchisme sur le retour avec Tancrède Ramonet," *La Grande Table idées*, France Culture, April 11, 2017, Part 2. [CS translation]

Chapter 2: Dissociating Anarchism from Anarchy

1 Bakunin, Mikhail, "God and the state," in *L'Empire knoutogermanique* (1871); quoted in Daniel Guérin, ed., *No Gods, No Masters: An Anthology of Anarchism*, trans. Paul Sharkey (Edinburgh: AK Press, 2005), p. 152.

2 Rancière, Jacques, "Ten theses on politics," *Theory and Event*, 5/3 (2001), p. 4.

3 García, Vivien, *L'Anarchisme aujourd'hui* (Paris: L'Harmattan, 2007), p. 87. [CS translation]

4 Ibáñez, Tomás, "Réflexions, approximativement philosophiques, sur l'anarchie, l'anarchisme et le néo-anarchisme," *Rebellyon.info*, March 7, 2011. [CS translation]

5 This is why Max Weber, for example, stopped using the word "domination" (*Herrschaft*) to refer to "power," limiting it to a more specific use. If domination were nothing but a mere synonym for power, he argued, the concept "could not constitute a scientifically useful category"; see Max Weber, *La Domination*, trans. Isabelle Kalinowski, ed. Yves Sintomer (Paris: La Découverte, 2013). This passage is cited by Sintomer in his introduction to the work, p. 20, referring to p. 45 in the text. Later we read: "Weber writes that by 'domination' we therefore mean the fact that an asserted will (an 'order') from one or more 'dominant parties' seeks to influence the action of others ('those who are dominated') and does so effectively in as far as to a significant degree from a social view point, this action takes place as if the dominated had made the content of this order, as such, the maxim of their action ('obedience')." [CS translation]

6 Goldman, Emma, "The tragedy of woman's emancipation": lecture given at the first meeting of *Mother Earth* in New York in March 1906, republished in *Anarchism and Other Essays* (New York: Dover Publications Inc, 1969 [1910]), p. 221.

7 Proudhon, Pierre-Joseph, *General Idea of the Revolution in the Nineteenth Century* (1851);

see Pierre-Joseph Proudhon, "The authority principle," in Guerin, ed., *No Gods, No Masters*, p. 81. Translator's note: the famous phrase is translated as "the prejudice in favor of government," in Iain McKay, ed., *Property is Theft! A Pierre-Joseph Proudhon Reader* (Edinburgh: AK Press, 2011), p. 561.
8 Proudhon, Pierre-Joseph, *Resistance to the Revolution: Louis Blanc and Pierre Leroux* (1849), in Guerin, ed., *No Gods No Masters*, pp. 482–3. Throughout this book, I use the spelling *archē* for the Greek term *arkhē*.
9 Proudhon, *General Idea of the Revolution in the Nineteenth Century*, in McKay, ed., *Property is Theft!*, p. 598.
10 Barnett, Derek C., "The primacy of resistance: Anarchism, Foucault, and the art of not being governed," University of Western Ontario, Graduate Program in Theory and Criticism, Electronic Thesis and Dissertations Repository, December 16, 2016.
11 Barnett, "The primacy of resistance," p. 42.
12 Aristotle, *Politics*, Book 3, Chapter 6, in *Aristotle's Politics*, trans. Carnes Lord (Chicago, IL: University of Chicago Press, 2013), p. 71.
13 Aristotle, *Politics*, Book 3, Chapter 7, p. 73.
14 Rancière, Jacques, *Disagreement: Politics and Philosophy*, trans. Julie Rose (Minneapolis: University of Minnesota Press, 1999), p. 16.
15 Schürmann, Reiner, *Heidegger on Being and Acting: From Principles to Anarchy*, trans. Christine-Marie Gros (Bloomington: Indiana University Press, 1987). Although he never articulates it as such, deconstruction for Schürmann is a synthetic term, encompassing both Heideggerian *Destruktion* and Derridean deconstruction. Throughout the body of my analysis in this English translation, I refer to Schürmann's book using the significant English subtitle, *From Principles to Anarchy*, which is closer to the main title in the French (*Le Principe d'anarchie*). In the references, however, I use the English main title, *Heidegger on Being and Acting*.
16 Schürmann, *Heidegger on Being and Acting*, p. 269.
17 See Chapter 3.
18 See Chapter 5.
19 Agamben, Giorgio, *The Use of Bodies*, trans. Adam Kotsko (Stanford, CA: Stanford University Press, 2016), p. 275.
20 Rancière, Jacques, "Politics, identification, and subjectivization" *October*, 61 (Summer 1992), pp. 58–64: p. 59. See also Chapter 7.
21 Schürmann, *Heidegger on Being and Acting*, p. 6.
22 Badiou, Alain, *The Communist Hypothesis*, trans. David Macey and Steve Corcoran (London: Verso, 2010), p. 155.
23 May, Todd, *The Political Philosophy of Poststructuralist Anarchism* (University Park: Penn State University Press, 1994), Introduction, p. 3.
24 May, *The Political Philosophy of Poststructuralist Anarchism*, p. 10.
25 May, *The Political Philosophy of Poststructuralist Anarchism*, p. 12.
26 May, *The Political Philosophy of Poststructuralist Anarchism*, p. 13.
27 May, *The Political Philosophy of Poststructuralist Anarchism*, p. 13.
28 Call, Lewis quoted in Duane Rousselle, *After Post-Anarchism* (Berkeley, CA: Creative Commons, LBC Books, 2012), pp. 126–7.
29 See Irène Pereira, "L'anarchisme face au paradigme de la colonisation," *Grand Angle*, May 6, 2018.
30 Newman, Saul, quoted in Rousselle, *After Post-Anarchism*, p. 119.
31 Proudhon, Pierre-Joseph, *What is Property?* The Anarchist Library. https://theanarchistlibrary.org/library/pierre-joseph-proudhon-what-is-property-an-inquiry-into-the-principle-of-right-and-of-governmen.

32 Linguist Jean-François Sablayrolles explains that a neologism is either a "new word or an existing word used with a new meaning." In fact, there is no substantial difference between a neologism and a revived archaism: "This paradox is discussed for several pages of *Histoire de la langue française* [history of the French language]. Neologism and archaism are presented as producing the same novelty effect as a foreign word ... For historical reasons, we artificially distinguish neologisms and archaisms. From a stylistic point of view, the effect on the reader is exactly the same": "Néologie et/ou évolution du lexique? Le cas des innovations sémantiques et celui des archaïsmes," *ELAD-SILDA*, 1 (2018). [CS translation]

33 Kropotkin, Peter, *Anarchism: Its Philosophy and Ideal* (London: J. Turner, 1897), p. 7.

34 This statement is widely attributed to Pierre-Joseph Proudhon, although it does not in fact figure in the oft-cited source, *Confessions of a Revolutionary, to serve as a history of the February Revolution* (1849).

35 French dictionaries date the creation of the word "anarchism" to 1839 or 1840. It was not added to the *Littré* dictionary until 1875.

36 Lechauve, Octave, "Histoire des mots anarchie, anarchiste et anarchisme" [History of the words anarchy, anarchist and anarchism], Coordination des Libertaires de l'Ain, published online February 10, 2015. Lechauve adds: "Yet dictionaries are utterly insufficient so far as it is concerned: *Littré* simply ignores it, while *Lexis* dates the first appearance to 1839 and TLF to 1840, without any of them mentioning, however, its use prior to 1892 (Goncourt, *Journal*), even though the word was already used in two titles from the 1880s: Courtois, *Anarchisme théorique et collectivisme pratique* (1885) and Deville, *L'anarchisme* (1887 and 1891). In fact, formed with the addition of the suffix -ism, which refers to a doctrine or political or cultural movement, the term is far older, since it is the contemporary of the neologisms socialism (1833) and communism (towards 1839): indeed, it figures in the seventh edition of Boiste's *Dictionnaire universel* (1835): 'System, anarchist opinions'." Later we read: "Since the Renaissance (for instance Rabelais gives the name Anarche to the ridiculous king of the Dipsodes who drowns in Pantagruel's piss), the word is generally taken with the same pejorative meanings as in Greece: 'A state that has no true leader' (Furetière, 1690) and 'disorder produced in a state by the lack of government or the weakness of the governors' (Cotgrave, 1611). We can therefore consider Bossuet's highly reactionary maxim (*Traité de la connaissance de Dieu et de soi-même*, 1741, I, 13) as representative of the conception of anarchy during the Ancien Régime: 'Given that order is better than confusion, I conclude that there is nothing worse than anarchy, that is, living without government or laws'." [CS translation]

37 1751. See also Rousseau, Jean-Jacques, *Considérations sur le gouvernement de Pologne*, Ch. 9 (1771).

38 Lechauve, "Histoire des mots anarchie, anarchiste et anarchism." [CS translation]

39 Proudhon, *What is Property?* The Anarchist Library.

40 Reclus, Élisée, *Discours à la séance solennelle de rentrée du 22 octobre 1895 de l'Université nouvelle de Bruxelles*. [CS translation]

41 Malatesta, Errico, *Anarchy*. Further, he writes: "So, since it was thought that government was necessary and that without government there could only be disorder and confusion, it was natural and logical that anarchy, which means absence of government, should sound like absence of order." https://theanarchistlibrary.org/library/errico-malatesta-anarchy.

42 Proudhon, *What is Property?* The Anarchist Library; *le vol* is translated as "robbery."

43 Proudhon, *What is Property?* The Anarchist Library.

44 Proudhon, Pierre-Joseph, *Système de la raison publique, ou système social*, in Œuvres, Classcompilé no. 63, XLIII.
45 Freud, Sigmund, "Negation" [*Die Verneinung*], in *The Standard Edition of the Complete Psychological Works of Sigmund Freud* 19, trans. James Strachey (London: The Hogarth Press, The Institute of Psycho-Analysis, 1961), pp. 233–40.
46 Freud, "Negation," p. 233.
47 See Chapter 4 below.
48 Hobbes, Thomas, "Of the Kingdom of God by Nature," in *Leviathan*, ed. J. Gaskin (Oxford: Oxford University Press, 1998), p. 235.
49 Freud, Sigmund, *Civilization and its Discontents*, trans. James Strachey (New York: Norton, 1962), p. 59.
50 Derrida, Jacques, *Archive Fever: A Freudian Impression*, trans. Eric Prenowitz (Chicago, IL: University of Chicago Press, 1996), pp. 10–11.
51 Lordon, Frédéric, *Imperium: Structures and Affects of Political Bodies*, trans. Andy Bliss (London: Verso, 2022), p. 58.
52 Foucault, Michel, "*Society Must Be Defended*: Lectures at the Collège de France, 1975–76," ed. Mauro Bertani and Alessandro Fontana, trans. David Macey (New York: Picador, 2003), pp. 89–90.
53 Barnett, "The primacy of resistance," p. 326.
54 Barnett, "The primacy of resistance," p. 304.
55 Agamben, Giorgio, *Stasis: Civil War as a Political Paradigm*, trans. Nicholas Heron (Stanford, CA: Stanford University Press, 2015), p. 53.
56 Tiqqun, *Contribution à la guerre en cours. Introduction à la guerre civile* (Paris: La Fabrique, 2009), p. 59. [CS translation] Barnett is quite right when he notes that this "unorthodox" reading of Hobbes is also found in the work of Pierre Clastres in the chapters "Archéologie de la violence" and "Malheur du guerrier sauvage," in *La Société contre l'État* (Paris: Minuit, 1977). Deleuze and Guattari refer to Clastres in *A Thousand Plateaus*: "Clastres ... [identifies] *war* in primitive societies as the surest mechanism directed against the formation of the State: war maintains the dispersal and segmentarity of groups ... Clastres can thus invoke natural Law while reversing its principal proposition: just as Hobbes saw clearly that *the State was against war, so war is against the State*, and makes it impossible. It should not be concluded that war is a state of nature, but rather that it is the mode of a social state that wards off and prevents the State." *A Thousand Plateaus: Capitalism and Schizophrenia*, trans. Brian Massumi (London: Continuum, 1987 [1980]), p. 394.
57 Foucault, Michel, *The Birth of Biopolitics: Lectures at the Collège de France, 1978–1979*, trans. Graham Burchell (New York: Picador, 2010).
58 Foucault, *The Birth of Biopolitics*, p. 297.
59 Foucault, *The Birth of Biopolitics*, p. 295.

Chapter 3: On the Virtue of Chorus Leaders

1 Aristotle, *Politics*, Book 7, Chapter 14, p. 211. Translation modified.
2 Pellegrin, Pierre, Preface to Aristotle, *Les Politiques* (Paris: Flammarion, 2015), p. 10. [CS translation]
3 Schürmann, Reiner, *Heidegger on Being and Acting: From Principles to Anarchy*, trans. Christine-Marie Gros (Bloomington: Indiana University Press, 1987), p. 87.
4 Pellegrin, Preface to *Les Politiques*, p. 15. [CS translation]
5 *Politics* is one of Aristotle's "acroamatic" treatises; in other words, it is a text that collates his teachings.
6 Pellegrin, Preface to *Les Politiques*, p. 15. [CS translation]

7 Pellegrin, Preface to *Les Politiques*, p. 10. [CS translation]
8 Pellegrin, Preface to *Les Politiques*, p. 15. [CS translation]
9 Translator's note: While *politeia* is translated into French as "constitution," here it is translated throughout as "regime," except in the discussion of *The Athenian Constitution*, where it is rendered as "constitution," and the few occasions where "constitutional regime" is used for clarity.
10 Aristotle, *Politics*, Book 3, Chapter 1, 1274b 33, p. 62.
11 Aristotle, *Politics*, Book 1, Chapter 1, 1252a 7–8, p. 1.
12 Aristotle, *Politics*, Book 3, Chapter 1, p. 62.
13 Aristotle, *Politics*, Book 3, Chapter 1, p. 62.
14 Aristotle, *Politics*, Book 3, Chapter 1, 1275a 7, p. 62.
15 Aristotle, *Politics*, Book 3, Chapter 1, 1275a 18, p. 63.
16 Aristotle, *Politics*, Book 3, Chapter 1, 1275a 20–21, p. 63.
17 Aristotle, *Politics*, Book 3, Chapter 1, 1275a 24, p. 63.
18 Translator's note: in contemporary French usage, the terms "magistrate" and "judicial authorities" used in the translation have a more limited meaning than in this context. The English translation cited here uses the wider terms "decision and office."
19 Aristotle, *Politics*, Book 3, Chapter 1, 1275a 24–25, p. 63.
20 Aristotle, *Politics*, Book 3, Chapter 1, 1275a 31, p. 63.
21 Aristotle, *Politics*, Book 3, Chapter 1, 1275b 18–19, p. 64.
22 Aristotle, *Politics*, Book 3, Chapter 1, 1275b, p. 64.
23 Aristotle, *Politics*, Book 3, Chapter 4, 1277b 7–9, p. 69.
24 Aristotle, *Politics*, Book 3, Chapter 4, 1277b 9–17, p. 69.
25 Derrida, Jacques, *Rogues. Two Essays on Reason*, trans. Pascale-Anne Brault and Michael Naas (Stanford, CA: Stanford University Press, 2005), p. 13.
26 Aristotle, *Politics*, Book 3, Chapter 4, p. 67.
27 Aristotle, *Politics*, Book 3, Chapter 4, 1277b 17, p. 69.
28 Aristotle, *Politics*, Book 3, Chapter 4, 1276b 20–26, p. 67.
29 Aristotle, *Politics*, Book 3, Chapter 4, 1276b 34–36, p. 67.
30 Cournarie, Laurent, "Commentaire du Livre IV des *Politiques*," *Philopsis*, 2012, pp. 1–87: p. 33. [CS translation]
31 See Aristotle, *Nicomachean Ethics*, trans. W. D. Ross (Kitchener: Batoche Books, 1999), Book 6.
32 Aristotle, *Politics*, Book 3, Chapter 4, 1277a 15–17, p. 68.
33 Aristotle, *Politics*, Book 3, Chapter 4, 1277b 26–29, p. 69.
34 Muglioni, Jean-Marc, "Intelligence et moralité selon Aristote," "Aristote," in *Historia Philosophiae* (Paris: L'Harmattan, 2000), p. 11. [CS translation]
35 Aristotle, *Politics*, Book 3, Chapter 18, 1288b, p. 96.
36 Aristotle, *Politics*, Book 7, Chapter 14, 1333a, p. 212.
37 Aristotle, *Politics*, Book 7, Chapter 14, 1332b 41–42, p. 211. Translation modified.
38 Aristotle, *Politics*, Book 3, Chapter 3, 1276b, p. 66.
39 Aristotle, *Politics*, Book 3, Chapter 6, 1278b 11–12, p. 71.
40 Aristotle, *Politics*, Book 3, Chapter 7, 1279a 26–27, p. 73.
41 Aristotle, *Politics*, Book 4, Chapter 14, 1297b 41 – 1298a 1–3, p. 120.
42 Pellegrin, Preface to *Les Politiques*, p. 61. [CS translation]
43 Aristotle, *Politics*, Book 3, Chapter 12, 1282b 15, p. 81.
44 Aristotle, *Politics*, Book 4, Chapter 14, p. 120.
45 The "best regime" is introduced in Book 3, Chapter 4, 1276b 38, p. 67.
46 Aristotle, *Politics*, Book 3, Chapter 1, 1274b 33, p. 62.
47 Aristotle, *The Athenian Constitution* (Harmondsworth: Penguin, 1984).

48 Pellegrin, Pierre, "Preface," in *Constitution des Athéniens*, trans. Pierre Pellegrin and Marie Joséphine Werlings, in *Œuvres complètes* (Paris: Flammarion, 2014), p. 11. [CS translation]
49 See Aubenque, Pierre, "Aristote et la démocratie," in Pierre Aubenque and Alonso Tordesillas, *Aristote politique. Études sur la* Politique *d'Aristote* (Paris: Puf, 1993), pp. 255–64: p. 256.
50 Aristotle, *Politics,* Book 6, Chapter 2, p. 173. Aristotle notes that the citizen, "is a citizen above all in a democracy; he may, but will not necessarily, be a citizen in the others. In some regimes there is no people, nor is an assembly recognized in law, but [only a consultative meeting of specially] summoned persons, and cases are adjudicated by groups of officials." *Politics,* Book 3, Chapter 1, p. 63. In conditions other than democracy, the unconstrained office holder is no longer an assembly member or judge, but the holder of a defined office. Outside democracy, participation in deliberative and judicial functions is relative or weakened.
51 Aristotle, *Politics,* Book 6, Chapter 3, 1318a, p. 174.
52 Aristotle, *Politics,* Book 1, Chapter 12, p. 21.
53 Aristotle, *Politics,* Book 1, Chapter 12, p. 21, fn58. Translator's note: The French translation uses the word "subordination" to describe the female relation to the male; the English translation veers away from that assertion, writing: "The male always stands thus in relation to the female," in which "thus" refers to "Amasis, an Egyptian king of lowly origin, [who] had his subjects worship a statue of a god fashioned from a golden foot pan." This is a euphemism for what the French also defines as a "regime that never alternates."
54 Aristotle, *Politics,* Book 3, Chapter 4, 1277a 33–35, p. 68.
55 Aristotle, *Politics,* Book 1, especially Chapter 7, p. 11.
56 Aristotle, *Politics,* Book 3, Chapter 4, 1276b 38–42, p. 67.
57 Aristotle, *Politics,* Book 3, Chapter 4, 1277a 6–11, 67–8.
58 Aristotle, *Politics,* Book 3, Chapter 4, 1277a 8–9, pp. 67–8.

Chapter 4: Ontological Anarchy

1 Schürmann, Reiner, *Heidegger on Being and Acting: From Principles to Anarchy*, trans. Christine-Marie Gros (Bloomington: Indiana University Press, 1987), p. 121
2 Schürmann, *Heidegger on Being and Acting*, p. 9.
3 See *Des Hégémonies brisées* (Zurich: Diaphanes, 2017 [1996]), as well as the articles collected in *Tomorrow the Manifold. Essays on Foucault, Anarchy, and the Singularization to Come,* ed. Malte Fabian Rauch and Nicolas Schneider (Zurich: Diaphanes, 2019).
4 Schürmann, *Heidegger on Being and Acting*, p. 17.
5 Schürmann, *Heidegger on Being and Acting*, p. 272.
6 Schürmann, *Heidegger on Being and Acting*, p. 4.
7 Schürmann, *Heidegger on Being and Acting*, p. 5.
8 Translator's note: a reminder that the subtitle of the English translation of Schürmann's *Heidegger on Being and Acting* is *From Principles to Anarchy*, reflecting the main title in the French, *Le Principe d'anarchie*.
9 Schürmann, *Heidegger on Being and Acting*, p. 6.
10 Schürmann, *Heidegger on Being and Acting*, p. 20.
11 Schürmann, *Heidegger on Being and Acting*, p. 20.
12 Schürmann, *Heidegger on Being and Acting*, p. 20.
13 Schürmann, *Heidegger on Being and Acting*, p. 21.
14 Schürmann, *Heidegger on Being and Acting*, p. 292. Schürmann cites Proudhon, *What is Property?* trans. Benjamin R. Tucker (Princeton, 1876), pp. 28, 34, and Bakunin, *Oeuvres*, vol. III. (Paris, 1893), p. 82.

15 Schürmann, *Heidegger on Being and Acting*, p. 292.
16 Schürmann, *Heidegger on Being and Acting*, p. 292.
17 Schürmann, *Heidegger on Being and Acting*, pp. 6–7.
18 Schürmann, *Heidegger on Being and Acting*, p. 38.
19 Aristotle, *Metaphysics*, Book 5, trans. W. D. Ross (Infomotions, 2001), p. 48.
20 Aristotle, *Metaphysics*, Book 5, p. 48.
21 Rauch, Malte Fabien, and Schneider, Nicholas, "Of peremption and insurrection: Reiner Schürmann's encounter with Michel Foucault" in *Tomorrow the Manifold*, pp. 151–81: p. 153.
22 Schürmann, *Heidegger on Being and Acting*, p. 39.
23 Schürmann, *Heidegger on Being and Acting*, p. 5.
24 Schürmann, *Heidegger on Being and Acting*, p. 5.
25 Schürmann, *Heidegger on Being and Acting*, pp. 39–40. See also *Aristotle: Posterior Analytics. Topica*, trans. Hugh Tredennick and E. S. Forster (Cambridge, MA: Harvard University Press, 1960); *Organon* 4, Section V, ch. 19, §5.
26 Rauch and Schneider, "Of peremption and insurrection," p. 153.
27 Schürmann, *Heidegger on Being and Acting*, p. 85.
28 Schürmann, *Heidegger on Being and Acting*, p. 99.
29 Schürmann, *Heidegger on Being and Acting*, p. 97. The reference to Aristotle is *Metaphysics* 5:1, 1012b 34 to 1013a 17.
30 Heidegger, Martin, *Introduction to Metaphysics*, trans. Gregory Fried and Richard Polt (New Haven, CT: Yale University Press, 2000), p. 67.
31 Beaufret, Jean, "Hegel et la proposition spéculative," in *Dialogue avec Heidegger* (Paris: Minuit, 1973), p. 137. [CS translation]
32 See Schürmann, *Heidegger on Being and Acting*, p. 87.
33 Schürmann, *Heidegger on Being and Acting*, p. 99.
34 Schürmann, *Heidegger on Being and Acting*, p. 103.
35 Schürmann, *Heidegger on Being and Acting*, p. 104.
36 Schürmann, *Heidegger on Being and Acting*, p. 104.
37 Schürmann, *Heidegger on Being and Acting*, p. 103.
38 See Schürmann, *Heidegger on Being and Acting*, p. 83.
39 Schürmann, *Heidegger on Being and Acting*, p. 100.
40 Schürmann, *Heidegger on Being and Acting*, p. 103.
41 Schürmann, *Heidegger on Being and Acting*, p. 87.
42 Schürmann, *Heidegger on Being and Acting*, p. 103.
43 Schürmann, *Heidegger on Being and Acting*, p. 140.
44 Schürmann, *Heidegger on Being and Acting*, p. 106.
45 Schürmann, *Heidegger on Being and Acting*, p. 106.
46 Schürmann, *Heidegger on Being and Acting*, p. 112.
47 Schürmann, *Heidegger on Being and Acting*, p. 115.
48 Schürmann, *Heidegger on Being and Acting*, p. 110.
49 Schürmann, Reiner, "Legislation-transgression: Strategies and counter-strategies in the transcendental justification of norms," in *Tomorrow the Manifold*, pp. 77–120: p. 100.
50 Schürmann, *Heidegger on Being and Acting*, p. 108.
51 Breton, Stanislas, *Du Principe* (Paris: Cerf, 2011), p. 242. [CS translation]
52 Aristotle, *Metaphysics*, Book 5, p. 48.
53 Schürmann, *Heidegger on Being and Acting*, p. 30.
54 Schürmann, *Heidegger on Being and Acting*, p. 30.
55 Schürmann, *Heidegger on Being and Acting*, p. 95.

NOTES TO PP. 47–52

56 Schürmann, *Heidegger on Being and Acting*, pp. 12–13.
57 Schürmann, *Heidegger on Being and Acting*, p. 120.
58 Schürmann, *Heidegger on Being and Acting*, p. 91.
59 Schürmann, *Heidegger on Being and Acting*, p. 96.
60 Schürmann, *Heidegger on Being and Acting*, p. 121.
61 Schürmann, *Heidegger on Being and Acting*, p. 37. Translator's note: the last sentence in this passage is my translation since it is omitted in the English published translation.
62 Schürmann, *Heidegger on Being and Acting*, p. 243.
63 Schürmann, *Heidegger on Being and Acting*, p. 6.
64 Schürmann, *Heidegger on Being and Acting*, p. 3.
65 Schürmann, *Heidegger on Being and Acting*, p. 3.
66 Schürmann, as cited in Rauch and Schneider, "Of peremption and insurrection," p. 156.
67 Schürmann, *Heidegger on Being and Acting*, p. 253.
68 Translator's note: Schürmann, *Heidegger on Being and Acting*, p. 46. My translation, since this sentence is omitted in the English published translation.
69 Schürmann, *Heidegger on Being and Acting*, p. 95.
70 Schürmann, *Heidegger on Being and Acting*, p. 37.
71 Schürmann, *Heidegger on Being and Acting*, p. 37. Translator's note: the last sentence in this passage is my translation since it is omitted in the English published translation.
72 Schürmann, *Heidegger on Being and Acting*, p. 95.
73 Schürmann, Reiner, "L'hénologie comme dépassement de la métaphysique" [henology as an overcoming of metaphysics], *Les Études philosophiques*, 3 (July–September 1982), 331–350 [CS translation]. This French article should not be confused with a different article in English with a similar title, published a year later "Neoplatonic henology as an overcoming of metaphysics," *Research in Phenomenology*, 13 (1983), pp. 25–41.
74 Schürmann, "L'hénologie comme dépassement de la métaphysique," p. 332. [CS translation]
75 Schürmann, "L'hénologie comme dépassement de la métaphysique," p. 332. [CS translation]
76 Schürmann, "L'hénologie comme dépassement de la métaphysique," p. 334. [CS translation]
77 Schürmann, "L'hénologie comme dépassement de la métaphysique," p. 337. [CS translation]
78 Schürmann, "L'hénologie comme dépassement de la métaphysique," p. 337. [CS translation]
79 Schürmann, "L'hénologie comme dépassement de la métaphysique," p. 336. [CS translation]
80 There is also a reference to Heraclitus: "'Lightning is the pilot of all things.' The One sets all things in place – not as supreme agent, but the way a flash of lightning does." Schürmann, *Heidegger on Being and Acting*, p. 178.
81 Schürmann, "L'hénologie comme dépassement de la métaphysique," p. 337. [CS translation] Schürmann cites Plotinus, *Ennéades*, Book 5, Chapter 5 [32], 8, 23.
82 Schürmann, "L'hénologie comme dépassement de la métaphysique," p. 333. [CS translation]
83 Schürmann, "L'hénologie comme dépassement de la métaphysique," p. 338. [CS translation]
84 See Schürmann, *Heidegger on Being and Acting*, p. 273. See "anarchy does not mean anomy," p. 290.
85 See the reference from Deleuze to Plotinus' ontological anarchism in Chapter 5.
86 Schürmann, *Heidegger on Being and Acting*, p. 111.

87 Schürmann, "Legislation-transgression," in *Tomorrow the Manifold*, p. 118. Rauch and Schneider rightly emphasize that Schürmann's philosophical trajectory has a dual orientation. The first is the "line of deepening fissure leading to the disintegration of the metaphysical field: 'Marx, Nietzsche, and Heidegger'" (p. 156). The second is a more contemporary orientation that leads Schürmann to read Derrida, Deleuze, and especially Foucault.
88 Schürmann, "Legislation-transgression," in *Tomorrow the Manifold*, p. 120.
89 Schürmann "Legislation-transgression."
90 Foucault, Michel, "What is Enlightenment?" in Paul Rabinow, ed., *The Foucault Reader*, amended trans. Catherine Porter (New York: Pantheon Books, 1984), pp. 32–50: p. 45.
91 Foucault, "What is enlightenment?" p. 46.
92 In the epigraph to his article, Schürmann cites Derrida ("La loi du genre/The law of gender," trans. Avital Ronell, *Glyphe* 7 (1980), p. 204): "What if there were, lodged within the heart of law itself, a law of impurity or a principle of contamination? What if the condition for the possibility of law were the *a priori* of a counter-law, an axiom of impossibility, maddening its sense, order and reason": "Legislation-Transgression," p. 77.
93 Schürmann, "Legislation-transgression," p. 100.
94 Schürmann, "Legislation-transgression," p. 118.
95 Schürmann, "Legislation-transgression," p. 120.
96 Schürmann, "On constituting oneself as an anarchistic subject," in *Tomorrow the Manifold*, pp. 7–30.
97 Schürmann, *Heidegger on Being and Acting*, p. 11.
98 Schürmann, *Heidegger on Being and Acting*, p. 131.
99 Schürmann, *Heidegger on Being and Acting*, p. 122.
100 See "A rose that does not bloom, an adolescent who refuses to become and adult, a house that remains a building site," Schürmann, *Heidegger on Being and Acting*, p. 258.
101 Schürmann, "Ultimate double binds," in *Tomorrow the Manifold*, p. 135.
102 Schürmann, *Heidegger on Being and Acting*, p. 92.
103 Schürmann, *Heidegger on Being and Acting*, p. 92.
104 Schürmann, "L'hénologie comme dépassement de la métaphysique," p. 140. [CS translation]
105 Schürmann, "Legislation-transgression," p. 122, note 2. Schürmann elucidates: "Obviously, I am not retaining these features as they are used in social psychology."
106 Schürmann, "Legislation-transgression," p. 126.
107 Schürmann, "Legislation-transgression," p. 126.
108 Schürmann, "Legislation-transgression," pp. 127–8.
109 Schürmann, *Heidegger on Being and Acting*, p. 156. Schürmann specifies that the expression comes from Max Weber, p. 352, note 8.
110 Schürmann, *Heidegger on Being and Acting*, p. 156.
111 Schürmann, *Heidegger on Being and Acting*, p. 156.
112 Schürmann, *Heidegger on Being and Acting*, p. 147. See also "the legitimation of the anarchic origin requires a deduction," and then a delegitimation, p. 157.
113 Schürmann, *Heidegger on Being and Acting*, p. 26.
114 Wachtel, Nathan, *La Vision des vaincus. Les Indiens du Pérou devant la conquête espagnole (1530–1570)* (Paris: Gallimard, 1971). In a later book, Wachtel demonstrated that "there is perhaps a group that is even worse off than these conquered peoples: the 'conquered of the conquered,' the Urus Indians, who, in the 16th century, were a quarter of the population of the high plains of Bolivia and who, marginalized by the majority Aymaras, still live today under a condition of indifference and scorn": *Le Retour des ancêtres. Les Indiens Urus de Bolivie, XXe–XVIe siècle. Essai d'histoire régressive*

(Paris: Gallimard, 1990). See Daniel Bermond, "Nathan Wachtel: l'écho des vaincus," *L'Histoire*, April 2009.
115 Schürmann, *Heidegger on Being and Acting*, p. 163.
116 Schürmann, *Heidegger on Being and Acting*, p. 166.
117 Schürmann, *Heidegger on Being and Acting*, p. 146.
118 Schürmann, *Heidegger on Being and Acting*, p. 29.
119 Schürmann, *Heidegger on Being and Acting*, p. 26.
120 Schürmann, *Heidegger on Being and Acting*, p. 27.
121 Schürmann, *Heidegger on Being and Acting*, pp. 26–7.
122 Schürmann, *Heidegger on Being and Acting*, p. 27. Schürmann describes the organization in considerable details, especially on pp. 27–8.
123 Schürmann, *Heidegger on Being and Acting*, p. 27.
124 Schürmann, *Heidegger on Being and Acting*, p. 28.
125 Schürmann, *Heidegger on Being and Acting*.
126 Schürmann, *Heidegger on Being and Acting*, p. 146.
127 Schürmann, *Heidegger on Being and Acting*, p. 163.
128 Schürmann, *Heidegger on Being and Acting*, p. 167.
129 Schürmann, *Heidegger on Being and Acting*, p. 167.
130 Schürmann, *Heidegger on Being and Acting*, p. 167.
131 Schürmann, *Heidegger on Being and Acting*, p. 29.
132 Schürmann, *Heidegger on Being and Acting*, p. 29.
133 Schürmann, *Heidegger on Being and Acting*, p. 35.
134 See in particular "Colonialidad y modernidad/racionalidad," *Perú indígena*, 13(29), 1922, available as "Coloniality and modernity/rationality," in Goran Therborn, ed., *Globalizations and Modernities* (Stockholm: Forksningsradnämnden, 1999). "Decolonial thought" is also the name of a group of Latin American theorists who originally collaborated in the "Modernity/coloniality" research program: Anibal Quijano, Enrique Dussel, Ramon Grosfoguel, Walter Mignolo.
135 Cited in Ramon Grosfogel, "Decolonizing Western uni-versalisms: Decolonial pluri-versalism from Aimé Césaire to the Zapatistas," *Transmodernity, Journal of Peripheral Cultural Production of the LusoHispanic World*, 1/3 (2012), pp. 88–104: p. 89. See also Enrique Dussel, *Filosofía de la liberación* (Edicol: Ciudad de México, 1977), and *1492: El encubrimiento del Otro: hacia el origen del "mito de la modernidad"* (La Paz: Plural Editores, 1994).
136 Schürmann, *Heidegger on Being and Acting*, p. 303.
137 Schürmann, *Heidegger on Being and Acting*, p. 236. Translator's note: the sentence in brackets in this quote is missing from the English translation of the French text.

Chapter 5: Ethical Anarchy

1 Levinas, Emmanuel, *Otherwise than Being, or Beyond Essence*, trans. Alphonso Lingis (Pittsburgh, PA: Duquesne University Press, 1981), p. 52.
2 Levinas, *Otherwise than Being*, p. 138.
3 Claudel, Paul, cited by Michel Autrand, "Les saisons noires du jeune Claudel, 1882–1895," *Revue d'histoire littéraire de la France*, 3/9 (1993): p. 400. [CS translation]
4 Levinas, *Otherwise than Being*, p. 194.
5 Abensour, Miguel, *Emmanuel Levinas, l'intrigue de l'humain. Entre métapolitique et politique. Entretiens avec Danielle Cohen Levinas* (Paris: Hermann, 2012), p. 47. [CS translation]
6 See the chapter "Walter Benjamin et l'anarchism," in Michael Löwy, *La Révolution est le frein d'urgence. Essais sur Walter Benjamin* (Paris: Éditions de l'Éclat, 2019).

7 This idea is present from the first lines of Emmanuel Levinas, *Totality and Infinity. An Essay on Exteriority*, trans. Alphonso Lingis (Pittsburgh, PA: Duquesne University Press, 1969).
8 Levinas, *Totality and Infinity*, p. 303.
9 Levinas, *Totality and Infinity*, p. 46; emphasis mine.
10 Levinas, *Totality and Infinity*, p. 293.
11 Levinas, *Otherwise than Being*, p. 99.
12 Levinas, *Otherwise than Being*, p. 8.
13 Levinas, *Otherwise than Being*, p. 11.
14 Levinas, *Otherwise than Being*, p. 118.
15 Levinas, *Otherwise than Being*, p. 188.
16 Levinas, *Otherwise than Being*, p. 106.
17 Levinas, *Otherwise than Being*, p. 119.
18 Levinas, *Otherwise than Being*, p. 7.
19 Levinas, *Otherwise than Being*, p. 113.
20 Levinas, *Otherwise than Being*, p. 115.
21 Levinas, *Otherwise than Being*, p. 113.
22 Levinas, *Otherwise than Being*, p. 101.
23 Derrida, Jacques, *Adieu to Emmanuel Levinas* (Stanford, CA: Stanford University Press, 1999), p. 70.
24 Derrida, *Adieu to Emmanuel Levinas*, p. 33.
25 Levinas, *Otherwise than Being*, p. 6.
26 See Jean-Luc Marion's talk at the international conference "René Girard – Emmanuel Lévinas: du sacré au saint," held on November 4, 2013 at the École normale supérieure in Paris. [CS translation]
27 Levinas, *Otherwise than Being*, p. 103.
28 Levinas, *Otherwise than Being*, p. 196.
29 Levinas, *Otherwise than Being*, p. 194.
30 Levinas, *Otherwise than Being*, p. 113.
31 Levinas, "Reflections on the philosophy of Hitlerism," trans. Sean Hand, *Critical Inquiry*, 17/1 (Autumn 1990), pp. 62–71: p. 63.
32 Levinas, "Reflections on the philosophy of Hitlerism," p. 63.
33 Levinas, "Reflections on the philosophy of Hitlerism," p. 63.
34 Levinas, *Otherwise than Being*, p. 87.
35 Levinas, *Otherwise than Being*, p. 13.
36 Levinas, *Otherwise than Being*, p. 148.
37 Levinas, *Humanism of the Other*, p. 54.
38 Levinas, *Otherwise than Being*, p. 13.
39 Levinas, *Otherwise than Being*, p. 100.
40 Levinas, *Totality and Infinity*, p. 228.
41 Levinas, "Reflections on the philosophy of Hitlerism," p. 64.
42 See Kant, Immanuel, *Foundations of the Metaphysics of Morals*, 2nd rev. ed., trans. Lewis White Beck (Upper Saddle River, NJ: Prentice Hall, 1997), pp. 57–8.
43 Levinas, Emmanuel, *Discovering Existence with Husserl*, trans. Richard A. Cohen and Michael B. Smith (Evanston, IL: Northwestern University Press, 1998). Translator's note: the English translation does not include all the essays in the French edition; notably, "La philosophie et l'idée de l'infini" [philosophy and the idea of the infinite] is not included.
44 Levinas, Emmanuel, *En découvrant l'existence avec Husserl et Heidegger* (Paris: Vrin, 2001), p. 178. [CS translation]
45 Levinas, *Totality and Infinity*, p. 46.

46 Levinas, *Totality and Infinity*, p. 45.
47 Robbins, Jill, ed., *Is It Righteous to Be? Interviews with Emmanuel Levinas* (Stanford, CA: Meridian, 2001), p. 165.
48 Levinas, Emmanuel, *Difficult Freedom: Essays on Judaism*, trans. Seán Hand (Baltimore, MD: Johns Hopkins University Press, 1990), p. 295.
49 Levinas, *Otherwise than Being*, p. 56.
50 Levinas, Emmanuel, "Humanism and An-Archy" in *Humanism of the Other*, trans. Nidra Poller (Champaign: University of Illinois Press, 2003), p. 52.
51 Levinas, Emmanuel, *God, Death and Time*, trans. Bettina Bergo (Stanford, CA: Stanford University Press, 2000), p. 152.
52 Levinas, *Otherwise than Being*, p. 54.
53 Levinas, *God, Death and Time*, p. 179.
54 Levinas, *Otherwise than Being*, p. 70
55 Levinas, *Totality and Infinity*, p. 88.
56 Levinas, *Otherwise than Being*, p. 148.
57 Levinas, *Otherwise than Being*, p. 10.
58 Levinas, "Humanism and an-archy," p. 53.
59 Levinas, *Otherwise than Being*, p. 135.
60 Levinas, *Otherwise than Being*, p. 105.
61 Levinas, "Freedom and command," in *Collected Philosophical Papers*, trans. Alphonso Lingis (Dordrecht: Martinus Nijhoff, 1987), pp. 15–23: p. 16.
62 Levinas, "Freedom and command," p. 16.
63 Levinas, "Humanism and an-archy," p. 52.
64 Levinas, "Humanism and an-archy," p. 52.
65 See the chapter "Possession and labor," in Levinas, *Totality and Infinity*.
66 See "Humanism and an-archy," p. 52: the slave "must keep a memory of the present when the determining determined it and was its contemporary." Further on, Levinas continues: "the part – be it infinitesimal – of freedom necessary for the condition of servitude."
67 Blanchot, Maurice, *The Infinite Conversation*, trans. Susan Hanson (Minneapolis: University of Minnesota Press, 1993), p. 173.
68 Blanchot, *The Infinite Conversation*, p. 175.
69 Levinas, *Totality and Infinity*, p. 300.
70 Levinas, Emmanuel, in the essay "Judaism and Revolution," in "From the Sacred to the Holy: Five New Talmudic Readings," in *Nine Talmudic Readings*, trans. Annette Aronowicz (Bloomington: Indiana University Press, 1990), p. 98.
71 Levinas, "Humanism and an-archy," p. 53.
72 Levinas, *Beyond the Verse*, p. 10.
73 Blanchot, Maurice, "Prophetic speech," in *The Book to Come*, trans. Charlotte Mandell (Stanford, CA: Stanford University Press, 2003), p. 80.
74 Levinas, Emmanuel, *In the Time of the Nations*, trans. Michael B. Smith (London: The Athlone Press, 1994): "The Jew is free *qua* affranchised: his memory is immediately compassion for all the enslaved or all the wretched of the earth, and a special flair for that wretchedness that the wretched themselves are prone to forget," p. 78.
75 Levinas, *Difficult Freedom*, p. 152.
76 Levinas, "From the sacred to the holy," p. 97.
77 Levinas, Emmanuel, *Beyond the Verse: Talmudic Readings and Lectures*, trans. Gary D. Mole (Bloomington: Indiana University Press, 1994), p. 10.
78 Levinas, *Beyond the Verse*, p. 10.
79 Levinas, "From the sacred to the holy," p. 115.
80 Levinas, "From the sacred to the holy," p. 98.

81 Levinas, "From the sacred to the holy," p. 98.
82 Derrida, *Adieu to Emmanuel Levinas*, p. 70.
83 Levinas, *Beyond the Verse*, p. 4.
84 Levinas, *Humanism of the Other*, p. 66.
85 Levinas, "From the sacred to the holy," p. 99.
86 Levinas, "Freedom and command," p. 17.
87 Levinas, *Totality and Infinity*, p. 303.
88 See Abensour, *Emmanuel Levinas*, p. 65. [CS translation]
89 Levinas, *Beyond the Verse*, p. 188.
90 Abensour, *Emmanuel Levinas*, p. 82. [CS translation]
91 Abensour, *Emmanuel Levinas*, p. 71. [CS translation]
92 Abensour, *Emmanuel Levinas*, pp. 30–1. [CS translation]
93 Cited in Abensour, *Emmanuel Levinas*, p. 55.
94 Levinas, *Otherwise than Being*, p. 4; see also Abensour, *Emmanuel Levinas*, p. 67.
95 Cited in Abensour, *Emmanuel Levinas*, p. 66. [CS translation]
96 Abensour, *Emmanuel Levinas*, p. 117; see also Levinas, *Beyond the Verse*, p. 184.
97 Abensour, *Emmanuel Levinas*, p. 117; see also Levinas, *Beyond the Verse*, p. 184.
98 Levinas, *Beyond the Verse*, p. 181.
99 Levinas, "Substitution" (1996), in *Basic Philosophical Writings*, ed. Adriaan Peperzak, Simon Critchley, and Robert Bernasconi (Bloomington: Indiana University Press, 1998), pp. 79–96: p. 91.
100 "Nouvelles lectures talmudiques" is the title of Chapter 2 in the French version of *Nine Talmudic Readings*. It is not included in the English translation.
101 Abensour, *Emmanuel Levinas*, p. 74. [CS translation]
102 Derrida, *Adieu to Emmanuel Levinas*, p. 76.
103 In the state of David as conceived by Levinas ("The state open to the best, always on the alert, always ready for renovation, always returning to a free people that delegate freedom subject to reason to it without separating themselves from it"), Abensour reads an example of politics that goes beyond the limits of the nation of Israel, beyond a territory to incarnate the universal promise of an emancipation from all domination. It throws a "bridge to utopia," p. 52. [CS translation]
104 Pierre Hayat, "Emmanuel Levinas: une intuition du social," *Le Philosophoire*, 32/2 (2009), pp. 127–37: p. 134. [CS translation]
105 Cited in Hayat, "Emmanuel Levinas," p. 136. [CS translation]
106 Cited in Hayat, "Emmanuel Levinas," p. 136. [CS translation]
107 Levinas, *Humanism of the Other*, p. 69.
108 Levinas, *Humanism of the Other*, note p. 76.
109 Levinas, *Humanism of the Other*, p. 69.
110 Levinas, *Humanism of the Other*, note p. 76.
111 http://www.larousse.fr/dictionnaires/francais/esclave/30979 [CS translation]. See also Convention to Suppress the Slave Trade and Slavery (1926) League of Nations: "Article 1: For the purpose of the present Convention, the following definitions are agreed upon: (1) Slavery is the status or condition of a person over whom any or all of the powers attaching to the right of ownership are exercised. (2) The slave trade includes all acts involved in the capture, acquisition or disposal of a person with intent to reduce him to slavery; all acts involved in the acquisition of a slave with a view to selling or exchanging him; all acts of disposal by sale or exchange of a slave acquired with a view to being sold or exchanged, and, in general, every act of trade or transport in slaves."
112 Aristotle, *Politics*, Book 1, 4, 1253b 33–1254a8.
113 Aristotle, *Politics*, Book 3, 1280a 33–34; Book 7, 1328a 37–38, 1331b 9.

114 Aristotle, *Politics*, Book 1, 1255b 11–12, 1254b 4–5.
115 Montesquieu, *The Spirit of the Laws*, trans. Thomas Nugent (Kitchener: Batoche Books, 2001 [1752]), p. 264.
116 Barro, Abdoulaye, "Phénoménologie des identités juives et noires," *Pardes*, 44/1 (2008), pp. 57–75: p. 58. [CS translation]
117 Barro, "Phénoménologie des identités juives et noires," p. 58. [CS translation]
118 Du Bois, W. E. B., *The Souls of Black Folk* (New Haven, CT: Yale University Press, 2015).
119 Barro, "Phénoménologie des identités juives et noires," p. 58. [CS translation]
120 Glissant, Edouard, *Poetics of Relation*, trans. Betsy Wing (Ann Arbor: University of Michigan Press, 1997), p. 8. Cited by François Noudelmann in "La Traite, la Shoah, sur les usages d'une comparaison" [the slave trade, Shoah, and the uses of a comparison], *Littératures*, 2, 174 (2014), pp. 104–13: p. 106.
121 Glissant, *Poetics of Relation*, p. 8.
122 Noudelmann "La Traite, la Shoah, sur les usages d'une comparaison," p. 105. [CS translation]
123 Noudelmann, "La Traite, la Shoah, sur les usages d'une comparaison," p. 105. [CS translation]

Chapter 6: "Responsible Anarchism"

1 Derrida, Jacques, "Deconstruction and the Other: An interview with Derrida," in Richard Kearney, *Dialogues with Contemporary Continental Thinkers: The Phenomenological Heritage* (Manchester: Manchester University Press, 1984), pp. 113–35: pp. 120–1.
2 Derrida, Jacques, *The Post Card: From Socrates to Freud and Beyond*, trans. Alan Bass (Chicago, IL: University of Chicago Press, 1987), p. 265. Translator's note: translation modified – *denegation* is translated throughout as "disavowal."
3 Derrida, Jacques, "Force of law: The 'mystical foundation of authority," trans. Mary Quaintance, *Cardozo Law Review*, 11/5–6 (July/August, 1990), pp. 920–1046: p. 995.
4 Derrida, "Force of law," p. 995.
5 Derrida, "Force of law," p. 995.
6 Derrida, "Force of law," p. 995.
7 Derrida, "Force of law," pp. 995–7.
8 Derrida, "Force of law," p. 995.
9 Derrida, "Force of law," p. 997. Derrida adds that this is why these "Benjaminian oppositions seem … to call more than ever for deconstruction."
10 Might the disavowal be found in some of Derrida's silences? His silence on Mallarmé's significant relation to anarchism, for example? Or on the place of *Heliogabalus or, the Crowned Anarchist* in Artaud's work? These silences are certainly surprising in such a meticulous reader. However, a listing of these shadowy phenomena would not be grounds for an accusation of disavowal, which his indefatigable anarchic shifts between yes and no would immediately refute. The anarchism of Mallarmé and Artaud, he would say, appears exactly in the spot where it's least expected and there's certainly no need to go looking for it only where it is named explicitly.
11 Derrida, *Resistances of Psychoanalysis*, trans. Peggy Kamuf, Pascale-Anne Brault, and Michael Naas (Stanford, CA: Stanford University Press, 1998), p. 116.
12 See Derrida, *Of Grammatology*, pp. 150–1.
13 See "Violence and metaphysics," in *Writing and Difference*, trans. Alan Bass (Chicago, IL: University of Chicago Press, 1978 [1967]), *Passions* (Paris: Galilée, 1993), and *Adieu to Emmanuel Levinas*, trans. Pascale-Anne Brault and Miochael Naas (Stanford, CA: Stanford University Press, 1996).
14 The discussion with Freud is a thread that runs throughout Derrida's work: in his

seminar "La vie la mort" (1975–77), then in "To speculate – on 'Freud'" in *The Post Card*, in *Resistances of Psychoanalysis*, and finally in *Archive Fever*, trans. Eric Prenowitz (Chicago, IL: University of Chicago Press, 1996) and *Psychoanalysis Searches for the States of Its Soul: Address to the States General of Psychoanalysis* (Stanford, CA: Stanford University Press, 2002).

15 Freud, Sigmund, *Beyond the Pleasure Principle* in *The Standard Edition of the Complete Psychological Works of Sigmund Freud*, trans. James Strachey, vol. 18 (1920–22) (London: Hogarth Press and the Institute of Psychoanalysis, 1955), pp. 7–64: p. 7.
16 Freud, *Beyond the Pleasure Principle*, p. 11.
17 Derrida, *Resistances of Psychoanalysis*, p. 33. See also the theme of the divisibility of the *archē*, in Derrida, *Archive Fever*, p. 2.
18 Derrida, Jacques, *Memoires for Paul de Man*, trans. Cecile Lindsay, Jonathan Culler, and Eduardo Cadava (New York: Columbia University Press, 1986), p. 72.
19 Derrida, *The Post Card*, p. 54.
20 Derrida, *Archive Fever*, pp. 10–11.
21 Derrida, "To speculate – on 'Freud'," p. 404.
22 Derrida, "To speculate – on 'Freud'," p. 399.
23 Derrida, *Resistances of Psychoanalysis*, p. 27.
24 Derrida, *Archive Fever*, p. 1.
25 Derrida, *Archive Fever*, p. 1.
26 Derrida, Jacques, "The *retrait* of metaphor," in *Psyche: Inventions of the Other* (Stanford, CA: Stanford University Press, 2007), p. 57.
27 Derrida, *Resistances of Psychoanalysis*, p. 26.
28 Derrida, *Resistances of Psychoanalysis*, p. 26.
29 Cited in Derrida, *Of Grammatology*, trans. Gayatri Chakravorty Spivak (Baltimore, MD: Johns Hopkins University Press, 2016), p. 136.
30 Derrida, *Of Grammatology*, p. 138.
31 A taste of power that he had not known before this intrusion. See the analysis by Pierre Clastres: "Hence there is no king in the tribe, but a chief who is not a chief of State. What does that imply? Simply that the chief has no authority at his disposal, no power of coercion, no means of giving an order. The chief is not a commander; the people of the tribe are under no obligation to obey. *The space of the chieftainship is not the locus of power,* and the 'profile' of the primitive chief in no way foreshadows that of a future despot. There is nothing about the chieftainship that suggests the State apparatus derived from it": *Society against the State*, trans. Robert Hurley in collaboration with Abe Stein (New York: Zone Books, 1989), pp. 131–2.
32 Derrida, *Of Grammatology*, p. 128.
33 Derrida, *Of Grammatology*, p. 143.
34 Cited in a letter written by Lévi-Strauss in *Of Grammatology*, p. 130.
35 Derrida, *Of Grammatology*, pp. 150–1.
36 Derrida, *Of Grammatology*, p. 151.
37 Derrida, *Of Grammatology*, pp. 142–3.
38 Derrida, *Of Grammatology*, p. 145.
39 Derrida, *Of Grammatology*, p. 152.
40 Derrida, *Of Grammatology*, pp. 141–2.
41 Derrida, *Archive Fever*, p. 2.
42 Derrida, Jacques, "Différance," in *Margins of Philosophy*, trans. Alan Bass (Chicago, IL: University of Chicago Press, 1982), p. 6.
43 Derrida, *The Truth in Painting*, trans. Geoff Bennington and Ian McLeod (Chicago, IL: University of Chicago Press, 1987), p. 118.

44 Derrida, "La parole soufflée," in *Writing and Difference*, p. 179.
45 Derrida, "La parole soufflée," in *Writing and Difference*, p. 175.
46 Derrida, *Of Grammatology*, pp. 75–6.
47 Derrida, *Of Grammatology*, p. 76.
48 Derrida, "To speculate – on 'Freud'," p. 405
49 Derrida, *Of Grammatology*, p. 66.
50 Derrida, *Of Grammatology*, p. 66.
51 Derrida, "Violence and metaphysics," in *Writing and Difference*, p. 123.
52 Derrida, *Adieu to Emmanuel Levinas*, p. 90.
53 Derrida, "Violence and metaphysics," p. 151.
54 Derrida, "Violence and metaphysics," p. 128.
55 Derrida, "Violence and metaphysics," p. 128.
56 Derrida, "Violence and metaphysics," p. 147.
57 Derrida, "Violence and metaphysics," p. 129.
58 Derrida, "Violence and metaphysics," p. 147.
59 Derrida, "Violence and metaphysics," p. 146.
60 Derrida, "Violence and metaphysics," p. 147.
61 Derrida, "Violence and metaphysics," p. 146.
62 Derrida, "Violence and metaphysics," p. 128.
63 Derrida, *Of Grammatology*, p. 67; emphasis mine.
64 Derrida, *Of Grammatology*, p. 66.
65 Derrida, *Of Grammatology*, p. 66.
66 Derrida, *Resistances of Psychoanalysis*, p. 103.
67 Derrida, "To speculate – on 'Freud'," p. 405.
68 Derrida, "To speculate – on 'Freud'," p. 404.
69 Derrida, "To speculate – on 'Freud'," p. 404.
70 Freud, *Beyond the Pleasure Principle*, p. 22.
71 Freud, *Beyond the Pleasure Principle*, p. 31.
72 Freud, *Beyond the Pleasure Principle*, p. 35.
73 Freud, *Beyond the Pleasure Principle*, p. 13.
74 Freud, *Beyond the Pleasure Principle*, p. 16.
75 Freud, *Beyond the Pleasure Principle*, p. 15.
76 Freud, *Beyond the Pleasure Principle*, p. 16.
77 Freud, *Beyond the Pleasure Principle*, p. 16. See Derrida's commentary in "To speculate – on 'Freud'," p. 318.
78 Freud, *Beyond the Pleasure Principle*, p. 35.
79 Freud, *Beyond the Pleasure Principle*, p. 36.
80 Freud, *Beyond the Pleasure Principle*, p. 36.
81 Freud, *Beyond the Pleasure Principle*, p. 36.
82 Freud, *Beyond the Pleasure Principle*, p. 38.
83 Freud, *Beyond the Pleasure Principle*, p. 38.
84 Freud, *Beyond the Pleasure Principle*, p. 54.
85 Freud, *Beyond the Pleasure Principle*, p. 55.
86 The Nirvana principle is described in an even more ambiguous manner in *Beyond the Pleasure Principle*. Freud in fact describes it as a principle of constancy, which may allow it to be confused with the pleasure principle. But in 1924, in *The Economic Principle in Masochism*, he clearly recognizes that "the Nirvana principle expresses the trend of the death instinct," and thus, as Laplanche and Pontalis put it, "something more than a law of constancy or homeostasis"; see Jean Laplanche and Jean-Bertrand Pontalis, *The Language of Psychoanalysis*, trans. Donald Nicholson-Smith (New York: Norton, 1973), pp. 272–3.

87 Laplanche and Pontalis, *The Language of Psychoanalysis*, p. 272.
88 Derrida, "To speculate – on 'Freud'," p. 325.
89 See Derrida, "To speculate – on 'Freud'," p. 400.
90 Derrida, "To speculate – on 'Freud'," p. 348.
91 Derrida, "To speculate – on 'Freud'," p. 269.
92 Derrida, "To speculate – on 'Freud'," p. 404.
93 Derrida, "To speculate – on 'Freud'," p. 318.
94 Derrida, "To speculate – on 'Freud'," p. 317.
95 Derrida, "To speculate – on 'Freud'," p. 283.
96 Derrida, "To speculate – on 'Freud'," p. 405.
97 Derrida, "To speculate – on 'Freud'," p. 404.
98 Derrida, "To speculate – on 'Freud'," p. 404.
99 Derrida, "To speculate – on 'Freud'," p. 356.
100 Freud, *Civilization and its Discontents*, pp. 65–6.
101 Freud, *Beyond the Pleasure Principle*, p. 39.
102 Derrida, "To speculate – on 'Freud'," p. 403.
103 Derrida, "To speculate – on 'Freud'," pp. 392–3.
104 Derrida, "To speculate – on 'Freud'," p. 283.
105 Freud, *Beyond the Pleasure Principle*, pp. 53–4.
106 Freud, *Beyond the Pleasure Principle*, p. 54.
107 Freud, *Civilization and its Discontents*, p. 66.
108 Freud, *Civilization and its Discontents*, p. 66.
109 Apparently, Freud never imagined for a minute that political-social state cohesiveness could be shaken by anything other than the destruction instinct.
110 Zaltzman, Nathalie, "La pulsion anarchiste," in *Psyche anarchiste. Débattre avec Nathalie Zaltzman* (Paris: Puf, 2011), p. 53. [CS translation]
111 See Zaltzman, "La pulsion anarchiste," pp. 56–7. [CS translation]
112 Scarfone, Dominique, "Besoin, emprise, 'régression' et anarchie," in Zaltzman, "La pulsion anarchiste," p. 117. [CS translation]
113 Derrida, *Resistances of Psychoanalysis*, p. 117.
114 Derrida, *Resistances of Psychoanalysis*, p. 117.
115 Derrida, *Resistances of Psychoanalysis*, p. 117.
116 Derrida, "To Speculate – on 'Freud'," p. 405.
117 Derrida, "Autoimmunity: Real and symbolic suicides: A dialogue with Jacques Derrida," in Giovanna Borradori, *Philosophy in a Time of Terror: Dialogues with Jürgen Habermas and Jacques Derrida* (Chicago, IL: University of Chicago Press, 2003).
118 Derrida, "Autoimmunity: Real and symbolic suicides," p. 93.
119 Derrida, "Autoimmunity: Real and symbolic suicides," p. 110.
120 Derrida, "Autoimmunity: Real and symbolic suicides," pp. 102–3.
121 Derrida reminds us that Einstein, in *Why War?*, demonstrated that a "'craving for power' … characterizes the governing class of every nation": "Psychoanalysis searches the states of its soul. Address to the states general of psychoanalysis," in *Without Alibi*, ed. and trans. Peggy Kamuf (Stanford, CA: Stanford University Press, 2002), p. 251.
122 Derrida, "Psychoanalysis searches the states of its soul," p. 241.
123 Derrida, "Psychoanalysis searches the states of its soul," p. 254.
124 Derrida, Jacques. *Faith and Knowledge: The Two Sources of Religion in Acts of Religion and the Limits of Reason Alone*, trans. Samuel Weber, in *Acts of Religion*, ed. Gil Anidjar (New York: Routledge, 2002), p. 55.
125 Derrida, "Psychoanalysis searches the states of its soul," p. 252.
126 See, for example, Derrida, *Rogues*, pp. 36–7, 76ff.

127 See Derrida, Jacques, *Specters of Marx*, trans. Peggy Kamuf (New York: Routledge, 1994); see in particular the discussion of Fukuyama's theses, pp. 68–95.
128 Derrida, *Rogues*, p. 10.
129 Derrida, *Rogues*, see pp. 36–9.
130 Derrida, "Autoimmunity: Real and symbolic suicides," p. 121.
131 Derrida, "Autoimmunity: Real and symbolic suicides," pp. 113–14.
132 Derrida, *Faith and Knowledge*, p. 94, translation modified.
133 Derrida, *Faith and Knowledge*, p. 94, translation modified.
134 Boudou, Benjamin, "La traversée du politique: Derrida et Ricœur entre pureté de la philosophie et tragique de l'action," trans. JPD Systems. *Raisons Politiques*, 45/1 (2012), pp. 211–33: p. 215.
135 Derrida, "The crisis in teaching," in *Who's Afraid of Philosophy? Right to Philosophy 1*, trans. Jan Plug (Stanford, CA: Stanford University Press, 2022), pp. 115–16.
136 Derrida, "The crisis in teaching," p. 115.
137 Derrida, "Mastery and measure," in *Rogues*, p. 43.
138 Translator's note: the English translation erases the word *liberté* (freedom) and downplays Derrida's admission still further. The expression "*mettre en veilleuse*" that Malabou emphasizes becomes nothing more than "with some caution" in the English.
139 Ramond, Charles, "Derrida, éléments d'un lexique politique," *Cités*, 30/2 (2007), pp. 143–51, p. 148. [CS translation]
140 Derrida, *Rogues*, p. 65.
141 Derrida, *Rogues*, p. 66.

Chapter 7: Anarcheology

1 Foucault, Michel, *The Government of Self and Others: Lectures at the Collège de France 1982–1983*, trans. Graham Burchell (New York: Palgrave Macmillan, 2010), p. 292.
2 Foucault, Michel, *On the Government of the Living, Lectures at the Collège de France 1979–1980*, trans. Graham Burchell (New York: Palgrave Macmillan, 2014), p. 36.
3 Foucault, Michel, "La vérité et ses formes juridiques," in *Dits et Ecrits* I (Paris: Gallimard, 2001), p. 1510. Translator's note: See "Truth and juridical forms," in *Power*, ed. James D. Faubion, trans. Robert Hurley et al. (New York: New Press, 2000), pp. 1–89; this quote does not appear in the English version, hence my translation.
4 Foucault, Michel, "The ethics of the concern for self as a practice of freedom" (1984), in *Ethics: Subjectivity and Truth*, ed. Paul Rabinow, trans. Robert Hurley et al. (New York: The New Press, 1997), pp. 281–301: p. 282.
5 Foucault, "The ethics of the concern for self," p. 282.
6 Foucault, Michel, "*Society Must Be Defended*: Lectures at the Collège de France, 1975–76," ed. Mauro Bertani and Alessandro Fontana, trans. David Macey (New York: Picador, 2003), pp. 89–90: p. 260. He adds: "Socialism was a racism from the outset, even in the nineteenth century. No matter whether it is Fourier at the beginning of the century or the anarchists at the end of it, you will always find a racist component in socialism," p. 261.
7 In "La vérité et ses formes juridiques," Foucault plays with his interlocutor, responding, when asked about revolution: "On that point, I would be far more anarchist," p. 1510. [CS translation]
8 Foucault, *On the Government of the Living*, p. 78.
9 Foucault, *On the Government of the Living*, p. 79.
10 Foucault, *On the Government of the Living*, p. 77.
11 May, Todd, "Anarchism from Foucault to Rancière," in *Contemporary Anarchist Studies. An Introductory Anthology of Anarchy in the Academy*, ed. Randall Amster et al. (London: Routledge, 2009), pp. 11–17: p. 11.

12 Newman, Saul, *From Bakunin to Lacan: Anti-Authoritarianism and the Dislocation of Power* (New York: Lexington Books, 2001), p. 157. Foucault's thought has thus become an essential point of reference for contemporary anarchism, as is also suggested by the emergence of Anarchist Studies and Resistance Studies, which have become independent disciplinary fields in social and political thought in the United States. See Randall Amster et al., "Introduction," in *Contemporary Anarchist Studies*, pp. 1–7.
13 Foucault, *Society Must Be Defended*, p. 88.
14 Foucault, *Society Must Be Defended*, p. 97.
15 Foucault, *Society Must Be Defended*, pp. 107–8.
16 Foucault, *Society Must Be Defended*, pp. 108–9.
17 Foucault, *Society Must Be Defended*, p. 16.
18 Foucault, Michel, "Sex, power, and the politics of identity," in *Ethics: Subjectivity and Truth*, pp. 163–73: p. 167; my emphasis.
19 Foucault, Michel, "The subject and power," in Hubert L. Dreyfus and Paul M. Rabinow, eds., *Beyond Structuralism and Hermeneutics* (Chicago: University of Chicago Press, 1983), pp. 208–26: p. 222.
20 Foucault, "The subject and power," p. 211.
21 Foucault, "The subject and power," p. 209.
22 Foucault, "The subject and power," pp. 220, 221.
23 Foucault, *Society Must Be Defended*, pp. 7–8.
24 Foucault, *On the Government of the Living*, pp. 77–8.
25 Foucault, *On the Government of the Living*, p. 78.
26 Foucault, *On the Government of the Living*, pp. 77–8.
27 Foucault, "History, discourse, discontinuity," trans. Anthony Nazzaro, *Salmagundi*, 20 (Summer–Fall 1972), pp. 225–48: pp. 229–30.
28 Foucault, Michel, "The hermeneutic of the subject," in *Ethics: Subjectivity and Truth*, pp. 93–106: p. 96.
29 Foucault, Michel, *Remarks on Marx: Conversations with Duccio Trombadori*, trans. R. James Goldstein and James Cascaito (Los Angeles, CA: Semiotext(e), 1991), p. 38.
30 Foucault, Michel, "Michel Foucault: An interview by Stephen Riggins" (1983), in *Ethics: Subjectivity and Truth*, pp. 121–33: p. 131.
31 Foucault, "Remarks on Marx: Conversations with Duccio Trombadori," pp. 38–9.
32 García, Vivien, *L'Anarchisme aujourd'hui* (Paris: L'Harmattan, 2007), p. 44. [CS translation]
33 Hubert Dreyfus and Paul Rabinow present what is probably the most accurate and useful study of the evolution of Foucault's thought in *Michel Foucault: Beyond Structuralism and Hermeneutics* (Chicago, IL: University of Chicago Press, 1983).
34 Bookchin, Murray, *Social Anarchism or Lifestyle Anarchism* (Edinburgh: AK Press, 1995).
35 See, for example, Mitchell Dean and Daniel Zamora, *Le Dernier Homme et la fin de la révolution. Foucault après mai 1968* (Montreal: Lux Éditeur, 2019).
36 Foucault, Michel, *The Courage of Truth. The Government of Self and Others II: Lectures at the Collège de France 1983–1984*, trans. Graham Burchell (New York: Palgrave Macmillan, 2011).
37 Foucault, Michel, "What is critique?" in *The Politics of Truth*, ed. Sylvère Lotringer and Lysa Hochroth, trans. Lysa Hochroth (Los Angeles, CA: Semiotext(e), 1997), p. 44.
38 Foucault, "What is critique?," p. 44.
39 Foucault, "What is critique?," p. 75.
40 Foucault, *On the Government of the Living*, p. 12.
41 Foucault, "Remarks on Marx: Conversations with Duccio Trombadori," p. 177.

42 Foucault, *On the Government of the Living*, p. 11. The spelling *parrēsia* is used throughout this chapter.
43 Foucault, *The Courage of Truth*, p. 135.
44 Foucault, "Governmentality," in *Power*, trans. Robert Hurley et al., ed. James D. Faubion (New York: New Press, 2000), pp. 201–22: p. 221.
45 Foucault, "Governmentality," p. 205. Foucault refers specifically to the work of Guillaume de la Perrière, *Le Miroir politique, concernant différentes manières de gouverner* (1555).
46 Foucault, "Governmentality," pp. 211, 217.
47 Foucault, "Governmentality," p. 216.
48 Foucault, "Governmentality," p. 203.
49 Foucault, "Governmentality," p. 213.
50 Foucault, "Governmentality," p. 210.
51 Foucault, "The subject and power," p. 208.
52 Foucault, "Governmentality," p. 211.
53 Foucault, "Governmentality," p. 210.
54 Foucault, "Governmentality," p. 221.
55 Foucault, "The subject and power," p. 212.
56 Foucault, "What is critique?" p. 47.
57 Foucault, "The subject and power," p. 208.
58 Foucault, "Remarks on Marx: Conversations with Duccio Trombadori," p. 144.
59 Foucault, "The Subject and power," p. 211.
60 Foucault, "The Subject and power," p. 211.
61 Foucault, "The Subject and power," p. 226.
62 Foucault, "What is critique?" p. 47.
63 Foucault, "What is critique?" p. 49.
64 Foucault, *On the Government of the Living*, p. 11.
65 Foucault, *On the Government of the Living*, p. 17.
66 From *aletheia*, alethurgy, truth.
67 Foucault, *On the Government of the Living*, p. 22.
68 Foucault, *On the Government of the Living*, p. 17.
69 Foucault, *On the Government of the Living*, p. 12.
70 Foucault, *On the Government of the Living*, p. 75.
71 Foucault, *The Government of Self and Others*, p. 66.
72 Foucault, Michel, *Herméneutique du sujet: Cours au Collège de France (1981–1982)* (Paris: Gallimard/Seuil), p. 54. Translator's note: translation is mine because this sentence is missing from the published English translation.
73 Foucault, Michel, *The Hermeneutics of the Subject: Lectures at the Collège de France, 1981–1982*, trans. Graham Burchell (New York: Palgrave Macmillan, 2005), p. 56.
74 Foucault, *The Hermeneutics of the Subject*, p. 56.
75 Foucault, *The Hermeneutics of the Subject*, p. 56.
76 Foucault, *The Hermeneutics of the Subject*, p. 252.
77 Foucault, *The Courage of Truth*, p. 62.
78 Foucault, *The Courage of Truth*, p. 60.
79 See the example of Pisistratus and the peasant in Foucault, *The Courage of Truth*, p. 59.
80 Foucault, *On the Government of the Living*, p. 14.
81 Foucault, *On the Government of the Living*, p. 14.
82 Butler, Judith, "What is critique? An essay on Foucault's virtue," in David Ingram, ed., *The Political: Readings in Continental Philosophy* (Oxford: Blackwell, 2002), pp. 212–28: p. 213.
83 Foucault, *On the Government of the Living*, p. 81.

84 Foucault, *The Government of Self and Others*, p. 150.
85 Foucault, *The Government of Self and Others*, p. 158.
86 Foucault, *The Government of Self and Others*, p. 158.
87 Foucault, *The Government of Self and Others*, p. 159.
88 Foucault, *The Government of Self and Others*, p. 175.
89 Foucault, *The Government of Self and Others*, pp. 175–6.
90 Foucault, *The Government of Self and Others*, p. 178.
91 Foucault, *The Government of Self and Others*, p. 181.
92 Foucault, *The Government of Self and Others*, p. 182.
93 Foucault, *The Government of Self and Others*, p. 184.
94 Foucault, *The Government of Self and Others*, p. 184.
95 Hardt, Michael, and Antonio Negri, *Empire* (Cambridge, MA: Harvard University Press, 2000), p. 28.
96 Hardt and Negri, *Empire*, p. 28.
97 Schürmann, "On constituting oneself as an anarchistic subject," in *Tomorrow the Manifold. Essays on Foucault, Anarchy, and the Singularization to Come*, ed. Malte Fabian Rauch and Nicolas Schneider (Zurich: Diaphanes, 2019), p. 27.
98 Deleuze, Gilles, *Foucault*, trans. Seán Hand (Minneapolis: University of Minnesota Press, 1988), p. 96.
99 Deleuze, Gilles, *Negotiations (1972–1990)*, trans. Martin Joughin (New York: Columbia University Press, 1995), p. 98.
100 Deleuze, *Negotiations*, p. 84.
101 Deleuze, *Foucault*, p. 100.
102 Deleuze, *Negotiations*, p. 91.
103 Deleuze, *Foucault*, p. 98.
104 Deleuze, *Foucault*, p. 102.
105 Deleuze, *Foucault*, p. 98.
106 Deleuze, *Foucault*, p. 120.
107 Deleuze, *Foucault*, p. 98.
108 Deleuze, *Foucault*, p. 99.
109 Deleuze, *Foucault*, p. 99.
110 Deleuze, *Foucault*, p. 118.
111 Deleuze, *The Deleuze Seminars: Foucault 13*, February 25, 1986.
112 Deleuze, *The Deleuze Seminars: Foucault 9*, January 7, 1986.
113 See Foucault, Michel, *The History of Sexuality, Volume I, The Will to Knowledge*, trans. Robert Hurley (New York: Vintage Books, 1990), p. 98. Foucault also declares: "Relations of power are not in a position of exteriority with respect to other types of relationships (economic processes, knowledge relationships, sexual relations), but are immanent in the latter," p. 94.
114 Deleuze, Gilles, *Foucault*, p. 37. See also Giles Deleuze, "What is a *Dispositif*?" in *Two Regimes of Madness: Texts and Interviews 1975–1995*, ed. David Lapoujade, trans. Ames Hodges and Mike Taormina (Los Angeles, CA: Semiotexte(e), 2006), pp. 338–48.
115 Deleuze, *Foucault*, p. 100.
116 Deleuze, *Negotiations*, p. 98.
117 Deleuze, *The Deleuze Seminars, Spinoza: The Velocities of Thought 4*, March 24, 1981.
118 Deleuze, *Spinoza: The Velocities of Thought: Lecture 3*, December 16, 1980.
119 Deleuze, "Zones of immanence," in *Two Regimes of Madness*, pp. 261–4, p. 261.
120 Deleuze, *Foucault*, p. 101.
121 Deleuze, *Foucault*, p. 101.
122 Foucault, *The Hermeneutics of the Subject*, p. 38.

123 Foucault, *The Hermeneutics of the Subject*, p. 53.
124 Foucault, *The Courage of Truth*, p. 274.
125 Foucault, Michel, "Technologies of the self." Interview by Luther H. Martin recorded on October 25, 1982, in *Technologies of the Self: A Seminar with Michel Foucault*, ed. Luther H. Martin, Huck Gutman, and Patrick H. Hutton (Amherst: University of Massachusetts Press, 1988), pp. 16–49: p. 19; emphasis mine.
126 Foucault, *The Courage of Truth*, p. 131.
127 Foucault, *The Courage of Truth*, p. 134.
128 Foucault, *The Courage of Truth*, p. 134.
129 Foucault, *The Courage of Truth*, p. 128.
130 Foucault, *The Courage of Truth*, p. 144.
131 Foucault, *The Courage of Truth*, p. 128.
132 Foucault, *The Courage of Truth*, p. 144.
133 Foucault, *The Courage of Truth*, p. 144.
134 Foucault, *The Courage of Truth*, p. 145.
135 Foucault, *The Courage of Truth*, p. 113.
136 Foucault, *The Courage of Truth*, p. 146.
137 Foucault, *The Courage of Truth*, p. 135.
138 Foucault, *The Courage of Truth*, p. 135.
139 In *The Courage of Truth*, Foucault specifies: "In the texts of the Hellenistic and Roman period … Diogenes, Laertius, [in] Dio Chrysostom, to a certain extent [in] Epictetus," p. 166.
140 Foucault, *The Courage of Truth*, p. 183.
141 Foucault, *The Courage of Truth*, p. 284.
142 Foucault, *The Hermeneutics of the Subject*, p. 69.
143 Foucault, *The Hermeneutics of the Subject*, p. 70. The same analysis is discussed in *The Courage of Truth*, p. 159.
144 Foucault, *The Hermeneutics of the Subject*, p. 71.
145 Foucault, *The Courage of Truth*, p. 160.
146 Schürmann, "On constituting oneself as an anarchistic subject," p. 30.
147 Schürmann, "On constituting oneself as an anarchistic subject," p. 15.
148 Schürmann, "On constituting oneself as an anarchistic subject," p. 24.
149 Schürmann, "On constituting oneself as an anarchistic subject," p. 22.
150 Schürmann, "On constituting oneself as an anarchistic subject," p. 28.
151 Schürmann, "On constituting oneself as an anarchistic subject," p. 10.
152 Foucault, *The Courage of Truth*, p. 224.
153 Foucault, *The Courage of Truth*, p. 243.
154 Foucault, *The Courage of Truth*, p. 265.
155 Foucault, *The Courage of Truth*, p. 265.
156 Foucault, *The Courage of Truth*, p. 241, "which will enable this coin to circulate with its true value," p. 227.
157 Foucault, *The Courage of Truth*, p. 227.
158 Foucault, *The Courage of Truth*, p. 227.
159 Foucault, *The Courage of Truth*, p. 227.
160 Foucault, *The Courage of Truth*, p. 227.
161 Foucault, *The Courage of Truth*, p. 227.
162 Foucault, *The Courage of Truth*, p. 232.
163 Foucault, Michel, *The Birth of Biopolitics: Lectures at the College de France, 1978–1979*, trans. Graham Burchell (New York: Palgrave Macmillan, 2008), p. 319.
164 Lagasnerie, Geoffroy de, "Néo-libéralisme, théorie politique et pensée critique," *Raisons*

politiques, 52 (2013–14), pp. 63–75: p. 74. See also Serge Audier, *Penser le "néolibéralisme." Le moment néolibéral, Foucault, et la crise du socialisme*, Lormont, Le Bord de l'eau, "Documents," 2015. [CS translation]
165 Foucault, *The Courage of Truth*, p. 336.
166 See Foucault, *The Birth of Biopolitics*, p. 242 *sq*.
167 Foucault, *The Courage of Truth*, p. 285.
168 See, for example, Marianne E. Maeckelbergh, "Doing is believing. Prefiguration as strategic practice in the alterglobalization movement," *Social Movement Studies*, 10/1 (2011), pp. 1–20.
169 Foucault, "What is Enlightenment?"
170 Foucault, *The Courage of Truth*, p. 245.
171 Foucault, *The Courage of Truth*, p. 245.
172 Foucault, "What is critique?" p. 45.
173 Foucault, "What is critique?" p. 75.
174 Butler, "What is critique?" p. 216.
175 Foucault, "The subject and power," p. 221.
176 Foucault, "The ethics of the concern for self as a practice of freedom," p. 285.
177 Foucault, "Sex, power, and the politics of identity," p. 165.
178 Foucault, "Utopian body," trans. Lucia Allais, in Caroline A. Jones, ed., *Sensorium, Embodied Experience, Technology and Contemporary Art* (Cambridge, MA: MIT Press, 2006), pp. 229–34: p. 233.
179 Foucault, "Utopian body," p. 233.
180 Foucault, "Remarks on Marx: Conversations with Duccio Trombadori" pp. 31–2.

Chapter 8: Profanatory Anarchy

1 Agamben, Giorgio, "Vers une théorie de la puissance destituante," lundimatin#45, January 25, 2016. [CS translation]
2 Agamben, Giorgio, *The Kingdom and the Glory: For a Theological Genealogy of Economy of Economy and Government, Homer Sacer II*, p. 622. Unless indicated otherwise, all page references to Agamben's work refer to *The Omnibus Homo Sacer* (Stanford, CA: Stanford University Press, 2017).
3 Agamben, Giorgio, "In praise of profanation," in *Profanations*, trans. Jeff Fort (New York: Zone Books, 2007), p. 73.
4 Agamben, Giorgio, *Homo Sacer: Sovereign Power and Bare Life*, trans. Daniel Heller-Roazen, in *The Omnibus Homo Sacer*, p. 27.
5 Agamben, *Homo Sacer I*, in *The Omnibus Homo Sacer*, p. 22.
6 Agamben, *Homo Sacer I*, in *The Omnibus Homo Sacer*, p. 9.
7 Agamben, *Homo Sacer I*, in *The Omnibus Homo Sacer*, p. 70.
8 Agamben, Giorgio "Vers une théorie de la puissance destituante," p. 1. [CS translation]
9 Agamben, *Homo Sacer I*, in *The Omnibus Homo Sacer*, p. 56.
10 Agamben, *Homo Sacer I*, in *The Omnibus Homo Sacer*, p. 72.
11 Agamben, *Homo Sacer I*, in *The Omnibus Homo Sacer*, p. 56.
12 Later, in Rome, "sacredness is [*sacertas* ...] the originary form of the inclusion of bare life in the juridical order, and the syntagm *Homo sacer* names something like the originary 'political' relation ... [T]he originary political formulation of the imposition of the sovereign bond": Agamben, *Homo Sacer I*, in *The Omnibus Homo Sacer*, p. 72.
13 Agamben, *Homo Sacer I*, in *The Omnibus Homo Sacer*, p. 11.
14 Agamben, *The Sacrament of Language: An Archaeology of the Oath*, trans. Adam Kotsko, in *The Omnibus Homo Sacer II*, p. 329.
15 Agamben, "In praise of profanation," p. 73

16 Agamben, *Homo Sacer I*, in *The Omnibus Homo Sacer*, p. 13.
17 Agamben, *The Use of Bodies*, trans. Adam Kotsko, in *The Omnibus Homo Sacer II*, pp. 1275–6. On the same page, Agamben also indicates that the various philosophies of anarchy failed: "It is this destituent power that both the anarchist tradition and twentieth-century thought sought to define without truly succeeding in it. The destruction of tradition in Heidegger, the deconstruction of the *archē* and the fracture of hegemonies in Schürmann, what (in the footsteps of Foucault) I have called 'philosophical archaeology,' are all pertinent but insufficient attempts to go back to a historical *a priori* in order to depose it." On Agamben's relation with Schürmann and Derrida, see the excellent article by Malte Fabian Rauch, "*An-archē* and indifference: Between Giorgio Agamben, Jacques Derrida, and Reiner Schürmann," *Philosophy Today*, 65/3 (Summer 2021), pp. 619–36.
18 Agamben, *Homo Sacer I*, in *The Omnibus Homo Sacer*, p. 13.
19 Agamben, *Homo Sacer I*, in *The Omnibus Homo Sacer*, p. 13.
20 Agamben, Giorgio, "What is an apparatus?" in *What is an Apparatus and Other Essays*, trans. David Kishik and Stefan Pedatella (Stanford, CA: Stanford University Press, 2009), pp. 1–25: p. 24.
21 Agamben, *Homo Sacer I*, in *The Omnibus Homo Sacer*, p. 64.
22 Agamben, *Homo Sacer I*, in *The Omnibus Homo Sacer*, p. 68.
23 Agamben, *Homo Sacer I*, in *The Omnibus Homo Sacer*, p. 64.
24 Agamben, *Homo Sacer I*, in *The Omnibus Homo Sacer*, p. 65.
25 Agamben, *Homo Sacer I*, in *The Omnibus Homo Sacer*, p. 66.
26 Agamben, *Homo Sacer I*, in *The Omnibus Homo Sacer*, p. 67.
27 Agamben, *Homo Sacer I*, in *The Omnibus Homo Sacer*, p. 64.
28 Foucault, Michel, "A preface to transgression," in *Language, Counter-Memory, Practice: Selected Essays and Interviews*, trans. Donald F. Bouchard and Sherry Simon (Ithaca, NY: Cornell University Press, 1977), pp. 29–52: p. 30.
29 Agamben, *Homo Sacer I*, in *The Omnibus Homo Sacer*, p. 94.
30 Agamben, *The Use of Bodies*, in *The Omnibus Homo Sacer*, p. 1067.
31 Agamben, "What is an apparatus?" p. 19. See also *Homo Sacer I*, in *The Omnibus Homo Sacer*, p. 94.
32 Agamben, *Profanations*, p. 81.
33 "In its extreme form, the capitalist religion realizes the pure form of separation ... an absolute profanation without remainder": Agamben, *Profanations*, p. 81.
34 The Invisible Committee, *The Coming Insurrection* (Los Angeles, CA: Semiotext(e), July 2009), p. 42.
35 Agamben, *The Uses of Bodies*, in *The Omnibus Homo Sacer*, p. 1276.
36 Agamben, *The Kingdom and the Glory*, trans. Lorenzo Chiesa with Matteo Mandarini, in *The Omnibus Homo Sacer II*, p. 369.
37 Foucault, Michel, *Security, Territory, Population: Lectures at the Collège de France 1977–1978*, ed. Michel Senellart, trans. Graham Burhell (New York: Palgrave Macmillan, 2009), p. 76.
38 Which appears for the first time in *Security, Territory, Population*.
39 Foucault, "The confession of the flesh" (interview with Alain Grosrichard et al.), in *Power/Knowledge: Selected Interviews and Other Writings*, trans. Collin Gordon, Leo Marshall, John Mepham, and Kate Soper, ed. Colin Gordon (New York: Pantheon Books, 1980), pp. 194–228: p. 194
40 In "What is an apparatus?" pp. 12–13, Agamben writes: "One of the methodological principles that I constantly follow in my investigations is to identify in the texts and contexts on which I work what Feuerbach used to call the philosophical element, that is to say, the point of their *Entwicklungsfähigkeit* (literally, capacity to be developed), the locus and the moment wherein they are susceptible to a development. ... [The

interpreter] knows that it is now time to abandon the text that he is analyzing and to proceed on his own."
41 Agamben, *The Kingdom and the Glory*, in *The Omnibus Homo Sacer*, p. 369.
42 "The problem is ... to move from political philosophy to first philosophy (or, if one likes, politics is returned to its ontological position)." Agamben, *Homo Sacer I*, in *The Omnibus Homo Sacer*, p. 40.
43 Agamben, Giorgio, "What is a command?" in *Creation and Anarchy: The Work of Art and Religion of Capitalism*, trans. Adam Kotsko (Stanford, CA: Stanford University Press, 2019), p. 51. Translator's note: Agamben's translator Adam Kotsko uses "origin" where we have opted for "beginning."
44 Agamben, "What is a command?" p. 52.
45 Agamben, "What is a command?" p. 54.
46 Agamben, "What is a command?" p. 56.
47 "'Not every discourse,' writes Aristotle in *De Interpretatione*, 'is apophantic, but only that discourse in which it is possible to say the true and the false [*alētheuein ē pseudesthai*]. This does not happen in all discourses: for example, prayer is a discourse [*logos*], but it is neither true nor false. We can dismiss these other discourses, since consideration of them belongs rather to the study of rhetoric or poetry; the present investigation deals solely with apophantic discourse": quoted by Agamben in "What is a command?" p. 55.
48 Agamben, "What is a command?" p. 56.
49 Agamben, "What is a command?" p. 54.
50 Agamben compares his move here with that of Schürmann. Although Schürmann also asserts this inscription of anarchy within power, he describes the *archē* as a metaphysical attempt to found *praxis* within being. According to Agamben this is "the limit of Schürmann's interpretation." Indeed, there is no point in attempting to free action from the tyranny of the *archē*, since the separation between being and acting is its secret structure: "playing off one pole against the other is not sufficient to halt their functioning": *The Use of Bodies*, in *The Omnibus Homo Sacer*, p. 1276.
51 Agamben, *The Kingdom and the Glory*, in *The Omnibus Homo Sacer*, p. 389.
52 Agamben, *The Kingdom and the Glory*, in *The Omnibus Homo Sacer*, p. 390.
53 In the 1977 lecture series, Foucault shows that the origin of the link between sovereignty and governmentality should be sought in medieval theological treatises, from Silvanus to Saint Thomas, rather than in the archives of political science. But although he does study the notion of the divine government of the world in Saint Thomas, he does not reveal its ontological foundations – which is precisely the task undertaken by Agamben.
54 Agamben, *The Kingdom and the Glory*, in *The Omnibus Homo Sacer*, p. 395.
55 Agamben, *The Kingdom and the Glory*, in *The Omnibus Homo Sacer*, p. 417.
56 Agamben, *The Kingdom and the Glory*, in *The Omnibus Homo Sacer*, p. 497.
57 Agamben, *The Kingdom and the Glory*, in *The Omnibus Homo Sacer*, p. 623.
58 Agamben, *The Kingdom and the Glory*, in *The Omnibus Homo Sacer*, p. 429.
59 Agamben, *The Kingdom and the Glory*, in *The Omnibus Homo Sacer*, p. 424.
60 Agamben, *The Kingdom and the Glory*, in *The Omnibus Homo Sacer*, p. 467.
61 Agamben, *The Kingdom and the Glory*, in *The Omnibus Homo Sacer*, p. 466.
62 Agamben, *The Kingdom and the Glory*, in *The Omnibus Homo Sacer*, p. 496.
63 Agamben, *The Kingdom and the Glory*, in *The Omnibus Homo Sacer*, p. 423.
64 Agamben, *The Kingdom and the Glory*, in *The Omnibus Homo Sacer*, p. 563.
65 Agamben, *The Kingdom and the Glory*, in *The Omnibus Homo Sacer*, p. 444.
66 See Agamben, "What is a command?" p. 58 and *The Kingdom and the Glory*, p. 35.
67 Agamben, *Opus Dei: An Archeology of Duty*, trans. Adam Kotsko, in *The Omnibus Homo Sacer II*, p. 697.

68 Agamben, *Opus Dei: An Archeology of Duty*, in *The Omnibus Homo Sacer*, p. 697.
69 Agamben, *The Kingdom and the Glory*, in *The Omnibus Homo Sacer*, p. 415.
70 Agamben, *The Kingdom and the Glory*, in *The Omnibus Homo Sacer*, p. 416: "The paradigm of government and of the state of exception coincide in the idea of an *oikonomia*."
71 Marin, Louis, "Le pouvoir et ses représentations," in *Politiques de la représentation*, ed. Alain Cantillon et al. (Paris: Éditions Kimé, 2005), p. 74. [CS translation]
72 Marin, "Le pouvoir et ses représentations," p. 73. [CS translation]
73 Agamben, "In praise of profanation," p. 76.
74 Agamben, Giorgio, *Pilate and Jesus*, trans. Adam Kotsko (Stanford, CA: Stanford University Press, 2015).
75 Agamben, *The Kingdom and the Glory*, in *The Omnibus Homo Sacer*, p. 549.
76 Agamben, *The Kingdom and the Glory*, in *The Omnibus Homo Sacer*, p. 580.
77 Agamben, *The Kingdom and the Glory*, in *The Omnibus Homo Sacer*, p. 580.
78 Agamben, *The Kingdom and the Glory*, in *The Omnibus Homo Sacer*, p. 551.
79 Agamben, *The Kingdom and the Glory*, in *The Omnibus Homo Sacer*, p. 551.
80 Agamben, *The Kingdom and the Glory*, in *The Omnibus Homo Sacer*, p. 552.
81 Agamben, *The Kingdom and the Glory*, in *The Omnibus Homo Sacer*, p. 549.
82 Agamben, *The Kingdom and the Glory*, in *The Omnibus Homo Sacer*, p. 559.
83 Agamben, *The Kingdom and the Glory*, in *The Omnibus Homo Sacer*, p. 555.
84 Agamben, *The Kingdom and the Glory*, in *The Omnibus Homo Sacer*, p. 594.
85 Agamben, *The Kingdom and the Glory*, in *The Omnibus Homo Sacer*, p. 594.
86 Agamben, *The Kingdom and the Glory*, in *The Omnibus Homo Sacer*, p. 595.
87 Agamben, *The Kingdom and the Glory*, in *The Omnibus Homo Sacer*, p. 549.
88 Agamben, *The Kingdom and the Glory*, in *The Omnibus Homo Sacer*, p. 580.
89 Agamben, *The Kingdom and the Glory*, in *The Omnibus Homo Sacer*, p. 532.
90 Agamben, *The Kingdom and the Glory*, in *The Omnibus Homo Sacer*, p. 529.
91 Agamben, *The Kingdom and the Glory*, in *The Omnibus Homo Sacer*, p. 547.
92 Agamben, *The Kingdom and the Glory*, in *The Omnibus Homo Sacer*, p. 525.
93 See Agamben, *The Kingdom and the Glory*, in *The Omnibus Homo Sacer*, p. 527.
94 Agamben, *The Kingdom and the Glory*, in *The Omnibus Homo Sacer*, p. 534.
95 Agamben, *The Kingdom and the Glory*, in *The Omnibus Homo Sacer*, p. 533.
96 Agamben, *The Kingdom and the Glory*, in *The Omnibus Homo Sacer*, p. 536.
97 Agamben, *The Kingdom and the Glory*, in *The Omnibus Homo Sacer*, p. 536.
98 Agamben, *The Kingdom and the Glory*, in *The Omnibus Homo Sacer*, p. 536.
99 Agamben, *The Kingdom and the Glory*, in *The Omnibus Homo Sacer*, p. 536.
100 Agamben, *The Highest Poverty: Monastic Rules and Form-of-Life*, trans. Adam Kotsko, in *The Omnibus Homo Sacer I*.
101 Agamben, *Opus Dei*, in *The Omnibus Homo Sacer*, p. 649.
102 Agamben, *Opus Dei*, in *The Omnibus Homo Sacer*, p. 657.
103 Agamben, *Opus Dei*, in *The Omnibus Homo Sacer*, p. 658.
104 Agamben, *Opus Dei*, in *The Omnibus Homo Sacer*, p. 658.
105 Agamben, *Opus Dei*, in *The Omnibus Homo Sacer*, p. 658.
106 Agamben, *Opus Dei*, in *The Omnibus Homo Sacer*, p. 664.
107 Agamben, *Opus Dei*, in *The Omnibus Homo Sacer*, p. 656, emphasis mine.
108 Agamben, *Opus Dei*, in *The Omnibus Homo Sacer*, p. 689.
109 Agamben, *Opus Dei*, in *The Omnibus Homo Sacer*, p. 664.
110 Agamben, *Opus Dei*, in *The Omnibus Homo Sacer*, p. 690.
111 Agamben, *Pilate and Jesus*, p. 55.
112 Agamben, *Pilate and Jesus*, p. 14, citing John, 19: 13.
113 Agamben, *Pilate and Jesus*, p. 36.

114 Agamben, *Pilate and Jesus*, p. 48.
115 Agamben, *Pilate and Jesus*, p. 20.
116 Agamben, *Pilate and Jesus*, p. 49.
117 Agamben, *Pilate and Jesus*, p. 51.
118 Agamben, *Pilate and Jesus*, p. 32.
119 Agamben, *The Use of Bodies*, in *The Omnibus Homo Sacer*, p. 1058.
120 Agamben, *The Use of Bodies*, in *The Omnibus Homo Sacer*, p. 1123.
121 Agamben, *The Use of Bodies*, in *The Omnibus Homo Sacer*, p. 1119.
122 Agamben, *The Use of Bodies*, in *The Omnibus Homo Sacer*, p. 1123.
123 Agamben, *The Use of Bodies*, in *The Omnibus Homo Sacer*, p. 1058.
124 Agamben, *The Use of Bodies*, in *The Omnibus Homo Sacer*, p. 1058.
125 "What Foucault does not seem to see, despite the fact that antiquity would seem to offer an example in some way, is the possibility of a relation with the self and of a form of life that never assumes the figure of a free subject – which is to say, if power relations necessarily refer to a subject, of a zone of ethics entirely subtracted from strategic relationships, of an Ungovernable that is situated beyond states of domination and power relations": Agamben, *The Use of Bodies*, in *The Omnibus Homo Sacer*, p. 1125.
126 Agamben, *The Use of Bodies*, in *The Omnibus Homo Sacer*, p. 1052.
127 Agamben, *The Use of Bodies*, in *The Omnibus Homo Sacer*, p. 1214.
128 Agamben, *The Use of Bodies*, in *The Omnibus Homo Sacer*, p. 1053.
129 Agamben, *The Use of Bodies*, in *The Omnibus Homo Sacer*, p. 1176.
130 Agamben, *The Use of Bodies*, in *The Omnibus Homo Sacer*, p. 1053.
131 Agamben, *The Use of Bodies*, in *The Omnibus Homo Sacer*, p. 1054.
132 Agamben, *The Use of Bodies*, in *The Omnibus Homo Sacer*, p. 1274.
133 Foucault, "What is Enlightenment?" p. 50.
134 Foucault, "What is Enlightenment?" p. 45.
135 "The Passion of Christ is no longer simply prefigured by the sacrifice of Abraham, but calls up all the prestige of torture and innumerable dreams associated therewith, so that Tubal, the blacksmith, and Isiah's wheel take their place around the cross, going beyond all the lessons about sacrifice to form a fantastical tableau of pain and relentlessly tortured bodies": Michel Foucault, *History of Madness*, trans. Jonathan Murphy and Jean Khalfa (New York: Routledge, 2006), p. 17.
136 Foucault, Michel, *Discipline and Punish: The Birth of the Prison* (New York: Random House, 1977), pp. 10–13.
137 Foucault, *The Courage of Truth*, lecture of 15 February 15, 1984, 2nd hour, pp. 95–116.
138 Foucault, *The Courage of Truth*, pp. 278–9.
139 Foucault, "A preface to transgression," p. 48.
140 Agamben, *Homo Sacer I*, in *The Omnibus Homo Sacer*, p. 94.
141 Agamben, *Homo Sacer I*, in *The Omnibus Homo Sacer*: "compromising Bataille's inquiries into sovereignty," p. 64.
142 Agamben, *Homo Sacer I*, in *The Omnibus Homo Sacer*, p. 94.
143 Agamben, *Homo Sacer I*, in *The Omnibus Homo Sacer*, p. 94.
144 Agamben, *The Use of Bodies* in *The Omnibus Homo Sacer*, p. 1216.
145 Agamben cites Bataille's *The Accursed Share*, in *Homo Sacer II*, in *The Omnibus Homo Sacer*, p. 94.
146 Nancy, Jean-Luc, "The unsacrificeable," in *A Finite Thinking*, ed. Simon Sparks (Stanford, CA: Stanford University Press, 2003), pp. 51–77. On Agamben, Nancy, and the critique of Bataille, see my article "Faut-il sacrifier Bataille?" [should we sacrifice Bataille?] in "Valeur d'usage de Georges Bataille" [the use value of Georges Bataille], *ArtPress*, 2/42 (2016), pp. 16–21.

147 Agamben, *Homo Sacer I*, in *The Omnibus Homo Sacer*, p. 95.
148 Agamben, *Homo Sacer I*, in *The Omnibus Homo Sacer*, p. 95.
149 Agamben, *Homo Sacer I*, in *The Omnibus Homo Sacer*, p. 95.
150 Nancy, "The unsacrificeable," in *A Finite Thinking*, p. 54.
151 Agamben, *Opus Dei*, in *The Omnibus Homo Sacer*, p. 752.
152 Agamben, *The Highest Poverty*, in *The Omnibus Homo Sacer*, p. 958.
153 The concept of "politicity" first appears in *Homo Sacer I*, in *The Omnibus Homo Sacer*, p. 6, and returns often in Agamben's texts.
154 Agamben, *The Use of Bodies*, in *The Omnibus Homo Sacer*, p. 1276.
155 Agamben, *The Use of Bodies*, in *The Omnibus Homo Sacer*, p. 1243.
156 Agamben, *Opus Dei*, in *The Omnibus Homo Sacer*, p. 726.
157 Agamben, *The Use of Bodies*, in *The Omnibus Homo Sacer*, p. 1084.
158 Agamben, *The Use of Bodies*, in *The Omnibus Homo Sacer*, p. 1084.
159 Agamben, *The Use of Bodies*, in *The Omnibus Homo Sacer*, p. 1277.
160 Agamben, *Opus Dei*, in *The Omnibus Homo Sacer*, p. 726.
161 Agamben, *The Use of Bodies*, in *The Omnibus Homo Sacer*, p. 1277.
162 Agamben, *The Use of Bodies*, in *The Omnibus Homo Sacer*, p. 1277.
163 Aristotle, *Physics*, Book II, in *The Complete Works of Aristotle*, Revised Oxford Translation, vol. 1, ed. Jonathan Barnes (Princeton, NJ: Princeton University Press, 1998), p. 20.
164 Agamben, *Homo Sacer I*, in *The Omnibus Homo Sacer*, p. 1243.
165 Agamben, *The Use of Bodies*, in *The Omnibus Homo Sacer*, p. 1237.
166 Agamben, *The Use of Bodies*, in *The Omnibus Homo Sacer*, p. 1026. It is not clear that Agamben succeeds in what he reproaches Guy Debord for failing to do, namely, making the distinction between private life and secret life, that is, form-of-life. See *The Use of Bodies*, pp. 1021–4.
167 Agamben, *Homo Sacer I*, in *The Omnibus Homo Sacer*, p. 63.
168 Agamben, *The Use of Bodies*, in *The Omnibus Homo Sacer*, p. 1277.
169 Agamben, *Homo Sacer I*, in *The Omnibus Homo Sacer*, p.11.
170 Agamben, *Homo Sacer I*, in *The Omnibus Homo Sacer*, p. 48.
171 Agamben, *Homo Sacer I*, in *The Omnibus Homo Sacer*, p. 48.
172 Agamben, "Life, a work of art without an author: The state of exception, the administration of disorder and private life," *German Law Journal*, No. 5, May 1, 2004.
173 Agamben differentiates himself from Heidegger and Schürmann on several occasions in regard to the essential question of the metaphysical status of *archē*. As Rauch comments quite rightly, for Agamben, "Metaphysics [...] has not been defined by foundations, but by the positing of a negative ground, an absence of foundation, a constitutive lack," Rauch, "*An-archē* and indifference," p. 623.
174 Agamben, *The Use of Bodies*, in *The Omnibus Homo Sacer*, p. 1242.
175 Agamben, *The Use of Bodies*, in *The Omnibus Homo Sacer*, p. 1243.
176 Agamben, *The Highest Poverty*, in *The Omnibus Homo Sacer*, p. 937.
177 Agamben, *The Kingdom and the Glory*, in *The Omnibus Homo Sacer*, p. 542.
178 Agamben, *Opus Dei*, in *The Omnibus Homo Sacer*, p. 720.
179 The proximity between Agamben's "zone of indifference" and Deleuze's "zone of indistinction," emphasized on several occasions, is not very helpful since Agamben does not engage in problematizing becoming. By contrast, in *A Thousand Plateaus* especially, Deleuze and Guattari define the "zone of indistinction" as a "zone of proximity," or a "block of becoming." A "block of becoming" is a common space of deterritorialization, in which the flower and insect, for example, are neither brought together nor mixed, but are rendered indistinct. See Deleuze and Guattari, *A Thousand Plateaus*, p. 323.
180 Agamben, *Homo Sacer I*, in *The Omnibus Homo Sacer*, p. 77.

181 The choice of the term "zone" and its frequency in the texts is all the more paradoxical given that, originally, the "zone" is the result of a governmental decision. Between 1841 and 1844, the French authorities decided to surround Paris with a network of defensive fortifications called "*l'enceinte de Thiers*" [Thiers Wall]. Against these ramparts, a 250-meter-wide strip of land was decreed a "*zone non constructible (non ædificandi)*." Subsequently, the "zone" became filled anarchically with shacks, caravans, parcels of land farmed by "zone-dwellers." The French expression "*C'est la zone!* [it's the zone]" derives from this history.

182 Agamben, *The Use of Bodies*, in *The Omnibus Homo Sacer*, p. 1244.

183 Derrida, "*Ousia* et *Grammè*," in *Margins of Philosophy*, p. 50.

184 Thus, the monastic rules and spiritual movements of the twelfth and thirteenth centuries, "which culminate in Franciscanism": Agamben, *The Highest Poverty*, in *The Omnibus Homo Sacer*, p. 888. Agamben writes: "What is in question in the monastic rules is … a transformation that seems to bear on the very way in which human action is conceived, so that one shifts from the level of practice and acting to that of form of life and living": p. 937.

Chapter 9: Staging Anarchy

1 Rancière, Jacques, *Hatred of Democracy*, trans. Steve Corcoran (London: Verso, 2006), p. 73.

2 Rancière, Jacques, *Disagreement: Politics and Philosophy*, trans. Julie Rose (Minneapolis: University of Minnesota Press, 1999), p. 16.

3 Rancière, Jacques, "Politics, identification, and subjectivation," *October*, 61 (Summer 1992), pp. 58–64: p. 59.

4 Rancière, Jacques "La démocratie est née d'une limitation du pouvoir de la propriété." Interview with Irène Pereira, *Alternative libertaire*, November 2007, p. 167. [CS translation]

5 Rancière, "La démocratie est née d'une limitation du pouvoir de la propriété." [CS translation]

6 Rancière, "La démocratie est née d'une limitation du pouvoir de la propriété." [CS translation]

7 Rancière, "La démocratie est née d'une limitation du pouvoir de la propriété." [CS translation]

8 "Insistances démocratiques. Entretien avec Miguel Abensour, Jean-Luc Nancy et Jacques Rancière," *Vacarme*, "Puissance de la démocratie," 48 (Summer 2009), pp. 8–17: p. 9. [CS translation]

9 "Insistances démocratiques. Entretien avec Miguel Abensour, Jean-Luc Nancy et Jacques Rancière," p. 9. [CS translation]

10 Rancière, "La démocratie est née d'une limitation du pouvoir de la propriété." [CS translation]

11 Rancière, "La démocratie est née d'une limitation du pouvoir de la propriété." [CS translation]

12 Rancière, "The people is a construction," *Ballast*, May 10, 2017. [CS translation, modified]

13 Dupui-Déri, François, "Black Blocs bas les masques," *Mouvements des idées et des luttes*, 25 (2003), pp. 4–17: p. 5. [CS translation]

14 Dupui-Déri, "Black Blocs bas les masques," p. 9. [CS translation]

15 Rancière, "The people is a construction."

16 Rancière, *Disagreement*, p. 28.

17 Rancière, *Disagreement*, p. 28.

18 Rancière, Jacques, "Ten theses on politics," *Theory and Event*, 5/3 (2001), p. 8.

19 Rancière, *Disagreement*, p. 17.

20 Rancière, "Du politique à la politique," in *Aux bords du politique* (Paris: Folio essais, 2004), p. III. [CS translation]
21 Rancière, *Disagreement*, p. 31.
22 Rancière, *Disagreement*, p. 31.
23 May, Todd, *The Political Thought of Jacques Rancière. Creating Equality* (Edinburgh: Edinburgh University Press, 2008).
24 May, *The Political Thought of Jacques Rancière*, p. 145.
25 May, *The Political Thought of Jacques Rancière*, p. 176.
26 Chambers, Simon, "The politics of the police. From neoliberalism to anarchism, and back to democracy," in Paul Bowman and Richard Stamp, eds., *Reading Rancière: Critical Dissensus* (London: Bloomsbury, 2011).
27 Chambers, *Reading Rancière*, p. 36. See also Rancière, "Ten theses on politics," p. 11: "Politics thus has no 'proper' place nor does it possess any 'natural' subjects. A demonstration is political not because it takes place in a specific locale and bears upon a particular object but rather because its form is that of a clash between two partitions of the sensible. A political subject is not a group of interests or ideas: it is the operator of a particular mode of subjectification and litigation through which politics has its existence. Political demonstrations are thus always of the moment and their subjects are always provisional. Political difference is always on the shore of its own disappearance: the people are close to sinking into the sea of the population or of race, the proletariat borders on being confused with workers defending their interests, the space of a people's public demonstration is always at risk of being confused with the merchant's *agora*, etc."
28 Chambers, *Reading Rancière*, p. 36, citing Rancière, Jacques, "Problems and transformations in critical art//2004," in Claire Bishop, ed., *Participation*, Documents of Contemporary Art (London: Whitechapel, 2006), pp. 83–93: p. 93.
29 Rancière "Ten theses on politics," p. 11
30 In politics, "representation was never a system invented to compensate for the growth of populations. It is not a form in which democracy has been adapted to modern times and vast spaces. It is, by rights, an oligarchic form," Rancière, *Hatred of Democracy*, p. 53.
31 Rancière, *Disagreement*, p. xi.
32 Lyotard, Jean-François, *The Differend: Phrases in Dispute*, trans. Georges Van Den Abbeele (Minneapolis: University of Minnesota Press, 1988), p. xi.
33 Rancière, *Disagreement*, p. x.
34 Rancière, *Disagreement*, p. xi.
35 Rancière, *Disagreement*, p. xii.
36 Rancière, *Disagreement*, pp. 22–3.
37 Lyotard, Jean-François, "La phrase-affect (D'un supplément au différend)," in *Misère de la philosophie* (Paris: Galilée, 2000), pp. 43–54. [CS translation]
38 In *Misère de la philosophie*, p. 50, Lyotard cites Aristotle, *Politics*, Book 1, Chapter 2, 1253, line 10.
39 Lyotard, *The Differend*, p. 138.
40 Lyotard, *The Differend*, p. 138.
41 Rancière, *Disagreement*, p. 39.
42 Rancière, *Disagreement*, p. 39.
43 See Rancière, *Disagreement*, pp. 39, 46ff.
44 Lyotard, *The Differend*, p. 8.
45 Rancière, *Disagreement*, p. 19.
46 Rancière, *Disagreement*, p. 2.
47 Rancière, *Disagreement*, p. 2.

48 Rancière, *Disagreement*, p. 2.
49 Rancière "Ten theses on politics," p. 1.
50 Rancière "Ten theses on politics," pp. 2–3.
51 Rancière "Ten theses on politics," p. 5.
52 Rancière "Ten theses on politics," p. 4.
53 Rancière, *Disagreement*, p. 5.
54 Rancière, *Disagreement*, p. 6.
55 Rancière, *Disagreement*, p. 5.
56 Rancière, *Disagreement*, p. 6.
57 Rancière, *Disagreement*, p. 6.
58 Rancière, *Disagreement*, p. 8. "So, what does the freedom of the people bring to the community? And in what is it peculiar to them? This is where the fundamental miscount rears its head … the freedom of the *demos* is not a determinable property but a pure invention … Simply by being born in a certain city, and more especially in the city of Athens once enslavement for debt was abolished there … The simple impossibility for the *oligoi*'s reducing their debtors to slavery was transformed into the appearance of a freedom that was to be the positive property of the people as a part of the community": p. 7.
59 Rancière, *Hatred of Democracy*, p. 64.
60 Rancière, Jacques, *The Politics of Aesthetics: Distribution of the Sensible*, trans. Gabriel Rockhill (London: Continuum, 2004), p. 10.
61 Rancière "Ten theses on politics," p. 8.
62 Rancière, *Disagreement*, p. 65. In this section of the text, Rancière introduces the three terms "archipolitics," "parapolitics," and "metapolitics."
63 In *Disagreement*, p. 7, Rancière cites Aristotle, *Politics*, "just as impure substance mixed with the pure": Book 3, Chapter 11, 1281b 36.
64 Rancière, *Disagreement*, p. 6.
65 Rancière, *Disagreement*, p. 7.
66 Rancière, *Disagreement*, p. 8.
67 Rancière, *Disagreement*, p. 11.
68 Rancière, *Disagreement*, p. 11, citing Aristotle *Politics IV*, 1294a 17–19.
69 Rancière, *Disagreement*, p. 28.
70 Rancière, Jacques, "Le partage du sensible." Interview with ALICE, *Multitudes* (Summer 1999. [CS translation]
71 Rancière, *Disagreement*, p. 73
72 Rancière, *Disagreement*, p. 73.
73 Rancière, *Disagreement*, p. 8.
74 Rancière, *Hatred of Democracy*, p. 36, citing Plato, *Republic*, VIII, 562d–563d.
75 Rancière, *Disagreement*, p. 65.
76 Rancière, *Disagreement*, p. 71.
77 Rancière, *Disagreement*, p. 74.
78 Rancière, *Disagreement*, p. 74.
79 Rancière, *Disagreement*, p. 16.
80 Rancière, *Disagreement*, p. 68: "So such an archipolitics is just as much a form of archipolicing that grants ways of being and ways of doing, ways of feeling and ways of thinking."
81 Rancière, *Disagreement*, p. 64.
82 Rancière, "The people is a construction."
83 Rancière, *Hatred of Democracy*, p. 52.
84 Rancière, *Hatred of Democracy*, p. 49.

85 Rancière, *Hatred of Democracy*, p. 46.
86 Rancière, *Disagreement*, p. 39.
87 Citing Lyotard, Rancière writes that the sublime "'is none other than the sacrificial announcement of the ethical in the aesthetic field' ... [I shall] return to the terms 'sacrifice' and 'disaster'": Rancière, *Aesthetics and its Discontents*, trans. Steve Corcoran (Cambridge: Polity, 2009), pp. 89–90.
88 Rancière, *Disagreement*, p. 65.
89 Rancière, *Disagreement*, p. 30.
90 Rancière, *Disagreement*, pp. 29–30.
91 Rancière, *Disagreement*, p. 36. [Translation modified: *subjectivation* in place of *subjectification*.]
92 Rancière, *Disagreement*, p. 36.
93 Rancière, *Aesthetics and its Discontents*, p. 40.
94 Rancière, *Disagreement*, p. 39.
95 Rancière, *Disagreement*, p. 40.
96 Rancière, *Disagreement*, p. 49.
97 Rancière, *Disagreement*, p. 16.
98 Rancière, *Disagreement*, p. 17, citing Aristotle, *Politics*, 1254b 22.
99 Rancière, *Disagreement*, p. 37.
100 Rancière, *Disagreement*, p. 50.
101 Lyotard, Jean-François, *Lessons on the Analytic of the Sublime: Kant's Critique of Judgement, 23–29*, trans. Elizabeth Rottenberg (Stanford, CA: Stanford University Press, 1994), p. 124.
102 Rancière, "Are some things unrepresentable?," in *The Future of the Image*, trans. Gregory Elliott (London: Verso, 2007), pp. 109–38: p. 109.
103 Rancière, "Are some things unrepresentable?," p. 111.
104 Rancière, "Are some things unrepresentable?," p. 110.
105 Rancière, "Are some things unrepresentable?," p. 117.
106 Rancière, "Are some things unrepresentable?," p. 123.
107 Rancière, "Are some things unrepresentable?," p. 117.
108 Rancière, "Are some things unrepresentable?," p. 115.
109 Rancière, "Are some things unrepresentable?," p. 110.
110 Rancière, "Are some things unrepresentable?," p. 118.
111 Rancière, "Are some things unrepresentable?," p. 120.
112 Rancière, "Are some things unrepresentable?", p. 120.
113 Rancière, "Are some things unrepresentable?," p. 118.
114 Rancière, "Are some things unrepresentable?," p. 118.
115 Rancière, "Are some things unrepresentable?," pp. 123–4.
116 Lyotard, *The Differend*, p. 13.
117 Lyotard, *The Differend*, p. 13.
118 Rancière, *Aesthetics and its Discontents*, p. 89.
119 Rancière, *Aesthetics and its Discontents*, pp. 89–90. Parataxis (*parátaxis*, coordination) is a grammatical construction in which words or phrases are juxtaposed using simple conjunctions (and, but, or, when ...) without syntactical relations of subordination. It is contrasted to hypotaxis, which uses subordinate propositions and logical connections. Paul Feyerabend analyzes the Greek "paratactic aggregate," particularly in Homer's poetry, in *Against Method: Outline of an Anarchist Theory of Knowledge* (New York: Verso Books, 2010), p. 173. Foucault refers to Feyerabend when proposing the concept of "anarchaeology" in *On the Government of the Living*, p. 79.
120 Rancière, "Le travail de l'image," *Multitudes*, 28/1 (2007), pp. 195–210. [CS translation]

121 Rancière, "Are some things unrepresentable?," p. 124.
122 Rancière, "Are some things unrepresentable?," p. 125.
123 Rancière, "Are some things unrepresentable?," p. 125.
124 Rancière, "Are some things unrepresentable?," p. 126; emphasis mine.
125 Rancière, "Are some things unrepresentable?," p. 124.
126 Rancière, "The intolerable image," in *The Emancipated Spectator*, trans. Gregory Elliott (London: Verso, 2011), p. 91.
127 Rancière, "Are some things unrepresentable?," p. 129.
128 Rancière, "The intolerable image," p. 91.
129 Blanchot, *The Infinite Conversation*, p. 134.
130 Levinas, Emmanuel, *L'Être et le neutre. À partir de Maurice Blanchot* (Paris: Verdier, 2001), p. 98. [CS translation]
131 Rancière, "Are some things unrepresentable?," p. 131.
132 Fédida, Pierre, "Un grand avenir derrière lui," in *Par où commence le corps humain. Retour sur la regression* (Paris: Puf, "Bibliothèque de psychanalyse," 2000), p. 100. [CS translation]
133 Rancière, Jacques, *The Ignorant Schoolmaster: Five Lessons in Intellectual Emancipation*, trans. K. Ross (Stanford, CA: Stanford University Press, 1991).
134 Foucault, Michel, "Le discours de Toul" (1972), *Dits et Écrits* I, 99 (Paris: Gallimard, 2001), pp. 1104–6. [CS translation]
135 Foucault, "Le discours de Toul," p. 1106. [CS translation]
136 Foucault, "Le discours de Toul," p. 1105. [CS translation]
137 See Cohn, Jesse, *Anarchism and the Crisis of Representation. Hermeneutics, Aesthetics, Politics* (Selinsgrove: Susquehanna University Press, 2006), p. 123ff.
138 Cited in Françoise Cachin and Marina Ferretti-Boquillon, *Signac: Catalogue raisonné de l'œuvre peint* (Paris: Gallimard, 2000), p. 52.
139 Signac, Paul, *Les Temps nouveaux* (1891). [CS translation]

Conclusion

1 Lesage de La Haye, Jacques, "Psychanalyse, anarchie, ordre moral," in Roger Dadoun, Jacques Lesage de La Haye, and Philippe Garnier, *Psychanalyse et anarchisme* (Lyon: Atelier de création libertaire, 2002), p. 32. [CS translation]
2 Zaltzman, Nathalie, "La pulsion anarchiste," in *Psyche anarchiste. Débattre avec Nathalie Zaltzman* (Paris: Puf, 2011), pp. 58–9. [CS translation]
3 "'Fork' is emblematic of the 'open source' community. It signals the creation of a new project from a previous project, that is, 'forking' from the project to create a new one from it." See the explanation at the end of this conclusion in Audrey Tang, "Fork the government" (February 2), *La 27e région*, posted by Magali Marlin on March 16, 2016. [CS translation]
4 Derrida, Jacques, "Privilege: Justificatory title and introductory remarks," in *Who's Afraid of Philosophy*, trans. Jan Plug (Stanford, CA: Stanford University Press, 2002), p. 61.
5 Derrida, "Privilege: Justificatory title and introductory remarks," p. 61.
6 Cited by García, Vivien, *L'Anarchisme aujourd'hui* (Paris: L'Harmattan, 2007), p. 18. [CS translation]
7 Cited in García, *L'Anarchisme aujourd'hui*, p. 110. [CS translation]
8 García, *L'Anarchisme aujourd'hui*, pp. 87, 194; cited from Mikhail Bakunin, *L'Empire knouto-germanique et la révolution sociale*, Œuvres, vol. II, 52. [CS translation]
9 See also Sébastien Faure: "Due to its plasticity, and as a result of the free play of all the elements, both individual and collective, that it assembles, this type of organization

grants each of these elements the entirety of the forces that belong to it, while through the associating of these forces, it achieve the maximum vitality for itself": "Anarchie, anarchisme, individualisme anarchiste," in *Encyclopédie Anarchiste*, Vol. 1 (Paris: La Librairie internationale, 1925–1934), pp. 69–80: p. 74.
10 Newman, Saul, *From Bakunin to Lacan: Anti-Authoritarianism and the Dislocation of Power* (New York: Lexington Books, 2001), p. 5; cited by García in *L'Anarchisme aujourd'hui*, p. 47.
11 Eisenzweig, Uri, *Fictions de l'anarchisme* (Paris: Christian Bourgois, 2001), p. 161. [CS translation]
12 Mallarmé, Stéphane, "Accusation," in *Divagations*, trans. Barbara Johnson (Cambridge, MA: Harvard University Press, 2009), p. 257.
13 Zaltzman, "La pulsion anarchiste," p. 56. [CS translation] See also the published proceedings of the conference: Jean-François Chantaretto and Georges Gaillard, eds., *Psychanalyse et culture. L'œuvre de Nathalie Zaltzman* (Paris: Ithaque, 2020).
14 Zaltzman, "La pulsion anarchiste," p. 57. [CS translation]
15 See my own analysis of the death drive in *The New Wounded: From Neurosis to Brain Damage*, trans. Steven Miller (New York: Fordham University Press, 2012), pp. 121–41.
16 Zaltzman, "La pulsion anarchiste," p. 54. [CS translation]
17 Zaltzman, "La pulsion anarchiste," p. 54. [CS translation]
18 Zaltzman, "La pulsion anarchiste," p. 50. [CS translation]
19 Zaltzman, "La pulsion anarchiste," p. 53. [CS translation]
20 Reclus, Élisée, "À Élie Reclus," undated, in the countryside around New Orleans, in Élisée Reclus (1830–1905), *Correspondance*, Vol. 1: *Elisée Reclus 1911–1925*, Bibliothèque Nationale de France, Gallica. [CS translation]
21 Malaurie, Jean, *The Last Kings of Thule: With the Polar Eskimos as They Face Their Destiny*, trans. Adrienne Foulke (London: Jonathan Cape, 1982 [1955]).
22 Zaltzman, "La pulsion anarchiste," p. 63. [CS translation]
23 Zaltzman, "La pulsion anarchiste," p. 63. [CS translation]
24 Zaltzman, "La pulsion anarchiste," p. 53. [CS translation]
25 Zaltzman, *L'Esprit du mal* (Paris: L'Olivier, "Penser/Rêver," 2007), p. 20. [CS translation]
26 Recourse to the concept of hegemony is strangely frequent among most philosophers of radical democracy, such as Ernesto Laclau and Chantal Mouffe, whose major work is titled *Hegemony and Socialist Strategy: Towards a Radical Democratic Politics* (London: Verso, 1985).
27 Tang states this on their profile on the platform *Medium.com*, where they regularly publish article-manifestos.
28 In a TED talk titled "How the Internet will (one day) transform the government," scholar Clay Shirky explains what "the world of *open source* programing can teach democracy": TEDGlobal, September 25, 2012.
29 "Reprogramming power: Audrey Tang is bringing hacker culture to the state," *Apolitical*, October 18, 2018.
30 Interview with Catherine Hebert, Blog "Hinnovic," Montreal, May 6, 1921.
31 Condominas, Baptiste, "Taiwan: g0v, les hackers qui veulent changer la démocratie," Radio France International, December 2, 2016.

Index

Abensour, Miguel 75, 76
  Greek democracy 179–80
  Levinas's "an-archy" 61
action, prefigurative 141
aesthetics
  art and life 197
  phoronomic conception of 184
  representation 199–202
Agamben, Giorgio 2
  on aporias of Foucault 166–7
  apparatus 153
  archē paradigm 22
  beginning and commanding 154–6
  "being" an anarchist 210–11, 213
  Christ's sacrifice 163–5
  Cynics and 170
  defining "sacred" 146–8
  deflation of the symbolic 149–53
  destituent power 18
  domination and property 179
  exception and 172
  on Foucault and immanence 166–8
  four knocks of transgression 171–4
  on glory 159–62
  The Highest Poverty 163
  on Hobbes 22
  Homo Sacer I 153, 174
  immanence 145
  The Kingdom and the Glory 153, 159, 160
  Opus Dei 159, 163–5
  Pilate and Jesus 159, 165–6
  political anarchism 7
  political deconstruction 12, 13
  potentiality 173–4
  power and anarchy 13
  praise of impotence 174
  profanation 145–9, 151–3
  the sacred and 158–9
  semantic inflation 149–50
  sovereignty and 170–1
  transgression 151–3
  The Use of Bodies 163, 168, 170, 172
  zone argument 174–7
Alcibiades (Plato) 124, 125, 136
  Foucault on 133–4
anarcheology defined 113
anarchism
  anarchist drive 102–4
  anti-globalist views of 3
  archē paradigm 13
  Aristotle's archic paradigm 10–12
  "being an anarchist" 210
  capitalism and 3–4
  communication 3
  critique of domination 8–10
  critique of representation x
  cyber- 220–1
  Cynics and 135–8
  deconstruction as 83–4
  definition of 2
  dissociation with anarchy 74
  ethics and 13
  Foucault's disavowal of 112–13
  Foucault's many forms of 117–19
  hegemony and 219–20
  indifference to power 215–16, 217–18
  life and being 218–19
  many forms of 5–6
  May 1968 uprisings 77–8
  messianic 107
  no philosophy of 7–8

INDEX

anarchism (*cont.*)
  the non-governable 217–18
  ontology of 212–13
  paradox of 205–7
  philosophical deconstruction of 12–14
  as philosophy 211–15
  plasticity of 214–15
  pointillist painting 208–9
  post- 14–15, 113
  resistance 113–16
  rethinking 178–81
  Schürmann critiques 39–41
  separate from anarchy 5, 53, 54–5
  spatialization 2
  thematized 85
  theory and practice 7
  true/traditional 148–9, 151, 152–3
  undeniable denied 108–10
  ungovernable and non-governable 142–3
  variety of concepts 15–18
  witnessing 202–9
L'Anarchisme aujourd'hui (García) 117
anarchists as rogues 180–1
anarchy
  Agamben and 172
  an-archaisms 16
  archic paradigm 65–6
  breaking bonds 103
  democracy as 193–4
  disavowal 19–20
  dissociation with anarchism 74
  ethical deconstruction 12–13
  execution of God 177
  Father and Son 157–8
  geography and 1–2
  Levellers and Diggers 114–15
  Levinas's "an-archy" 61–2
  metaphysics and *archē* 89–90
  ontological 12–13, 131–2
  political deconstruction 12–13
  as a political question 48
  as *praxis* 39
  separate from anarchism 5, 53, 54–5

terrorism and 106–8
theft from anarchists 19
thematized 85
"thematizing" 89–90
transcendental 94
without transgression 171–4
animals
  compared to humans 186
  Cynics and 137–8
Antelme, Robert
  The Human Race 203, 204
anti-globalization 3
apparatus
  Foucault 153–4
  oikonomia 156–7
archē 10–13
  agonistic politics 21–2
  Aristotle 28, 42
  beginning and commanding 154, 155
  Christianity and 156–7
  Heidegger's deconstruction and 38–9
  home/*oikonomia* 12
  language and 65–6
  Levinas and 63
  metaphysics and 89–90
  to *principium* 45–7
  principle and 47
  writing and 93
Archive Fever (Derrida) 88, 92
Aristotle
  on anarchy 17
  archē ix, 10–12, 35
  The Athenian Constitution 33, 191–2
  choice of governors 190, 191–2
  commanding and obeying 190, 191
  the constative and imperative 155
  first aporia: citizens, ruler, ruled 26, 27–31
  logos 43
  Metaphysics 41–5
  The Nichomachean Ethics 191–2
  oikos and *polis* 35–7, 147
  parapolitics 194
  Poetics 155–6

INDEX

politeia 25
Politics 11, 24, 25–37, 188
potentiality 173–4
privation 174
rulers and ruled 25, 188
second aporia: regime/governing body 26, 31–2, 33
on slave understanding 198–9
state sovereignty 190
third aporia: subject of *Politics* 26, 33–5
art
  pointillist painting 208–9
  Rancière on 200–2
  realism 201–2
Artaud, Antoine
  "La parole soufflée" 93
artificial intelligence x
The Athenian Constitution (Aristotle) 33, 191–2
Au temps d'harmonie (Signac) 209
auto-affection
  concept of government and 145
  Cynicism 136–8
  Deleuze and 168
  Foucault and 129–32, 141
autonomy
  consequential 68–9
  Foucault and 167

Badiou, Alain 13
Bakunin, Mikhail 13
  exploitation and government 7
  inaccessibility 15
  plastic force of anarchism 214
  science and 40
Balthasar, Urs von
  The Glory of the Lord 160
Barnett, Derek 113
Barro, Abdoulaye
  "Phénoménologie des identités juive et noire" 80
Bataille, Georges 151
  sacrifice 171
  transgression 170–1

Bateson, Gregory 54
Bemächtigungstrieb: *see under* drives
Benveniste, Emile
  Dictionary of Indo-European Concepts and Society 150
Benjamin, Walter
  general or proletarian strikes 84
  translation and representation x
Bey, Hakim
  Post-Anarchism Anarchy 14
Beyond the Pleasure Principle (Freud)
  Derrida on 85–9, 96–9
The Birth of Biopolitics (Foucault) 24, 118, 140
Black Blocs 180–1, 206
Black Lives Matter 206
Black people, slavery and 78–81
Blanchot, Maurice 204
  Hebrew slaves in Egypt 73
  The Infinite Conversation 71–2
Bookchin, Murray 13
Breton, Stanislas 46
Britain: Levellers and Diggers 114–15
Buddhism, Nirvana principle and 99
Burnett, Derek C. 10
Butler, Judith
  "What is critique?" 142

Caillois, Roger 170
Call, Lewis 14, 15
Camus, Albert 203
capitalism
  downfall of 178
  transgression and 151
  ultraliberalism 3–4
  wounds of x
cause, immanent 168
Chambers, Simon 183
Char, René 60
childrearing 134–5
chrestai 167–8
Christianity
  dual anarchy of Father and Son 157–8

INDEX

Christianity (*cont.*)
  Judaism and 164
  oikonomia 156–7
citizenship
  access and 188
  Aristotle on 33
  ruling and ruled 26, 27–31
civil society 24
  distribution of parts 188–90
  hierarchy 114
Civilization and its Discontents (Freud) 20
Claudel, Paul 61
Cleisthenes of Athens 179–80
climate crisis x
Colli, Giorgio 176
colonization
  imperial "*ego conquiro*" 59–60
  Pizarro and Incas 56–60
Colson, Daniel 214
The Coming Insurrection (The Invisible Committee) 152
communication, alternative modes of 3–5
communism, anarchists and 180–1
Corneille, Pierre
  Oedipus 201
The Courage of Truth (Foucault) 118, 119, 133–4, 167, 169
  Cynics and 135–6, 140–1
cryptocurrency 4
cyber-anarchism 4
Cynics
  "alter your currency" 138–9
  anarchism and 135–8, 140–1
  Foucault on 169–70

Damasio, Alain 4
death drive 88, 98–9, 101
  as anarchism 86–7
  power and 103
deconstruction
  as anarchism 83–4
  delegitimizing 55–6, 57
  of metaphysics 212
Deleuze, Gilles 167
  analysis of the fold 168
  auto-affection 129–32
  Foucault's response to 132–3
  immanence 128–32
  post-anarchism 113
democracy
  ancient Greece 127–8
  apportioning parts 188–90
  Aristotle and 27, 33, 34–5
  concept of representation 196–8
  Derrida's critique of 107–8
  drawing of lots 195–6
  not a living space 183
  Plato on 193
  radical 179–80
  status of 193–4
  ungovernability 195
  the unrepresentable 183–4
  see also equality
Derrida, Jacques 2
  "anarchy drive" 20, 102–4
  anarchy-anarchism thematized 85
  archē paradigm 22
  arche-writing 18
  Archive Fever 88, 92
  "being" an anarchist 210–11
  deconstruction and anarchism 83–4
  deconstruction of metaphysics 89–90
  différance of mastery 100–2, 105–6
  "Force of law" 84
  Foucault and 104–5
  on Freud's *Beyond the Pleasure Principle* 96–9
  Of Grammatology 85
  on Greek citizens 28
  on Israel 77
  on Lévi-Strauss's "Writing Lesson" 90–3
  on Levinas and the transcendental 94–6
  mastery/*Bemächtigungstrieb* 100–2

on mastery drive 104–5
ontological deconstruction 12
pluralizing 6
political anarchism 7
The Post Card 20
on power 92
"Psychoanalysis Searches the States of its Soul" 107
on representative democracy 107–8
Resistances of Psychoanalysis 87
on responsibility 83
substitution 65
see also death drive
Dictionary of Indo-European Concepts and Society (Benveniste) 150
Diderot, Denis
"Anarchy" from *Encyclopedia* 17
Diogenes the Cynic 138, 139
Plato and 111
see also Cynics
Disagreement (Rancière) 184–7
Discipline and Punish (Foucault) 169
"Discours de Toul" (Foucault) 207–8
distribution
apportioning parts 188–90
having a part 187–8
occupations 192
domination
aggressiveness 111
masters 46
metaphysics and 47
obedience and 52–3
property and 179
double bind
anarchy and anarchism 54–5
obedience and command 66–7
drives
anarchistic 102–4, 216–17
compared to principles 99–100
compulsion and 97–8
death 88, 98–9, 101
mastery/*Bemächtigungstrieb* 88–9, 96–9, 104–5
pleasure principle 85–9
power and 143–4
the proper 101–2
Zaltzman on 216–17
Du Bois, W. E. B.
The Souls of Black Folk 80
Duchamp, Marcel 200
Duns Scotus, John 45
Dupui-Déri, François 181
Dussel, Enrique 59–60

The Earth and Its Inhabitants (Reclus) 1
ecology/environment 3, 218–19
Egypt, slavery in 72–3
election
heteronomies 70, 74
Levinas on 72–4
revolution and 73–4
and slavery 69–70
emancipation
of liberties under surveillance 49
En découvrant l'existence avec Husserl et Heidegger (Levinas) 68–9
L'Entraide, un facteur de l'évolution (Kropotkin) 1
equality
democracy as expression of 34–5
isonomia and *isēgoria* 126–7
mathematical vs political 189–90
radical 182
Rancière's active concept of 183
Ernout-Meillet *Dictionnaire étymologique de la langue latine* 150
essentialism, political problem of 15
ethics
anarchy and 13
excessive 75
Foucault and 117
obedience and command 67
evil, National Socialism and 66
exception
Agamben and 172
of God 156–7, 158
mechanism of 146–8, 176

exception (*cont.*)
　religion, law, and politics 148
　structure of 156–7
exclusion, domination and 179

Fédida, Pierre 206–7
feminism, domination and 8–9
Fénéon, Félix 208–9
Flaubert, Gustave 201
　Madame Bovary 203, 204
"Force of law" (Derrida) 84
Foucault, Michel 2
　agonism 115–16
　apparatus 153, 153–4
　autonomy 167
　"being" an anarchist 211
　The Birth of Biopolitics 24, 118, 140
　The Courage of Truth 118, 119, 133–4, 135–6, 140–1, 167, 169
　Cynics and 135–40
　Deleuze on immanence 128–32
　Derrida and 104–5
　Diogenes and Plato 111
　disavowal of anarchism 112–13
　Discipline and Punish 169
　"Discours de Toul" 207–8
　On the Government of the Living 112–13
　"governmentality" 118–23
　The Hermeneutics of the Subject 124, 132–3, 134, 166–7, 167
　History of Madness 169
　History of Sexuality 129
　on Hobbes 21
　immanence 166–8
　the instrumentalist soul 124–6
　isonomia and *isēgoria* 126–7
　many forms of anarchy 117–19
　on not being governed 10
　observations of nations 121
　parrēsia 122–3
　on *Phaedo* 169
　political anarchism 7
　political anarchy 13
　political authority 52–3

　political deconstruction 12
　power has no truth 111–12
　"A preface to transgression" 151
　resistance 113–16, 120–1
　response to Deleuze 132–3
　Schürmann and 49, 51–3, 137
　sovereignty and 170–1
　transformation 116–17
　on transgression 169
　"The Utopian Body" 144
　"What is Enlightenment?" 141, 169
　witnessing 204
France
　alternate politics 3
　May 1968 uprisings 77–8, 196
　Paris Commune 196, 206
freedom
　difficulty of 69
　relative 109
　state commitment 75
　transgression and 169
"Freedom and command" (Levinas) 71
Freud, Sigmund
　ambiguity of *Bemächtigungstrieb* 97–9
　Beyond the Pleasure Principle 85–9
　Civilization and its Discontents 20
　compulsion and 97–8
　deconstructive reading of 87–9
　Derrida looks beyond 107
　Derrida on anarchism and 85–9
　mastery/*Bemächtigungstrieb* 100–2, 105
　"Negation" 19
　pleasure principle 102–4
　role of transcendental predicate 105
　thanatological unlinking 218
　Totem and Taboo 150
　trauma 206
　see also death drive

g0v civic hackers 220–1
Gandillac, Maurice de 131
García, Vivien

INDEX

anarchism outside philosophy 214
L'Anarchisme aujourd'hui 117
theory and practice 7
German workers' councils 206
Glissant, Edouard
Poetics of Relation 80, 81
globalization, anti- 3
glory
　Agamben on 159–62
　the apparatus of 161
The Glory of the Lord: A Theological Aesthetics (von Balthasar) 160
God
　exception and 152
　execution 177
　Father and Son 157–8
　order and 46
Goldman, Emma 13
　tyrannies and feminism 8–9
Gould, Glenn 173
governmentality
　Foucault and 142
governability
　Aristotle on 43
　of slaves 81–2
government/rulers
　absence of 2
　architects and 44–5
　Aristotle on 190–5
　Aristotle's regime and governing body 31–2, 33
　choosing the governors 190, 191–2
　civil war 114–15
　commanding and obeying 121–2, 195
　dominating the non-governable 23–4
　drawing of lots 195–6
　Foucault on 118–23, 143
　hierarchies 32
　non-governable 23–4
　oligarchies 182
　problem with the problem 119–23
　self- 145
　truth and 122–3

the ungovernable 23
utopia 125
"governmental prejudice" 51
Greece, ancient
　anarkhia 16, 17
　slavery 78

"Hack the pandemic" (Tang) 220–1
hacking, Audrey Tang and 220–1
Hardt, Michael 128, 145
health 3
Heidegger, Martin 213
　being and life 218
　deconstruction 12
　obedience 62
　theoretical teleocracy 44
　time of anarchy 48–9
Heidegger on Being and Acting: From Principles to Anarchy (Schürmann) 12, 13
　critiques of anarchism 39–41
　on deconstruction 38–9
henology
　negative 54
　Plotinus' One 50–1
The Hermeneutics of the Subject (Foucault) 124, 132–3, 134, 166–7, 167
　care of the self as resistance 125–6
Herodotus, on anarchy 17
heteronomies
　of election 74
　the Other 95
　slavery and 70, 71, 74, 78–81
The Highest Poverty (Agamben) 163
Hippolytus 157
History of Madness (Foucault) 169
History of Sexuality (Foucault) 129
The History of the Peloponnesian War (Thucydides) 127
Hobbes, Thomas
　Foucault on 21
　human nature 115
　Leviathan 20–3

INDEX

Hobbes, Thomas (*cont.*)
  Levinas and 76–7
  social hierarchy 114
  state of nature 106–7
Homo Sacer (Agamben)
  Christian *oikonomia* 156–7
  execution of God 177
  zones of 175, 177
Homo Sacer I (Agamben) 153
horizontality
  in crises 2–3
  Lordon on 21
  politics of 2
Hubert, Henri
  Sacrifice: Its Nature and Function (with Mauss) 150
human nature
  animals and 186
  Hobbes and 115
The Human Race (Antelme) 203, 204
"Humanism and an-archy" (Levinas) 71
Husserl, Edmund 94

Ibáñez, Tomás 7–8
The Ignorant Schoolmaster (Rancière) 207
immanence
  auto-affection 129–32
  Deleuze 168
  Foucault and 128–32, 141, 166–8
Inca Empire
  authority 58
  intelligibility 58
  Pizarro and colonization 56–60
The Infinite Conversation (Blanchot) 71–2
information "silos" 3
interventionism 4
Inuit people 217
Italy: workers' councils 206

Jesus of Nazareth
  glory and 159–60
  sacrifice of 163–5

Jewish people
  David's state 76–7
  the Holocaust and 171
  Judaism and Christianity 164
  Levinas's Zionism 62
  representing Holocaust 201, 203–5
  revolution and 73–4
  slavery in Egypt 72–3, 78–81
John, Gospel of 165

Kant, Immanuel
  autonomy 68–9
  beautiful and sublime 199–200
  Foucault and 52–3
  the transcendental 94
The Kingdom and the Glory (Agamben) 153, 159, 160
Kropotkin, Peter 13
  concept of anarchy 16
  inaccessibility 15
  L'Entraide, un facteur de l'évolution 1
  mutual aid 219

labor, division of occupations 192
Laches (Plato) 133–5
Lacoste, Yves 1
Lagasnerie, Geoffroy de 140
language
  paratactic 203, 204–5
  the Saying and the Said 65
  understanding and obedience 198–9
  witnessing 203–5
Laplanche, Jean 99
The Last Kings of Thule (Malaurie) 217
law, structure of exception and 148
Lectures on the Religion of the Semites (Smith) 150
Leibniz, Gottfried Wilhelm 45
Lesage de la Haye, Jacques 210
Lévi-Strauss, Claude 85
  Derrida on "Writing Lesson" 90–3
  "Man's Exploitation by Man" 91–2
  Tristes Tropiques 90–1
Leviathan (Hobbes) 20–3

INDEX

Levinas, Emmanuel 2
  anarchic responsibility 18
  anarchism of the state 74–8
  "an-archy" 61–2, 94
  archē paradigm 22
  "being" an anarchist 210
  consequential autonomy 68–9
  election 72–4
  En découvrant l'existence avec Husserl et Heidegger 68–9
  ethics 12, 63
  "Freedom and command" 71
  heteronomies 67–71
  "Humanism and an-archy" 71
  May 1968 uprisings 77–8
  on National Socialism 66, 68
  non-governable slaves 81–2
  the Other 63–6, 205
  Otherwise than Being 64
  "La philosophie et l'idée de l'infini" 68–9
  political anarchism 7
  the proletarian 71–2
  on the state 76–7
  "Substitution" 63–6
  The Theory of Intuition in Husserl's Phenomenology 62
  Totality and Infinity 68
  on the transcendental 94–6
  Zionism of 62
libertarianism 91, 180
logos
  apophantic/non-apophantic 155
  humans and animals 185–6
  understanding and 198–9
Lordon, Frédéric 21
Luxemburg, Rosa 125
Lyotard, Jean-François
  dissensus and differend 184–7
  Rancière and 184, 196–7
  unrepresentable and unpresentable 199–200, 202
  the unthinkable 206
  witnessing 202–3

Machiavelli, Niccolò 46
  function of glory 160
Madame Bovary (Flaubert) 203, 204
Malatesta, Errico 13, 18
Malaurie, Jean
  The Last Kings of Thule 217
Malevitch, Kazmir 200
Mallarmé, Stéphane 215
"man's exploitation by man" 91–2
Marin, Louis 159
Mark, Gospel of 165
Marxism
  Lévi-Strauss and 91
  rethinking 178–9
  sacred authority 149
Matthew, Gospel of 165
Mauss, Marcel 160
  Sacrifice: Its Nature and Function 150
May, Todd
  on Foucault 113
  The Political Philosophy of Poststructuralist Anarchism 14
  The Political Thoughts of Jacques Rancière 183
metaphysics
  forms of domination 47
  ontological anarchy 39–40
  value of *archē* 89–90
Metaphysics (Aristotle) 41–5
migration 3
Montesquieu
  "Of the slavery of the Negroes" 79
More, Thomas 40
mutual aid 1–2, 219

Nambikwara people 90–1
Nancy, Jean-Luc 109
  "The unsacrificeable" 171
National Socialism, evil and 66
nature
  anarchy and 20–3
  Hobbes and 106–7
"Negation" (Freud) 19

Negri, Antonio 128, 145
neoliberalism, governability and 24
Newman, Saul
  anarchism and power 215
  on Foucault 113
  poststructuralist anarchism 14
The Nicomachean Ethics (Aristotle) 191–2
Nirvana principle 99
non-governable
  animals and 139
  concept of 142

obedience
  beginning and 154–6
  collective manifestation 188
  command and 53, 66–7, 121–2
  to laws 121
  transgression and 169
  understanding and 198–9
Occupy movements 3, 196
Oedipus (Corneille) 201
Of Grammatology (Derrida) 85
"Of the slavery of the Negroes" (Montesquieu) 79
oikonomia
  Aristotle on 35–7, 192
  Foucault on 153
  meaning of 154
  oligarchy and 193
oligarchy 182, 193
On the Government of the Living (Foucault) 112–13
ontology
  anarchist's orientation 131
  "egotism" of 62–3
  "ontological anarchy" 38–40, 48
  phenomenology of 40
  potentiality 158
Opus Dei (Agamben) 159, 163–5
the Other
  beginning of philosophy 69
  heteronomies 67–8
  Levinas and 63–6, 95

  slavery and 95
  witnessing and 204–5
Otherwise than Being (Levinas) 64–6

Paepe, César de 5
"La parole soufflée" (Artaud) 93
Paul, Christianity and Judaism 164
Pellegrin, Pierre 26
the people, welfare of 120
Peterson, Erik 162
Phaedo (Plato) 169
"Phénoménologie des identités juive et noire" (Barro) 80
phenomenology of ontology 40–1
"La philosophie et l'idée de l'infini" (Levinas) 68–9
philosophy
  anarchism as 211–15
  as "archipolitics" 190–5
  see also metaphysics; ontology
Philosophy in a Time of Terror (Derrida) 106
Pilate and Jesus (Agamben) 159, 165–6
Pizarro, Francisco, Inca Empire and 56–60
Plato
  Alcibiades 124, 125, 133
  on anarchy 17
  on democracy 193
  and Diogenes 111
  the instrumentalist soul 124–6
  Laches 133
  occupations 192
  Phaedo 169
  The Republic 71, 124
pleasure principle
  the anarchist drive 102–4
  the *archē* of the psyche 85–9
  mastery and 100
  sense experience 187–8
Plotinus 59
  the One 49, 50–1
Poetics of Relation (Glissant) 80, 81
Poland, Foucault and 121

police
  politics and 184, 195
  Rancière 181–3
The Political Philosophy of Poststructuralist Anarchism (May) 14
The Political Thoughts of Jacques Rancière (May) 183
politics
  Agamben and 172
  apportioning parts 189–90
  "archipolitics" 190–5
  Aristotle's *archē politike* 25–37
  dunasteia 126
  as event 50–1
  "metapolitics" 196–7
  origin in resistance 115
  parapolitics 194
  police and 184, 195
  and the political 49
  question of anarchy 48
  reconfiguration 196–8
  structure of exception 148
  without parties 13
Politics (Aristotle) 11, 25–37, 190–5
  aporias of 24
  commanding and obeying 190, 191
  humans and animals 186
Pontalis, Jean-Bertrand 99
Post-Anarchism Anarchy (Bey) 14
The Post Card (Derrida) 20, 106
poststructuralism, post-anarchism and 14–15
potentiality 156
  Aristotle 173–4
  ontology 158
  refusal to act 173–4
poverty 3, 179
power
  anarchism's indifference to 215–16, 217–18
  différance and 100–2, 105–6
  domination 8–10, 92
  of drives 86
  dunasteia 126

Foucault and 143
glory and 161–2
hierarchization 92
legitimizing 115–16
mastery/*Bemächtigungstrieb* 88–9, 96–7, 105
political authority 52–3
potentiality 156
resistance 120–1
sadism and 99, 143–4
symbols of 162–3
unjust 92
witnesses and 207–8
"A preface to transgression" (Foucault) 151
principium
  archē to 45–7
  principle of the principle 45
principles
  compared to drives 99–100
  of nothing 47–8
profanation
  Agamben and 159
  meaning of profane 146
the proletariat
  democratic representation 197
  Levinas and 71–2
  strikes and 84
property
  domination and 179
  as theft 16, 18
protest movements, non-governable and ungovernable 24
Proudhon, Pierre-Joseph x, 13
  Artaud's allusion to 93
  governmental prejudice 9–10
  inaccessibility 15
  property as theft 48
  property is theft 18
  science and domination 40
  theory and practice 7
  use of term "anarchy" 16
  What is Property? 16
prudence, Aristotle on 29–30

"Psychoanalysis searches the states of its soul" (Derrida) 107
"La pulsion anarchiste" (Zaltzman) 103–4

Quesnay, François 125
Quijano, Anibal 59

Ramond, Charles 109
Ramonet, Tancrède 6
Rancière, Jacques 2
   anarchism of 182
   anarchy of politics 178
   archē paradigm 22
   "archipolitics" 194–5
   "being" an anarchist 211, 213
   democracy 18, 179–80
   dissensus and differend 184–7
   distribution of the sensible 187–90
   on domination 7
   drawing of lots 195–6
   The Ignorant Schoolmaster 207
   Lyotard and 196–7
   "metapolitics" 196–7
   oikos 12
   police and politics 181–3
   political anarchism 7
   reconfiguring politics 12, 196–8
   rethinking Marxism 178–9
   unrepresentable and unpresentable 183–4, 200–2
   witnessing 202–9
Reclus, Élisée 217
   anarchy as expression of order 18
   The Earth and Its Inhabitants 1
religion, structure of exception and 148
representation
   art 199–202
   unrepresentable and unpresentable 199–202
   witnesses 202–9
   women and proletarians 197
repression
   facing the ungovernable 23
   of secularization 159

The Republic (Plato) 71, 124
resistance, Foucault and 120–1
Resistances of Psychoanalysis (Derrida) 87
responsibility
   Derrida on 83
   freedom and 69
revolution, Jewish people and 72–3
Rifkin, Jeremy
   "Collaborative Commons" 5
right-libertarianism, anarchism and 5
Rojava, Western Kurdistan 206
Rose, Edith 207–8
Roussel, Raymond 129

the sacred
   Agamben's definition of 146–8
   ecce homo 165–6
   homo sacer 148, 163–5
   the mythologeme of 150
   sacer and 148, 158–9
   symbolic brilliance 158–9
   symbolic deflation of 172
   touching 172–3
Sacrifice: Its Nature and Function (with Hubert) 150
sadism, power and 103
Saint-Simon, Henri de 125
Scarfone, Dominique 104
Schopenhauer, Artur 99
Schürmann, Reiner 2
   the anarchist being 212–13
   archē paradigm 22, 45–7, 46–8
   on Aristotle 25, 41–5
   "being" an anarchist 210
   critiques of anarchism 39–41
   deconstructing anarchy 12
   delegitimizing deconstruction 55–6
   double bind 54–5
   on Foucault 137
   Foucault and 51–3
   Heidegger 56
   Heidegger on Being and Acting: From Principles to Anarchy 12, 13, 38–9
   henology 50–1

ontological anarchism 18
Pizarro and the Incas 56–60
political anarchism 7
praxis to *theōria* 39
time of anarchy 48–9
science 40
secularization as repression 159
Security, Territory, Population (Foucault) 153
self
  action of 168
  care of as resistance 125–6
sense experiences
  pleasure and suffering 187–8
separation, critique of 171–2
Seurat, Georges 208–9
sexual instinct
  sadism and 99, 103
Shoah (film) 204
Signac, Paul
  on pointillism 208–9
  Au temps d'harmonie 209
slavery
  in Egypt 72–3
  election and 69–70
  heteronomies of 70, 71, 74
  Jewish people in Egypt 78–81
  non-governable slaves 81–2
  the Other 95
  slave trade and 78–81
  understanding and obedience 198–9
Smith, William Robertson
  Lectures on the Religion of the Semites 150
social authenticity 91
Sophocles, on anarchy 17
The Souls of Black Folk (Du Bois) 80
sovereignty
  Aristotle on 190–1
  exception 147
  Foucault on 119–21
  new types of 120–1
  obedience to laws 121
  transgression and 170–1

Spanish Civil War 206
Spinoza, Baruch
  immanent cause 168
  third mode of knowing 131
states
  anarchist terrorism and 106–8
  counter-*archē* 21
  freedom and 75
  Levinas on 76–7
  Levinas on anarchism of 74–8
  sovereignty of 9–10
strikes, general or proletarian 84
subjectivization, Foucault and 117
suffering, sense experience and 187–8
Sweden, Foucault and 121
symbols and the symbolic
  deflation of 172
  floating signifiers 150
  performative force 162–3
  of power 162–3
  sacred and 158–9
  signs of power 159

Taiwan
  Tang's "civic hackers" 220–1
Tang, Audrey
  Sunflower Movement 220–1
teleocracy, Aristotelian 41–5
terrorism 106–8
  September 11 attacks 106
Tertullian 157
"The unsacrificeable" (Nancy) 171
theft
  of anarchy from anarchists 19
  colonization and 57
  property as 114
  Proudhon on 18–19
  Schürmann on 46–8
The Theory of Intuition in Husserl's Phenomenology (Levinas) 62
Thiers, Adolphe 153
Thucydides
  The History of the Peloponnesian War 127

Tiqqun journal
　history of modern state 22
Totality and Infinity (Levinson) 68
Totem and Taboo (Freud) 150
touching, Agamben on 172–3
trade unions 180
　revolutionary 206
transcendental power 96–7
transformation, Foucault on 116–17
transgression
　critique of 168–71
　four knocks of 171–4
　profanation and 151–3
　sovereignty and 170–1
trauma, psychic energy and 97
Trebatius: defines "profane" 146
Tristes Tropiques (Lévi-Strauss) 90–1
Trump, Donald, as anarchist 4
truth
　parrēsia 119, 122–3, 124, 126–8
　power without 111–12
　utopia and 125
Tunisia, Foucault and 121

the unconscious as governing body 20
universalism
　disappearance of 15
The Use of Bodies (Agamben) 163, 168, 172
utopia
　government by truth 125
　Schürmann on 40

"The Utopian Body" (radio broadcast) 144

violence
　an-archic nonviolence 95
　writing and 92–3
virtue
　Aristotle's "good man" 28–31
The Vision of the Vanquished (Wachtel) 56–7

Wachtel, Nathan
　The Vision of the Vanquished 56–7
welfare state 3
"What is critique?" (Butler) 142
"What is Enlightenment?" (Foucault) 141, 169
What is Property? (Proudhon) 16
women, democratic representation 197
writing, power and 92–3
Wundt, Wilhelm 150

Xenophon, on anarchy 17

Yellow Vests/*Gilets Jaunes* 3

Zaltzman, Nathalie
　the anarchistic drive 216–17
　"Long Live Death" motto 210
　"La pulsion anarchiste" 103–4
Zola, Émile 203
Zones to Defend (ZAD) 3, 206
"Zones of immanence" (Deleuze) 131